French Revolutions

Tim Moore's writing has appeared in the *Daily Telegraph*, the *Observer*, the *Sunday Times* and *Esquire*. He lives in west London with his wife and their three children.

FRENCH REVOLUTIONS

Tim Moore

Yellow Jersey
London

Published by Yellow Jersey Press 2001

2 4 6 8 10 9 7 5 3 1

First published in Great Britain in 2001 by
Yellow Jersey Press
Random House, 20 Vauxhall Bridge Road,
London SW1V 2SA

Random House Australia (Pty) Limited
20 Alfred Street, Milsons Point, Sydney,
New South Wales 2061, Australia

Random House New Zealand Limited
18 Poland Road, Glenfield,
Auckland 10, New Zealand

Random House South Africa (Pty) Limited
Endulini, 5A Jubilee Road, Parktown 2193, South Africa

Random House UK Limited Reg. No. 954009
www.randomhouse.co.uk

A CIP catalogue record for this book
is available from the British Library

ISBN 0-224-06095-3

Papers used by Random House UK Limited are natural,
recyclable products made from wood grown in sustainable forests;
the manufacturing processes conform to the environmental
regulations of the country of origin

Typeset by SX Composing DTP, Rayleigh, Essex
Printed and bound in Great Britain by
Mackays of Chatham PLC, Chatham, Kent

To Tom Simpson

Acknowledgements

Thanks to Rachel Cugnoni, Paul Ruddle, Martin Warren, Simon O'Brien, Matthew Lantos, Richard Hallett, *procycling*, Pyrenean Pursuits, Thordis Olafsdottir and my family. Not forgetting the Tour de France press office, without whom none of this would have been difficult.

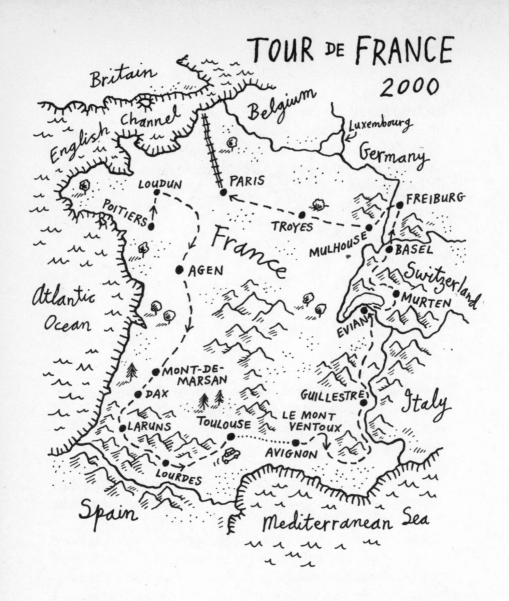

Prologue

Parasailing, pot-holing, the luge: even those sporting activities that appear to require no skill invariably demand an abundance of human qualities that I might only hope to acquire if the Wizard of Oz was in a particularly generous mood. But we can all ride a bike. We have all known what it is to grind agonisingly up a steep hill and freewheel madly down the other side. In its unique dual capacity as mode of transport and childhood accessory, the bicycle has played a formative role in all our lives.

But thinking back, I find that my cycling memories are imbued less with a nostalgic sepia glow than a stark fluorescent glare of fear and failure. Reading the back cover of *Rough Ride*, the autobiography of former Irish professional cyclist Paul Kimmage, I feel profoundly chastened. Describing a portentous first ride at the age of 6, Kimmage fondly recalls his father immediately removing the stabilisers before plonking his son on the saddle and pushing him off across the car park in front of their Dublin flat. 'I wobbled, but basically had no trouble and was delighted with myself.' Replace 'trouble' with 'balance', and 'delighted with myself' with 'repeatedly injured', and you have the encapsulation of my own debut.

I lived in the tricycle age for far too long, squeaking about Walpole Park on a maroon three-wheeler, its capacious tin boot flamboyantly emblazoned with a royal coat of arms my father had mysteriously acquired from somewhere. It may be that in this fashion I appeared a ghastly little ponce. After all, I hadn't learned to ride without that shaming third wheel until I was almost 8, being pushed again and again across our back garden on a hand-me-down girl's bike by an increasingly frustrated mother. I was not a natural. I lacked the reckless bravado that propelled other boys to pedal across Ealing Common with their arms ostentatiously aloft, or, worse, nonchalantly folded.

My first real bike was an ancient machine whose name had a stolid, Empire twang, something like Wayfarer or Valiant, and whose cast-iron forthrightness of design you could never quite shake off by removing the mudguards and fitting a pair of cow-horn handlebars. I should by rights have aspired to a Raleigh Chopper, but then Tomas Kozlowski got one, and seeing those already burgeoning Slavic buttocks unappealingly cleaved by that slender bench saddle I understood with a youthful prescience of which I am still quietly proud that Raleigh Choppers were laughably awful. So it was with Valiant between my pistoning young knees that I breathlessly eluded park-keepers seeking to enforce the new 'Sling Your Hook, Eddy Merckx' no-cycling rule; his were the wheels that shot across mad Mrs Lewis's feet and prompted her to send my parents an admonitory letter that famously included the word 'delinquent'. My Valiant was there outside Gunnersbury Park when a trainee psychopath treated me to my first encounter with a number of other new but much shorter words; there too when, perhaps four seconds later, I accepted that fondly remembered inaugural smack in the mouth.

A succession of inherited shopping models followed, and I had to wait until my sixteenth birthday for my first new bicycle, a ten-speed racer of East German origin. On the way to pick it up, my poor father felt obliged to usher his youngest son into manhood with a dilatory lecture on birth prevention, one whose more poignant euphemisms would recur to me whenever I rode it thereafter. Mercifully almost every component shattered, buckled or split within weeks – I had never previously thought of corrosion as a process you could actually sit down and watch happen. On the other hand, its demise did mean that the balance of those important mid-teenage years was spent wobbling about on my father's foldable Bickerton.

My girlfriend at that time, in fact my wife at this time, had a recurring dream in which I would pedal away from her house naked on the Bickerton. If I tell you that the Bickerton resembled two dwarf unicycles clumsily welded together you will understand that this was not an erotic dream. The Bickerton was a ludicrous machine with the handling characteristics of a human pyramid. Its unique selling point was portability, an asset summarised by a long-running television commercial in which a haughty executive defied a platform full of generously trousered commuters to snigger as he laboriously hauled a huge sack of metallic angles through the ticket barrier, chased and chivvied by taunting voiceover whispers of 'Bickerton! Bickerton!'

Nevertheless, as it became difficult to affect the piping tenor necessary to procure a child ticket from ever more sceptical bus conductors, so the Bickerton's social utility increased. I began riding it to pubs and parties, generally returning well-lit and yet, in a hilarious twist of irony, without lights. I crashed into road works and garden fences, and finally broke the Bickerton's back in the grand manner, careering into a parked car with such force that I snapped his number plate in half and ended up on the roof.

It was long years before I cycled again, so long that I almost forgot how to ride. Attending an auction of unclaimed stolen

3

property I felt sorry for a conspicuously pre-teenage girl's bicycle and acquired it for three quid; after a stimulating exchange of views with my wife Birna concerning the practical worth of this item I committed myself to riding it to and from my place of work, the offices of Teletext Ltd.

Six months on, a commuter's familiarity with my route was beginning to breed contempt, and one bright summer's morning I spectacularly overcooked it coming into the Old Ship chicane. Arriving at work with the coagulation process still very much an ongoing one, I was summoned to an impromptu meeting with senior management. Bleeding without permission was added to a catalogue of similar outrages against corporate discipline and four minutes later I was being escorted from the premises. This was a shame, for as well as stymieing a well-developed plan to substitute the main Teletext menu with an animated graphic of an ejaculating penis on 24.7 million television screens across the land, it meant I also faced the demanding challenge of storming furiously past the assembled terminators of my contract on a little pink bicycle.

When the girl's bike was stolen from outside my house, probably by Birna, it had already decayed into a state that would have made for a drawn-out round of Animal, Vegetable or Mineral; its eventual replacement, a brakeless old Peugeot touring bike bought from a man who I'm fairly certain hadn't paid for it, was used only as occasional urban transport for the slightly drunk. I'd hit 30 and had never successfully repaired a puncture, overtaken anything faster than a milk float or ridden hands-off without eating kerb. The faint, arthritic squiggle that was my career path as a cyclist had slipped unnoticed off the bottom axis.

That is until I arrived in the north Icelandic town of Blönduós at 9.32 p.m. on 28 June 1997. It's difficult to imagine cycling across Europe's second-largest desert by mistake, but this seemed the only fair description of the events of that day and its three predecessors. In the company of Birna's brother Dilli I emerged from two-wheeled retirement in glorious fashion, traversing the land of my in-laws on a day-trip that somehow ran out of control into a critic-confounding odyssey. During those long, lonely hours watching Dilli on my forward horizon as he squinted around to locate me on his hindward one, I had found myself mumbling an epic commentary, a tale of water-carriers and wheel-suckers, of bonks and breakaways, a vocabulary learned from ten years of seasonal obsession with the world's largest annual sporting event.

In fact, I'd first become aware of the Tour de France during the home leg of my elder brother's 1976 French exchange. Our house guest Denis spent almost every waking hour of those three weeks with his conspicuous facial features pressed up against a transistor radio on which he had managed to locate faint medium-wave coverage of the event. It was a display of stamina and dedication to parallel that of the riders themselves – clearly, here was an event which gripped a nation like no other, and didn't relax its grasp for twenty-one whole days.

Sadly, Denis was an awful boy who cheated at Monopoly and avenged yet another Belgian victory in that year's race by running amok in our flower-beds with the big lawnmower, so I did not at the time ascribe positive attributes to the focus of his obsession. My own interest lay dormant until the late Eighties, when Channel 4 began covering the event at a time when my lifestyle made getting up to switch channels after *Countdown* an onerous task beyond contemplation. By default I became one of the billion people who watch the Tour de France on telly.

It was Phil Liggett's memorably raw commentary on the epic Alpine performance of Irishman Stephen Roche ('There's someone coming through the mist . . . it can't be . . . *it is*! It's Roche! *It's Stephen Roche!*') during his triumphant 1987 Tour that initiated my fascination. I came to marvel at the heroic scale of the event and its incredible demands, the murderous climbs and

90-k.p.h. descents that sometimes defied death but, tragically, sometimes didn't. I realised that each stage was a race within a race, and that with the ox-like sprinters and bird-like climbers there were even different species within each race. I mastered the terminology – the humble *domestiques* who fed, watered and protected their team leaders; the *peloton*, the main bunch of riders that careered along, elbow to elbow and wheel to wheel, at ridiculous speed; the *gendarmes* assigned to keep tabs on rival breakaways; the humiliations of the broom wagon, on call to sweep up those who cracked in the Alps. I learned to distinguish the multi-coloured hooped jersey of the world champion from the appealing polka-dotted affair worn by the current leader in the Tour's King of the Mountains competition. And, after two years, I finally witnessed a rider hoicking up the leg of his shorts and peeing waywardly into the spectators at 50 k.p.h.

That those soiled by this incident reacted with baptismal joy suggested the feats of the enormous crowds were, in their way, no less remarkable than those of the riders. One third of the entire population of France watches the Tour from the hard shoulders and hillsides, occupying a long wait in the mad sun by daubing their favourites' names on the tarmac, then maximising their brief contact with the riders by swarming over the road, emptying warm Evian on the front runners, bellowing encouragement and occasionally knocking the unwary off their bikes. The rest of Europe provided a typical assortment of 'characters': a trident-waving, cloven-hoofed German Devil; the fabulously drunken flag-faced Danes. It was the only sporting event I had come across with its own personality.

For ten years my keen interest in the Tour had spawned no greater desire than a vague intention to join one day the exuberant roadside festivities among the largest sporting crowd in the world. But after my Icelandic triumphs, achieved without preparation and at the cost of only peripheral permanent injury, a bolder ambition was born. I might be too old to join the cast of sport's greatest drama, but maybe I could still stand on the same stage. Ride the route of the Tour de France, even on my own, even at a moderate pace, and I'd have achieved something remarkable, the sort of achievement that made men. Standing at the window with a recently drained bottle of millennial Moët dangling waywardly from my hand I added my own silent, vainglorious vow to the millions swirling blurrily through fizz-fuddled minds around the globe. As the final lonely firework hissed up into the drizzle I accepted that with a thriving thicket of unpigmented hairs in the temple region and three children old enough to swear in two languages, Old Father Time was catching up with old father Tim. If I didn't do it this year I wouldn't, because maybe next year I couldn't.

Unlike most professional sporting events, the Tour de France is more about taking part than it is about winning. Only two or three of the 180 starters would begin the race with any real hope of victory; for most, just completing what people (or anyway journalists) call La Grande Boucle – the Big Loop – is enough. Make it back to Paris – and in some years less than half the starters do – and you're a Giant of the Road. The last finisher, the *lanterne rouge*, is given a particularly rousing hero's reception and can look forward to a year of lucrative race offers and sponsorship.

A race where you get a huge cheer and large cash sums for coming last sounded like my kind of race. 'Giant of the Road': I could live with that. Maybe I could get some calling cards made up. OK, we were talking about a lot of cycling – but I mean how bad could a lot of cycling really be? I was starting to get quite cocky until I read about Tom Simpson.

'Put me back on the bloody bike.' As last words go, these are about as likely to pass my lips as 'It's time someone taught those ostriches a lesson.' But they did good service for Simpson, rasped out defiantly after he collapsed while challenging for the leader's yellow jersey on the dreadful Mont Ventoux climb in the 1967 Tour de France.

By dying, and by dying from heart failure brought about by overzealous consumption of the amphetamines that were later found both in his liver and jersey pocket, Simpson became the first Englishman to make a newsworthy contribution to the Tour since its debut in 1903. His fate showed both that the Tour's uniquely monstrous demands were requiring men to perform beyond their limits, and that despite this they would willingly gamble their lives in exchange for one of sport's greatest prizes.

Tommy's tragedy was the focus of an article I once read in a weekend supplement. Its theme was that though the lesson of his death was clear enough, it had not been learnt. I was particularly struck by the accompanying textbook-style illustration which suggested that, in an age where the demands of professional sport spawn outlandish physiques, there is no more grotesque specimen than the Tour de France cyclist. His oiled, hairless thighs are basted Christmas hams; those stringy, wizened arms last night's leftover chipolatas. Strip him, as the artist had down one half, and it gets worse – lungs so enlarged that they can squeeze out below his ribcage like a nascent pot belly, abrupt tan-line tidemarks delineating sun-broiled flesh from the ghostly, pallid areas forever sheathed beneath shorts and jersey. Inside his body, years of drug abuse have thickened his blood to the consistency of toothpaste, extruded laboriously through the leathery ventricles of a heart distended by relentless cardiovascular activity.

It isn't a good look, overall, but at least they don't have to put up with it for long. Given the ludicrous demands of the event and its associated history of dangerously pioneering chemistry, it wasn't surprising to learn that those who have competed in years gone by can look forward to the briefest retirement in professional sport. A life expectancy more than a decade and a half below the average means anyone seeking to organise a cycling Seniors Tour would struggle to recruit a quorum.

These were all terrible tidings. I had begun to imagine my own

Tour as a long jaunt through vineyards and sunflowers; maybe I'd get sunburn and a sore arse, but I didn't fancy going into an Alpine pharmacy with one hand holding my lungs in and the other flicking through the phrasebook for 'my organs are distended'. If these things happened to healthy young jocks in their sporting prime, what about a man theoretically old enough to have fathered children who remembered Adam and the Ants?

I needed succour, and I found it in the achievements of Firmin Lambot. By winning the Tour at the age of 36, 'The Lucky Belgian' offered genuine hope that I, an entire year younger, might feasibly complete the course without doing a Tommy.

One

'Oh, it's you again.'

It's never wise to phone a Frenchwoman more than once in any given fortnight, even if – or perhaps especially if – she happens to work on a help desk. Asking the Tour de France press office for details of the race route was clearly ranked on the scale of telephonic enquiries somewhere between 'Have you ever considered the benefits of pet insurance?' and 'What colour knickers are you wearing?' No matter that the route had clearly been decided well before the release of the basic outline in September, some six months previously.

'We do not announce zis informations,' said the voice defiantly, 'until fifteen May.' The line went dead; you could just imagine her flinging the phone down in petulant exasperation as a sympathetic press-office colleague looked up from her *Paris Match* and, slowly unwrapping another bon-bon, said, 'Don't tell me – another journalist.'

Anyway, it was a date. The plan, as it stood, was to complete the Tour route before the race itself set off on 1 July. Departing on 15 May gave me six weeks in which to do so – double the time allotted to the professionals; it also meant I would be 35 for three whole days of the period. On the other hand, all I now had to plot and prepare for my odyssey were a month and a postcard-sized map of the country with a squiggly line linking the start and end points of each stage, torn from the October issue of *procycling*.

Each Tour has a new route – travelled clockwise one year, anticlockwise the next. The 2000 Tour was an anticlockwise one. Starting in the centre-west of the country, the line meandered briefly north into Brittany before turning back on itself, sweeping down to the Pyrenees, then across Provence via Simpson's Ventoux to the Alps. Here it flailed madly about for a disturbing amount of time, working its way circuitously northwards: 'The entire length of the French Alps from the south, a route last taken in 1949, with the Cols d'Allos, Vars and Izoard, all over 2,000 metres high,' panted *procycling* eagerly. Then it was two days in Switzerland and Germany, crossing back over the Rhine in Alsace and working westwards to the traditional Parisian finish.

The accompanying map had the benefit of being small, but most of the important figures in a box alongside did not.

5 July, stage five: Vannes–Vitré, 198 km.

6 July, stage six: Vitré–Tours, 197 km.

7 July, stage seven: Tours–Limoges, 192 km.

Six hundred kilometres in three days, as near as 'dammit' is to swearing, though not quite as near as 'fuck that'. Can I have a rest now?

8 July, stage eight: Limoges–Villeneuve-sur-Lot, 200 km.

9 July, stage nine: Agen–Dax, 182 km.

10 July, stage ten: Dax–Lourdes/Hautacam, 205 km.

11 July, stage eleven: Bagnères-de-Bigorre–Revel, 219 km.

Apparently I could not. In seven days, the riders would cover a distance that in different and rather foolish circumstances would see them pedalling up to the outskirts of Warsaw. Worse, I knew from my television experiences that a lot of these kilometres would be breezed through by riders idly chatting to team-mates with their arms off the handlebars as they maintained speeds which even the ugliest exertions would leave me some way short of.

Not that there'd be any of that when the mountains got going. The route might change, but every Tour is won and lost in the second week, when the Pyrenean and Alpine climbs meet an angry sun halfway, the last stragglers wobbling over the line in graphic distress after eight scorched and airless hours in the saddle. Footballers whine if they're asked to play more than a single ninety-minute game a week. Olympic athletes demand a day of rest after running half a lap of the track. But when the Tour de France hits the mountains, its competitors have to haul themselves to the ragged edge of exhaustion from dawn to dusk, day after day, inching agonisingly up the highest roads in Europe and then careering lethally down them.

To this end, *procycling* had also helpfully included a 'gradient profile' of stage twelve, Carpentras–Le Mont Ventoux. As learning curves go, they didn't come much steeper: an alarming succession of peaks and troughs that looked like the printout of a lie-detector test. Two impressive 3,000-foot cols caused jerky fluctuations of the sort you'd expect from Jeffrey Archer comparing O-level results with Pinocchio, then – whoosh! – there was Jonathan Aitken booking Baron von Munchausen into the Ritz as up to Ventoux the line soared crazily off the scale.

All in all, there were 3,630 kilometres (which may be more familiar to you as 2,256 miles) and sixteen mountains to be conquered in three weeks. It was the equivalent of cycling from London to Bristol every day, only with Swindon wreathed in cold mist atop a towering peak so steep you'd be kneeing yourself in the face if you walked up it.

Slowly, certainly, the wrongheadedness of my initial pledge was dawning on me. With two weeks to go and my train ticket to Dover already rashly purchased, I knuckled down. I took out temporary membership of a gym, bought *Chris Boardman's Complete Book of Cycling*, and tried to fix the Peugeot's brakes.

I didn't take too much notice of the text side of Mr Boardman's volume after reading of the importance of training on Christmas Day to establish a psychological advantage over one's rivals, and coming across phrases such as 'The Tour came close to destroying me because it slowly drained my spirit . . . The Tour is the limit. It is the Olympics, Wimbledon and the World Cup all rolled into one. It is the highest level of sport . . . That feeling in the pit of your stomach that the next three weeks are going to hurt.'

On this basis, it didn't seem ideal that with less than a fortnight before departure I didn't actually own a roadworthy bicycle. Jogging for half an hour up and down the towpath every evening was a step in the right direction, but not a very big one. I needed to do some cycling. Or anyway some cycling-type exercises.

Chris Boardman, a former Olympic gold medallist and the first Englishman since Tom Simpson to wear the yellow jersey in the Tour, might reasonably be expected to know something about preparatory exercises. Holding a hand over the accompanying words (the mere mention of 'the muscle group at the front of your thighs' made me feel squeamish), I was soon mimicking Mr Boardman's line-drawn simulacrum on a twice-daily basis. Pressing a heel back to a buttock, pushing a wall, even lowering nose to (or anyway towards) thigh with my leg up on a chair (I'd work up to the illustrated table option just as soon as the sensation that my knees were about to snap forward the wrong way seemed less compelling): these at least had an authentic air, the kind of thing you might see footballers doing on the touch-line, albeit with fewer daughters hanging on to their legs and necks. Others, notably the spinal mobility and gluteus maximus stretches, cajoled me into whimsical poses last struck when Miss Pillins asked 2Y to imagine we were spring's first snowdrops emerging from the frosted soil.

In recent years, those snowdrops have invariably been accompanied by a savage and ridiculous new gym fad, and they don't come much more savage or ridiculous than spinning. Melding an exercise bicycle to the traumatic peer-pressure, barked commands and hysterical hi-NRG soundtrack of aerobics, I'd been told that spinning was to a jog around the river what bear-baiting was to yoga. It seemed sufficiently drastic. With a week left I went off and spun.

The airless spinning room at my local gym consisted of a claustrophobic mass of exercise bicycles arranged in tight, respectful semicircles before the instructor's machine; settling myself indelicately into the lofty saddle amid two dozen sinewy women in their forties and a fat, red Irishman, it occurred to me that if (or ideally when) we were all vaporised by Martian invaders the first member of the mopping-up squad to poke his little green head round the door would imagine he had discovered some hallowed chamber where obscure rotary homage was paid to King Spin. Only later did I realise that with all that tiresome bellowed encouragement, those clashing elbows, the soul-destroying, out-of-the-saddle, give-no-quarter competitiveness, a spinning class was a static peloton, the closest approximation to a desperate bunch finish I would ever experience.

I'd sat next to the Irishman in the hope of faring well by comparison, but after ten minutes of hectoring, Flashdance and increased wheel resistance ('Crank it up a notch, and one and two and UP on the pedals and give me ten and GO!') the sweat was already cascading in an unbroken stream from lowered chin to pumping knees, flying off the uselessly whirring front wheel and splattering toned, hairless flesh in a generous radius. Part of the deal in gyms, and indeed in professional cycling, is never to exhibit real pain or distress. Consequently, when we got into the uphill double-time sprinting the instructor, perhaps noting my uncanny visual impersonation of a man being exorcised in a sauna, slipped quietly off his bike and sidled over. 'Take it easy, eh?' he whispered soothingly as Donna Summer began to feel love. The phlegmy, rutting grunt that was all I could manage by way of response did not help my case.

After that I started lowering the resistance control a notch whenever he said to turn it up, but, even so, winding down at the end of the forty-minute session I felt very, very bad; worse, in fact, than I had ever felt. The techno thump of a shell-shocked heart filled my head; most of my muscle groups had disbanded and a leather-aproned medieval butcher was clumsily yanking my hamstrings. As I shakily dismounted into an unsightly puddle of body fluids, I had a strong sensation that my feet had somehow been stretched and extruded into platform-soled appendages.

'First time?' said the Irishman, who somehow looked further from death than he had before.

'Last time?' tinkled a hollow-cheeked, hawser-armed woman, her lilac crop top blemished with the merest sprinkling of perspiration that in any case was probably mine.

I didn't (or rather couldn't) say anything in reply, but explained myself to the instructor after the following day's session. 'That's quite an undertaking,' he said, implying that I would need quite an undertaker. One of 'his' women had recently returned from cycling over the Andes; another was off to the Himalayas. 'Don't worry,' he said, noting that this news had failed to comfort or inspire, 'that was a pretty big hill we just simulated. About 22 kilometres. And you'll only need to work at maybe 20 per cent of that rate.'

I nodded wetly. All I could think was that I'd just wasted 22 kilometres going nowhere in a room full of hot Lycra. There would be times, I imagined, when I would dearly want those 22 kilometres back, saving them up as a joker to be played in some epic Alpine crisis. 'Except,' he said, squinting thoughtfully, 'I suppose you'll need to be at it for about eight hours a day.'

Somehow blanking out the enormity of this task, I managed one more spinning class and two jogs. Then, gingerly consulting Chris Boardman, I came across the startling revelation that 'with one week to go, training should be finished . . . It is highly unlikely that you will generate more form in this time.' With five days left, interpreting this theory of 'tapering' a regime as a competition approached ('the volume of work is slowly reduced as the objective approaches'), I tapered my training rather more abruptly to a standstill. Everyone knows what the tough are said to do when the going gets tough. But I went shopping.

The sporting-goods industry prospers from the eternal truth that people who are not very good at something would rather blame a lack of expensive equipment than their own physical failings. Certainly rectifying the former is a lot quicker. Every time I looked at those little line drawings of Mr Boardman down on all fours howling silently at an unseen moon or getting his leg over the dining table, I felt an itching desire to slam his scary book shut and go into town to buy things made out of carbon fibre.

Not knowing anything about bikes, or at least bikes costing more than fifteen quid, flicking helplessly through the cycling-magazine adverts in Smith's was a sobering experience. It seemed to be quite easy to spend considerably over £1,500 just on a frame, a wheelless, chainless, pedalless diamond-shaped assemblage of metal tubes. Almost randomly, I came up with a figure of half this amount as my budget for a complete bicycle. Venturing much below this price raised fears of another two-wheels-on-my-Trabant DDR special, meaning that metal fatigue would set in after four days, and that on the way to pick it up my father would appear out of nowhere to place a kind, worldly hand on my shoulder and explain that the male menopause was nothing to be scared of. Beyond £750, I would be too crap to notice the difference, as well as potentially falling foul of the general rule that very expensive pieces of machinery require regular expert maintenance. I didn't want a Fiesta or a Ferrari. A nice Golf would do me.

I can't quite remember why the GT ZR3000 first appealed. It may have been the memory of the slanting GT logo flashed along many of the peloton's crossbars; it may have been because that crescendo of numerals and digits conjured images of an enormously overpowered motorcycle, thereby suggesting great speed with minimal human effort. When a call to GT's Martin Warren revealed that the ZR3000 was last year's model and could therefore be offered at an attractive discount, the deal was done. 'Do you want to assemble it yourself, or . . .?' he asked, ending the whimper-punctuated silence that followed with, 'Or . . . yes, I'll, um, put you down for the "or" option.'

The bike, of course, was only the start of it. An astonishing 4,000 people make up the Tour's travelling entourage – journalists, officials, members of the crap-chucking publicity caravan – and 600 of them are there to support the twenty teams who each enter nine riders. Ferried about in over a thousand official vehicles, they carry food, drink, spare parts, spare clothing, vitamins and, er, 'vitamins'. I would have to get all this stuff, and carry it myself in panniers.

There are plenty of people whose dark, dull lives are lit up by opportunities to patronise and humiliate those they encounter in their professional capacity. Although most of these people work in the police force or Paris, while acquiring the peripherals for my trip I was intrigued to note the number that had made their horrid little homes behind the counters of bicycle retailers.

I'd avoided them up to now, but with time running out I had to get help where I could. In tones normally reserved for asking small children to pop down the shops for a tin of elbow grease, I was scathingly informed that the ZR3000, as well as being last year's model and therefore on a competitive par with a swingbin full of fag-ends and used teabags, was risibly inappropriate for my task. The lugs, whatever and wherever they might be, would snap clean through as soon as I attached panniers, and actually the pannier rack wouldn't fit anyway, and in any case only a really major prannet would ever use panniers – and listen to this, Dave, there's a bloke here reckons he's doing the Tour de France, right, and he doesn't even know if his bike's got Presta valves or Schraders.

It was Martin Warren, perhaps mindful of the extraordinary number of wankers I would be encountering, who had suggested I talk to Richard Hallett, technical editor of *Cycling Weekly*, a man apparently much sought after for his rare ability to offer advice on clothing and equipment without snorting in helpless derision. I hadn't really wanted to trouble him, but being told by two awful men in a shop on the Fulham Road that I didn't walk like a cyclist was the last straw and I gave the man Hallett a call. He listened patiently while I explained my quest, then, rather sharply, asked his only question.

'Are you fat at all?'

The fact that I am not had, in all honesty, been my sole source of solace while surveying the library of cycling-related literature I was steadily building up. The big sprinters might be bollard-thighed bruisers, but the climbers – those whose bikes skipped lightly up the terrible bare slopes of Ventoux and the Izoard – were often frail-looking and pigeon-chested in a way I could cheerfully relate to. In fact, ludicrous as it may sound, in more expansive moments I had allowed myself to entertain fantasies, based on the recurrent assertion that 'good climbers are born, not made', that even without preparation I might belatedly emerge as an Alpine specialist of some note.

'No,' I replied, making the most of a scarce opportunity to express pride. (Later I wondered how he would have reacted if I'd said, 'Why, yes, I am! I'm a great big lardy pie-man!')

'Well, you probably won't die then. Now let's talk kit.'

18

If I had wanted answers like 'Well, it depends what you're looking for', Richard Hallett would not have been the man to ask. I did not know what I was looking for; I wanted to be told. Richard was more of a 'Selle Italia Turbomatic 3; Michelin Axial Pro 25Cs; Shimano SH-MO36' kind of guy, and as such deserves my heartfelt gratitude. Saddle, shoes, tyres, type of lock, tools and many of the other issues I had failed to consider were resolved in a brief series of staccato sentences. '. . . Then you'll need to take four inner tubes, one spare outer casing, hex keys, three pairs of bib shorts, two bottle cages . . . oh, and plenty of Savlon.'

'For when I fall off?'

'No. Well, yes, but not mainly. Stops boils and infections. Need to apply it every morning to anywhere that's in contact with the saddle. Do you know where your perineum is?'

He paused, perhaps sensing that with this phrase our conversation had moved into unacceptable territory. But perhaps not. 'Smear it all over your arse and bollocks, basically.'

I'm sorry, Mr Hallett, but there is nothing basic about smearing anything all over your arse and bollocks. I had a wretched premonition of sitting naked on a hotel bidet, morosely anointing my loins like a husband-to-be on a one-man stag night.

'It's just a fact. Your bollocks will sweat; infection will set in.' Richard Hallett was now sounding like a forthright sergeant major giving his platoon a lecture on the perils of consorting with the local girls. Then, drifting briefly out of character, he added in an odd, dreamy voice, 'So, yeah . . . really *slather* it on.'

A succession of delivery men arrived at my door over the days ahead, bringing Ortlieb panniers, Parrot waterproof clothing, wraparound Oakley shades and other equipment intended to make it look as if I knew what I was doing. To atone for this, I had eschewed a state-of-the-art Tour jersey for a monochrome Peugeot one of archaic design, similar to those worn both by the young Eddy Merckx and Tom Simpson. If it hadn't been for the aggressively synthetic composition – 'to wick away the sweat', said the website I ordered it from – I could have grown to love it, certainly more so than the lewdly comic Lycra shorts, whose gusset featured a thick, ventilated pad like a sanitary towel from the pre-'wings' era. It did not take my children long to establish that the rigidity of this structure allowed the shorts to stand up by themselves when placed on a flat, firm surface.

Finally, with my departure three days away, I opened the door to be greeted by a cardboard box the size of a mattress. ZR3000 had landed. In a state of childish excitement I tore open the packaging: inside was a very blue, very light machine with tyres as thin and hard as Hula-Hoops. Counting the sprockets (as I have since learned to call the cogs at either end of the chain) revealed that, with three sizes on the front and nine at the back, I would have twenty-seven gears at my disposal. These, I discovered after protracted panic and a phone call to Martin Warren that began with aggrieved gabbling and ended in a painfully embarrassed whisper, were selected by pressing the brake levers in and out.

With barely less difficulty I fitted Richard Hallett's recommended sit-upon – a no-mercy buttock-cleaver that recalled the old *Yellow Pages* ad where a young lad pedals off into a Yorkshire dawn on his birthday present while dad, peering out of the net curtains, mutters indulgently to himself, 'I were right about that saddle.' There had been much debate about the saddle. Some had advised me to go for a podgy, gel-filled number; Hallett, his complicated psyche awash with infected testicles and Stakhanovite toil, insisted that such a saddle would do me no favours in the long run. 'You'll be comfortable for three days, but then the sores will start,' he'd said, illustrating this theme with the parable of Holland's Joop Zoetemelk, who had silenced a press conference during the 1976 Tour by rolling up his shorts to reveal an intimate boil the size of an egg.

I'd been warned to expect trouble with the pedals, or more particularly the ski-type binding mechanism that is nowadays employed to attach them to the shoes. I'd never even ridden with toe clips, which had lashed every Tour rider's feet to his pedals from 1903 until the mid-Eighties. As someone who never feels truly at ease on a bicycle unless I can put both feet flat on the floor when waiting at traffic lights, the idea of being strapped tightly to the pedals was unsettling to say the least. But at least you could see toe clips, big stainless-steel bands round the top of the shoe. And when you had seen them, all you had to do to free the foot was to pull it back. The essential trouble with the newer system was that the cleat (a word whose leg-iron, penal twang would come to haunt me) which slotted into the pedal was on the sole of the shoe, utterly out of sight. And so utterly out of mind.

Having wobbled gingerly along the pavement to Kew Bridge on my debut ride (in cleated shoes but not the jersey and shorts, which I didn't yet feel qualified to wear), I was deeply disturbed by the head-down, humpbacked riding position, which as well as being instantly uncomfortable was also dangerous: to look where you were going rather than where you'd just been required an unnatural – and additionally uncomfortable – craning of the neck. None of this was assisted by the drop handlebars: so narrow and rigid that every slight hump or lump made my whole frame vibrate like a tuning fork; so featherweight and fickle that riding off a kerb was like barrelling out of some rodeo pen on an unbroken steer. Experimenting with the surfeit of gears I clanked and clunked down into gear twenty-seven: my feet spun manically, a dozen resistance-free rotations for a couple of car lengths' progress. Monstrous as this seemed, a small part of my brain acknowledged that there would be times when I'd be pressing down with the full weight of my breaking body to get gear twenty-seven creaking agonisingly round, times when twenty-seven wouldn't be enough, not nearly enough.

Seconds later, however, none of this seemed to matter. Clicking back into gear fifteen or so I was astonished by ZR3000's effortless straight-line performance: on other bicycles

I have owned, the drawn-out, rising span of Kew Bridge has always been an out-of-the-saddle lung-burster. I swept majestically past two schoolgirls on mountain bikes and immediately began to feel rather successful.

What is it pride comes before? Ah, yes. Cresting the bridge at a canter, and speeding down the other side, I was suddenly confronted with a long queue of stationary traffic; caught off-guard by the abrupt efficiency of the brakes, I inevitably forgot to perform the viciously pigeon-toed ankle twist required to liberate shoe from pedal. The good news was that I had come to a halt at a bus stop and by embracing the eponymous concrete post was able to avoid keeling gently over into four lanes of rush-hour traffic. The bad news was that there were a good two dozen people in the queue, and that the vaudevillian première of Mister Drunkpedal offered unexpected but welcome entertainment to every one of them, except perhaps the schoolboy who had been leaning against the bus stop.

As inauspicious starts go, this was right up there with Captain Scott peering out of his tent across the tundra and saying, 'Well, I don't know about the rest of you, but this isn't anything like how I imagined South Poland.' There were less than a hundred hours to go and the more people I talked to, the more disheartened I became. Martin Warren went very quiet when I phoned him to ask how often you were supposed to oil the brake pads, and my friend Matthew was clearly appalled by the grandiose scale of my ignorance and incompetence during a hands-on tutorial on removing the rear wheel. A call to another friend, Simon O'Brien, who will thank me for mentioning his Liverpool bike-shop/café, The Hub, but probably won't for referring to his distant notoriety in the role of *Brookside*'s Damon Grant, was regularly interrupted by prolonged gales of incredulous laughter.

During the small gaps in between these, Simon did at least impart what seemed like useful advice. Don't try to average more than about 80 kilometres (50 miles) a day; pre-book yourself into a nice hotel every ten days or so to give you a target to aim at and a reward for meeting it; shovel in carbohydrates. 'You cannot eat too much,' he stressed, which are just the words you want to hear when you're about to set off for a month in France, assuming you don't hang around for Simon's next sentence. 'Especially prunes and bananas.'

However saddening is the thought of filling a dry mouth with warm brown fruit, this prospect was at least preferable to the nutritional options suggested when I searched the Internet discussion forums. 'For a 200k ride, I usually pack four Power Bars and twelve Fig Newtons,' wrote one Canadian endurance enthusiast. I tried to imagine what a Power Bar might look like, and tried not to imagine what a Fig Newton might taste like. Fig Newton. It sounded like a result in that old game of deriving a porn-star alter ego from adding the name of your first pet to the street you lived in as a child.

The stuff was starting to accumulate. My Ortlieb panniers were soon complemented by a neat little bag that clipped to the handlebars and would eventually become my best friend, and having fitted all these, a process which probably needn't have involved quite so many hours, or indeed hissing at pieces of dismantled bicycle like a cornered stoat, I filled them.

Looking now at the list I compiled then, I can see the word 'shaver' crossed out, rewritten and crossed out again. I'd been agonising for weeks in advance about methods of saving weight, ever since reading Mr Boardman's assertion that even a couple of kilos could make the difference between whistling up the Giant of Provence and floundering grimly in the Valley of Death. My faithful Braun electric (175 grams) had assumed a crucial symbolic significance: by substituting it for a featherlight but wretched Bic disposable razor (7 grams), I would prove I was taking this thing seriously. I even pondered not shaving, before reaching the conclusion that after a month of harsh sun and prunes I'd be looking enough like Robinson Crusoe as it was.

Only when I made a heap of the essentials did I accept the hopelessness of it all. Maps, spares, tools, lock, all-weather clothing and, however often I tried to hide it beneath the multivitamins and toothbrush, a huge, leering tube of Savlon: with all that shoved into the panniers, ZR3000, once such a flighty will-o'-the-wisp that you could pick it up with two fingers, now required two people to perform the same task.

Oh, what was the point. In for a penny, in for a pound, I thought – or, more accurately, in for a pound, in for ten stone. I'd restricted my après-cycling evening wardrobe to one T-shirt, a pair of pants, thin cotton trousers and the selfsame footwear I would have been cleated into all day, but now threw in three additional shirts and the same of pants, baggy beach shorts, a load of socks and a pair of espadrilles. A couple of hefty guidebooks were promoted from the standby list, along with half a dozen back copies of *procycling* Matthew had lent me. The Braun joined them, though as a token gesture I didn't take the plastic head cover or the funny little cleaning brush. I also cut my nails down to the quick, took off my signet ring and had a very severe haircut. Then I sat down and watched a video.

Tour de France 1903–1985 did exactly what it said on the box, until the end. After a studiously forthright appraisal of the Tour's great riders, the badly dubbed, nasally British voiceover clicked clumsily off to be replaced by a rousing, if slightly approximate burst of *Onedin Line*-style orchestration. Then, over a visual backdrop of grainy Sixties Tour footage, a man who sounded a lot like Charles Aznavour trying to do Orson Welles began to speak in a voice charged with portent.

'Like one of Napoleon's soldiers, a racer in the Tour de France need only say, "I was there," to provoke the respect and admiration given to one who is ranked among exceptional human beings, part of an élite who seeks to excel through effort and suffering, and like Guillaumet, mechanic to the aviator Mermoz, he can say, "I have done what no animal can do."'

24

There was a short pause here, presumably while the narrator imagined two sheep standing flummoxed before an aeronautical tool kit. Then the epic soundtrack blared waywardly again and the commentary recommenced.

'In an apparent paradox, the racer achieves transcendence of himself, and his sense of the absolute, by reaching deep into himself and dreaming himself, as animals do when the survival instinct orders them to walk, to run, to fight. The racer in the Tour has his place somewhere between the animals and the gods, sometimes one, sometimes the other, often both, always oscillating between these two opposite poles of his destiny.'

Well, that was something to look forward to. Perhaps I'd got it all wrong. Instead of building up muscle bulk, or anyway making feebly half-hearted efforts at doing so, I should instead have been fine-tuning my sense of the absolute. A good, hard session on the transcendental treadmill and I'd be destiny-oscillating with the best of them.

Regrettably, my one extended training run – to Harrow and back, perhaps a 20-mile round trip – suggested that my place would be rather closer to the animals than the gods, and indeed within that former category rather closer to the invertebrates than the mammals. Bucking along the North Circular Road's bike-path pavement past Gunnersbury Park, I had to brake sharply, and therefore painfully, to avoid contact with a large cyclist emerging at speed through the park gates alongside. Mercifully uncleated, I had come to a lopsided halt with our wheels barely an inch apart. Feeling as if I had mistaken Deep Heat for Savlon, I looked up to see that the large cyclist was the type of middle-aged, Harrington-jacketed skinhead that everyone apart from newspaper cartoonists assumed had long since moonstomped off our high streets.

'Sorry, mate,' he said, but the eager sneer snagging his thin, cold-sored lips suggested there would be strings attached to this apology. It was no particular surprise, having cycled wordlessly on my way, to hear the loud shout of 'PRICK!' ringing out from behind.

Later, I marvelled at the wretched chemistry apparently created by combining me and a bicycle with Gunnersbury Park. Almost thirty years on, here I was again, being curtly abused by an ugly, bored male. Now that I consider the two events, it is in fact easily possible that both involved not just the same stage but the same actors.

The brain makes rapid calculations in moments like this, and as I trumped his insult in terms of both volume and profanity I was barely aware of having established that my enemy's bulk and inferior machinery made a successful pursuit unlikely. Certainly this calculation took no account of my own fitness, nor the fact that my sudden stop had left me in an appropriately high gear. If there is one thing more debilitating than running away, it is doing so while pretending not to. Striving to find a balance between life-saving flight and face-saving nonchalance, I ground in private agony up the North Circular Road, not daring to look round until I topped Hanger Hill two miles up the road.

This effort, coupled perhaps with an unwisely piquant supper that had paid extravagant homage to a lifelong fondness for Tabasco, malt vinegar and grapefruit juice, so disturbed my body's pH balance that freewheeling down towards the Hanger Lane Gyratory System I began to feel very unwell. It started as a stitch, I suppose, but the little man with the needle soon got carried away. Wincing, I dismounted alongside a huddle of pavement smokers outside a large office building, with the sensation of being internally tattooed. During my many subsequent distress stops, I established that temporary relief could be procured by bending double and stoutly pushing the left side of my stomach in with both hands. This was not a pose one would choose to sustain by the side of a public highway, and I would guess that my resultant impersonation of a man attempting to remove his own spleen attracted some interest among the rush-hour commuters of northwest London.

I arrived at the Harrovian residence of my friend Paul Rose looking like Stephen Roche at la Plagne and sounding like Stephen Hawking at la Scala. Helping me over his threshold, he set about my rehabilitation. This process incorporated three beers, six Rennies and several dozen viewings of a crafts-channel cable TV video clip wherein an erstwhile innocuous sculptor expresses abrupt and radical disgust for his half-finished feline creation by decapitating it with a single, lusty uppercut. It had taken me two hours to get there; the return leg required a quarter of this time.

Even so, it had not been an encouraging maiden voyage. In fact, if I had been planning to cycle to, say, Oxford or Brighton, I'd probably have called it off. In a strange way, only the sheer scale of my itinerary stopped me from losing heart: that daftly inflated figure of 3,630 kilometres was difficult to take seriously.

The night before leaving, very slightly drunk, I'd wandered down my road to the river. It was balmy; a group of girls sat around a cheerily crackling bonfire on the foreshore; before I'd even left, the elements and environment were in cahoots to engender homesickness. Almost inevitably there was a little crowd of French students on and around a towpath bench, and almost inevitably they were talking with some excitement about the Tour de France. Though I only got the odd noun – 'Armstrong', 'Virenque', 'EPO' (the notorious haemoglobin-boosting drug) – the relish was unavoidable. The race was still over a month off and already the expatriate youth of Gaul were on amber alert.

ZR3000 was propped by the front door, and on the way back in I squeezed round it, wondering how I felt about my bicycle now and how those feelings would have changed after 2,256 miles. Bowed down with baggage, the machine's lean, hungry look was gone: it was like putting a roof-rack on a Lotus. My children had fulsomely decorated the saddle's diminutive surface area with Cinderella stickers (you *shall* go to the balls, Cinders); there were already long scratches and an ugly dent where my trailing cleat had failed to clear the crossbar when I repeatedly dismounted in clumsy agony en route to Harrow.

Was I really going to cock my leg over that crossbar and not uncock it for a month and a bit? As a perennially shiftless slacker I had been urged more than once to get on my bike. To think that it should come to this.

Two

Cycling is the national sport of France, so I'm slightly annoyed with myself for failing to predict that it is consequently impossible to take bicycles on French trains. Or, even more appropriately, that it *is* possible, but only on randomly selected local services, and then on condition that the bicycle is dismantled, boxed, put on a freight train scheduled to show up seventy-two hours after your own before being thrown into the canal by a mob of opticians protesting about biscuit subsidies.

Newly acquainted with this reality brief hours before departure at least gave me something else to think about as my family pushed me out through the door into a glorious morning. Seven stages began some distance from where the previous one had ended; I'd hoped to take trains between these points. More immediately – in fact in, um, six hours' time – I'd hoped to be on a train from Calais to Futuroscope, the technological theme park near Poitiers where the Tour was to start.

Organisation is not my strongest suit. When I look down from aeroplane windows at the complex urban landscapes below it is in slack-jawed admiration for the people who create and maintain them, with a parallel gut-punching terror at the thought of the cack-handed, jerry-built anarchy that would reign if I myself had been involved at anything approaching an executive level. It had been an overwhelming enough task just to gather together the equipment for my tour (I'd give that a capital T at the same time as I felt I'd earned the right to wear the shorts and jersey); here I was, loaded up like a camel, and the news about the French trains was the straw that broke my back.

My sons' classmates were being taken to school, and as I cycled laboriously by, trying to haul all those panniers up to some sort of cruising speed, a couple of mothers recognised me and waved in a manic, give-'em-hell sort of way. I wasn't about to lift any part of my hand from the unsteady bars to return the greeting, and in any case lacked the spiritual wherewithal.

Fussing fretfulness about the transport situation, compounded by Birna's failed last-minute attempts to drum up a volunteer force to accompany me, had left me vulnerable to more elemental fears: I was beginning to feel like a blithe young conscript being sent off for a brutal, filthy death at the front; a butterfly to be broken upon two wheels. Even people who knew nothing about cycling, nothing about sport, seemed to be aware that the Tour de France was a grim and vicious ordeal. The reality had been postponed and ignored for as long as possible, but now there it was, staring in spiteful digits from the little multi-function odometer at the front of the crossbar. 0.97 . . . 0.98 . . . are my shoulder blades supposed to be feeling like this already? . . . 0.99 . . . Jesus, that van just missed my elbow with its wing mirror . . . 1.0. Pain and danger in one kilometre. Three thousand six hundred and twenty-nine to go.

Battered and clattered about in the otherwise empty guard's van – a proper old one lined with planks and many generations of fag-jaundiced gloss paint – ZR3000 and I made our irregular progress to Dover. Someone had left behind a copy of the *Daily Telegraph*; I got to the sports section as we rattled across the green belt and there, staring out across some bleak-looking mudflats with his elbows resting on the lofted saddle of a muddy-wheeled mountain bike, was a man I recognised as Mr Christopher Boardman. Even in Britain the Tour hype had started already. Mr Boardman, not a man given to hyperbole, described the forthcoming challenge as 'physically very unpleasant'; to drum up something more appropriately dramatic, the writer had introduced the interview with a quote from Greg LeMond, an American who in 1990 won the last of his three Tours. 'At the end of the first stage your lungs are on fire, your legs feel as though they have been plunged into molten tar, your arms burn, your chest, your shoulders, your back, are aflame. Even your eyelashes ache. And ahead of you . . .' We whooshed into a tunnel and I stood there in the deafening dark, doing a couple of half-hearted back stretches and picturing Greg wincing over his Fig Newtons as the Savlon kicked in. We whooshed out again and the italics juddered before my eyes. 'And ahead of you lie another three weeks of Tour de France.'

He couldn't even bring himself to give it a 'the'. Without a definite article he'd made it sound like a ghastly punishment: 'I sentence you to three weeks of Tour de France.' Imagining it as a penal institution, I could understand why Chris Boardman had never fulfilled his potential in the Tour. All the pictures I'd seen of the Tour's greats showed the kind of expressions you could imagine gracing the Daddy of C-Wing. Jacques Anquetil, winner five times in the Sixties, had narrow, weasely features and a sarcastic sneer; baby-faced legend Eddy Merckx surveyed the world with a terrible, blank-eyed froideur that helped earn him the nickname Cannibal; Miguel Indurain, who dominated in the early Nineties, was a huge, silent Terminator. Scariest of all was Bernard Hinault, winner five times in the Seventies and Eighties.

His nickname was Badger, which sounds a bit *Wind in the Willows* unless you happen to have seen one in action against two Jack Russells in a video seized by the RSPCA. Hinault's default demeanour on a bicycle suggested he'd just been told that some bloke up the road was prancing around in a wedding dress singing, 'Bernard, Bernard, je m'appelle Bernard'. It was an unbridled, primal rage that one could quite easily imagine being sated only by a fight to the death with a load of dogs.

Chris Boardman, however, was just a friendly bloke with a big nose, peering mildly into the Southport mist with an expression that said, 'On a clear day I can see me mam's house from here.' He was an exceptional cyclist, but he was no Cannibal. If you had to give him a nickname it would be The Grocer.

Half-heard snatches of notably less flattering epithets jeered down from French-exchange shoplifters on the sundeck as I freewheeled down the gangplank at Calais. But with ZR3000 weaving perilously through the articulated mayhem and on to French soil, I didn't really care. It had been a splendid crossing: I'd been the only cyclist on the ferry, and had ridden in through the cavernous bow doors exhilarated by the peculiarity of doing so, lashing my bike to a rusty railing beside those huge trailers of whatever it was of ours that the French could possibly admit to wanting. No less significantly, my mood had been lightened by the successful realisation of The Daytrip Gambit: twelve-hour returns are invariably much cheaper than singles, and I'd managed to blag the bike and me on to the boat for a fiver. Things had improved further with the mid-Channel epiphany that my logistical woes could of course be neatly resolved by hiring a car in Calais, dismantling the bike (stick that one on the back burner just for the moment), shoving it in the boot and dropping the car off in Poitiers.

'You are not maybe a mechanical man,' said the Avis official at the ferry terminal, watching as I made a mockery of the expressions 'quick-release hub', 'folding rear seat' and 'big boys don't cry'. 'Affirmative, master,' I said, in an idiotically camp C3-PO trill that failed to deter him from easing the now alarmingly cockeyed ZR3000 out of my battered hands. 'A beautiful vélo', he continued, working with neat efficiency as he filled my Volkswagen Polo with bicycle parts. 'You do a tour?'

I knew it was going to sound ridiculous, but I said it anyway. 'No. I do *the* Tour.'

Having mentally purged this exchange of its denouement, wherein Monsieur Avis turned slowly to showcase a cheesy 'that's the spirit, Tiger' wink of the sort normally reserved for young nephews who have expressed an intention to pilot the Space Shuttle, I set off for Poitiers in a portentous state of mind. With ZR3000's front wheel grazing my neck, I barrelled down a succession of autoroutes, many of them heading the right way, feeling like the Danish cyclist at the end of the 1973 Tour of Italy video I'd watched the night before, cheerily shoving his bike into the boot of a Peugeot 504 and speeding off into the Rome rush-hour with a farewell scratch of those big sidies. Off to the next race; wherever I lay my bike, that's my home; have bike, will ride; this bike's for hire – it's a tough job being a pro, but someone's got to do it. And here I was, flashing past old farmers dangling their leathery left arms out of Citroën van windows, my cleats clicking the clutch, doing it.

Sustaining this spirit for the six and a half hours it took me to get to Futuroscope was a challenge, but shuffling into the painstakingly anonymous reception of the Ibis hotel I was still clinging on to a thread. It was 10.15 p.m., and I caught the restaurant by the skin of my teeth; feasting alone among the impatient staff, I singlemindedly stocked up on carbohydrates before stumbling up to bed for a mercifully dreamless sleep.

Six hours later I was awake and peering blearily out of the window at the dawn-fringed outlines of some of the huge, mirrored tower blocks housing the enormous virtual-reality rides that are Futuroscope's raison d'être. Being flung down ski slopes,

33

hurtling through the Milky Way ('a vertigo-inducing 3-D nightmare' said the *Rough Guide to France* [620 grams], which was more than enough to put me off): there are cheaper ways of losing a pair of sunglasses and making yourself feel sick. Indeed, I was about to do one of them.

With its hordes of picnicking families and unashamed commercialism, the Tour de France is somehow a very Fifties event. It's appropriate, then, that the Tour regularly visits Futuroscope, whose breathless glorification of technological progress is the epitome of post-war, Dan Dare enthusiasm. There's something almost Communist about the desperation to showcase all this space-age know-how. The Concorde shambles didn't put them off: France still wants to have the fastest trains in the world, and the most nuclear power stations, and an active space programme. The hi-tech jet fighter that screamed terrifyingly over my helmet later that day provided the first of many saddle-soiling experiences with low-level training runs. While Britain's motor industry (silence at the back there, please) looks to past glories with retro-style Rovers and Jags, France is forever pushing out weirdly futuristic concept cars. The funny-faced Renault Twingo was considered so outré that they didn't even bother making a right-hand-drive model for our benefit.

After breakfast (another lock-up-your-croissants face-stuffer), I spread my Michelin maps on the table. The first stage prologue around Futuroscope was only 16 kilometres; even I could presumably manage this fairly smartly, then shove the bike in the boot, drop off the car in Poitiers and cycle back to rejoin the route for the next day's stage, Futuroscope to Loudun. Two stages in a day – stick that up your yellow jersey, boys.

There was a genial, flabby Dale Winton at reception; together we spent a short time plotting the progress of a column of ants across his desk before I asked him where, precisely, the Tour de France began.

It was 16 May, the day after the press office were to announce the route details. If nothing else, I thought, they'd have been looking forward to telling me exactly where to get off. Presently, however, it emerged that Dale had no idea what I was talking about, partly because despite mentally rehearsing the question several dozen times it had dribbled fitfully from my lips in an intriguing blend of languages – it would be two weeks before I stopped saying the Icelandic 'nei' instead of 'non' – and partly because of his preoccupation with the ants, and in particular the fact that the lead group had penetrated his switchboard. At length he presented me with a 1:5 billion scale map of western France and said, 'You try ze Futuroscope, ah, service de presse?'

Ten minutes later I was knocking gently on a little door by the park's entrance, surrounded by jabbering coachloads of schoolchildren waiting in the windy sunshine for the main gates to open for the day. I waited for a moment, then tried the handle. The door blew inwards and I crossed the threshold; before me stood a crisply presented young woman with an enamelled name badge detailing the flags of those countries whose nationals she was authorised to belittle.

The up-and-down look she poured slowly over me could have withered a vase of carnations at twelve paces, but in fairness it was difficult to take her to task. Back at the hotel I'd tried out my full Tour outfit for the first time: jersey, shorts, mirrored wraparounds, white Nike ankle socks, gloves, cleats. In the mirror it was surprisingly convincing, a symphony of lissom logos. It did not take me long, however, to establish that it was in fact too convincing. If you're going to walk the walk, you've got to talk the talk, but having already demonstrated incompetence at both disciplines I felt a fraud. If I was to avoid being shown up as the worst kind of inept poseur, the look would have to be diluted.

The Peugeot shirt made the cut, but was now teamed with a rather noticeable pair of baggy tartan shorts that sheathed those panty-linered Lycras. I kept the gloves, though the shades had gone, replaced as a facial accessory by a daftly bulbous white

35

helmet eerily reminiscent of the look pioneered by Woody Allen when playing the role of a spermatozoa. Big, fat, morning-campers panniers completed the picture. In the hotel mirror I'd looked the part; outside the Futuroscope press office I looked the prat.

Spying a Union Jack on her badge I piped up, 'I'm following the Tour de France, and it would be very useful if . . . if . . .' Something was wrong; I looked down and saw what it was. Her hand was on my chest – she was pushing me out of her office. Not quite knowing what else to do I carried on talking as she eased me outside and slammed the door behind us: '. . . If you . . . could . . .'

'Zis is a press office. It is perhaps more . . . correct to talk with you out of side.'

'No, no, I think it might be more correct to talk . . . in there, because I am a journalist, or anyway a writer, although I do look a bit of a bottom right now, but that's because I, um . . .'

'You 'ave a card? A press card?'

'Yes! No.'

It was looking bad, but I had an idea. I unhooked a pannier and began rummaging about, withdrawing a toothbrush, three socks and an E1–11 EC healthcare certificate that instantly blew away as the wind abruptly picked up. Aware that henceforth I would be treating my own compound fractures with a puncture-repair kit, I finally pulled out a copy of *procycling*.

'Here! This is the UK's premier publication for bikists,' I said in what had at least begun as an authoritative drawl. 'We run all sorts of features on pedals, handlebars, Savlon . . .'

She took the magazine and, having perfunctorily flicked through it, began examining the staff list on the masthead with the suspicious intensity of an Israeli border guard.

'Last month we blew the lid off Fig Newtons.'

'And your poste . . .?' she enquired briefly.

Well, that was easy. 'Technical Editor.'

'So you are . . . Steeeeve Robinson?'

'That's my name – don't wear it out.'

'Well, Monsieur Robinson, you 'ave a question?'

I looked at my hands and realised I'd put the gloves on the wrong ones. 'Yes. It's quite easy, actually: I'd just like to know the route of the first stage of the Tour de France.'

Her face lit up. 'No, no, no! I'm sorry, but it is not possible to say zis!'

'But the exact details were announced yesterday.'

She laughed horribly. 'No, no! It's a beeeeeeeg secret!'

'The Tour de France press office told me that—'

This was a serious tactical error, opening up whole new avenues down which bucks could be leisurely passed. 'Eh bien, well, you must talk wiss zem about it. Beeeeg secret 'ere!'

'It's not a very *good* secret, though, is it? The stage is only 16 kilometres long.'

We were now deep into shrug territory.

'But I'm almost certainly more important than you,' I said as the door eased shut in my face.

Cycling the long way round the enormous car parks into an already dispiriting headwind I took stock. My diminutive *procycling* Tour map implied that the prologue looped northwards from Futuroscope; only one road appeared to head off in this direction and after circling the roundabout in front of the Ibis about seven times I found it.

In less than five minutes I was in peasants-and-poppies rurality, an astonishing contrast with Futuroscope, but no doubt part of the reason the still heavily agricultural French are so obsessed with flaunting their technology. As a TGV powered steadily across a distant field as if being reeled in – the antithesis of that Thomas the Tank Engine affair aboard which I'd rattled through Kent – I remembered reading somewhere that as recently as 1965 only 15 per cent of French homes had telephones.

In less than ten minutes, of course, I was lost. I'd expected the route to be in some way obvious, lined with floral displays and

bunting, but, standing at a windswept hilltop crossroads surrounded by a billion acres of oil-seed rape and lowing cattle, I
realised it was not. Feeling lonely and ridiculous, I allowed myself
to be blown back to Futuroscope, where I again circled the
roundabout while wondering how to salvage something from this
towering anticlimax.

Forty minutes later, I braked to a slightly messy halt in a corner
of one of Futuroscope's desolate overspill car parks. In several
dozen clockwise circuits, before an understandably curious
audience of two gardeners and a coach driver, I had completed
my prologue; managing to focus on my odometer between
ragged exhalations I established that the 16 kilometres had been
undertaken at an average speed of 27.7 k.p.h., with a maximum
speed of 36.5. I knew the pros would average twice that, but it
didn't matter. My Tour had begun.

I was hot then and a lot hotter when I dropped the car off in
Poitiers and cycled back to find the route of stage two. The wind
had blown itself out, and as I assembled first ZR3000 and then a
complex baguette sandwich in the fascinatingly hideous car-
rental lot, the sun sat on me with its full weight. I'd never been to
Poitiers, and thought the old town seemed worth a look, but with
Brie being fondued in my lap and the bike's blue crossbar almost
too hot to touch I just wanted to hit the road and get some wind
in my hair.

Richard or Matthew or Simon or someone had told me the
heat wouldn't be a problem until I stopped or went uphill, and
they were right. The road northeast out of town offered views of
some arrestingly attractive châteaux, but when, at Dissay, I
stopped to look at one I found myself sagging into involuntary
siesta almost immediately. Besides, I wanted to get some
kilometres under my belt. After all, by now the real riders would
be . . . yes, actually, where would they be? I kept forgetting I was
making the route up as I went along. The best I could divine from
the *procycling* map was a sweeping spiral, up to the east of

Futuroscope, then north to Loudun, but trying to extrapolate anything cartographically meaningful from this was like giving someone directions from my house to Sainsbury's using a child's globe.

Still, I was heading in the right general direction and it was a splendid day if you kept on the move. Birds and crickets shrieked manically from roadside copses that exuded a strong smell of hot tea; old women in straw hats and housecoats prodded hoes at gaudily immaculate beds of irises. During a white-knuckle descent through Saint-Cyr I broke the 50 k.p.h. speed limit – a defining moment in my fledgeling career as a cyclist – and swallowed my first fly. I don't know why I swallowed a fly. Perhaps I'd die.

And curiously enough, in accordance with the generally accepted rule that steep downward hills are followed by steep uphill ones, after five minutes I almost had.

Simon had urged me to take advantage of the clear-plastic map-envelope thing on top of my handlebar bag, which permitted time-saving on-the-move navigation (albeit at the expense of taking another large step towards visual association with the worst sort of beardy hiking-socked cyclo-dullard). He had also recommended taking a set of hugely detailed ramblers' maps, but because this scheme involved the traumatic logistical undertaking of saving weight by mailing relevant batches of maps to poste-restante boxes in pre-booked hotels and sending the old ones home, I hadn't bothered. A more generously scaled map might have been more forthright in identifying the ascent of Beaumont as a labour straight out of Classical mythology; an illegibly minuscule couple of chevrons was all Monsieur Michelin had to say for himself, other than 'Please don't hurt me – I'm really stupid-looking and fat.'

As those with more experience than I had predicted, the heat soon become a very real issue as the road narrowed and rose; dropping my hazy gaze to the pitted asphalt immediately before me I was soon blinking body brine out of my eyes. I had not yet begun to master ZR3000's embarrassment of gears, forever clunking down at the front dérailleur when I meant to go up one at the back, but it had seemed inconceivable that I'd have any occasion to engage bottom gear, number twenty-seven, until I crossed the Pyrenean tree line. But though Beaumont was no doubt a mere pimple in professional cycling terms, here I was, grinding jerkily down into gear twenty-seven with the gradient still rising and the summit nowhere in sight.

'Spin the pedals,' I'd been told by Martin Warren. 'Get in an easy gear and keep the revs high.' Mr Boardman had been more specific. 'Maintain an average pedal cadence of around 80 revs per minute,' he'd said. The small parts of my brain not blaring manically like klaxons calculated this was more than one turn a second; surveying the humid, tortuous progress of my damp and reddening legs it seemed obvious that I was nearer 80 revs per hour.

Looking like Bernard Hinault giving birth to a cement mixer I made it to the village at the top, distantly grateful that because this was a mid-afternoon in France there was no one around to see me. At Poitiers I'd filled both my 750-millilitre bottles – or *bidons*, as I would quickly be bullied into calling them – and already they were empty. It was 40 broiled and brainless kilometres before I found anywhere to refill them, a grotty bar in Angliers through whose nicotined net curtains I could see a clutch of Tuesday-afternoon regulars sitting before little glasses of fluorescent aperitifs.

Until the Seventies it was a Tour tradition for riders to conduct lightning beverage raids in bars like this when the race passed through, tolerated and even eagerly awaited by the proprietors. As a silly-looking English tourist I hadn't anticipated the same reception, but as soon as I stumbled in with an empty in each hand the place came to life. Dogs barked; a vein-faced farmer raised his glass and muttered some well-meaning alcoholism;

the fulsomely moustached barman wrestled the bottles from me and filled them with a blend of iced water and orange juice ('Pour les vitamines,' he said with a genially conspiratorial wink). After a long draught of this mixture I realised the presence of humanity offered a belated opportunity to establish whether my made-up route to Loudun was in any way accurate.

'La Tour de France passe par ici?' I said, another rehearsed phrase that would be given regular daily outings – though not quite regular enough for me to establish that by not saying '*Le* Tour' I was in fact enquiring whether the tower of France would be passing through. Either way, however, the barman was not lying when, by means of the shaking head, the shimmied hand, the clucked palate and many more of the Frenchman's considerable armoury of negative expressions, he indicated that this was not so. 'La Roche-Rigault,' he said, slightly wistful for both our sakes at the near miss. It was a name I'd been seeing on signposts all afternoon.

Villages lobby for months or even years to be included in the itinerary: the towns that host the start or end of a stage pay the Tour organisers vast sums for the privilege. There is enormous prestige in being on the Tour route, but after the endless preparations – wholesale civic redecoration, new car parks – race day itself, as evidenced in the various reports I'd watched on Channel 4 over the years, seemed wilfully harrowing. First comes the grotesque cavalcade of promotional vehicles – mobile cereal packets and giant oranges manned by merchandise-hurling, garage-calendar blondes – before the riders themselves hurtle through in seconds, an alarming multicoloured swarm bookended by hooting and swerving support vehicles, police vans and motorcycle cameramen. It's like spending a year getting dressed up for a big date and then being showered with tacky gifts, rudely groped and roughly dumped all in the space of an afternoon.

The poor French. Cycling was their national sport, and they'd become rubbish at it: no winners since 1985; not even a stage victory for the last two years. I'd laughed about it before, but looking at the faces around me I realised how painful the last fifteen years must have been. 'To a country obsessed with a fear of demographic decline, economic failure and military defeat,' I'd read in an American account of the 1984 Tour, 'the Tour de France offered a comforting image of Frenchmen as tenacious, strong and swift.' Those were the days. In recent years their foot-ballers had won the World Cup and the European Champion-ships, but the average homme in the rue would have traded both of those for a native Tour champion.

Payment was proffered but flamboyantly shunned, and driven on by the dank, electrical whiff of a brewing thunderstorm I reached Loudun so quickly I almost rode straight through the place. Beginning at stage two's start point and ending at the right finish, I had done 104 kilometres – 65 miles – including my 16-kilometre stage-one car-park prologue. As the actual total for stage two alone was 191 kilometres, this did suggest that the corners I'd cut in between were generously angled, but at the time I really couldn't have cared less. I'd gone from A to B, exceeded my recommended daily 80 kilometres, and I had survived. Despite spurning the Savlon, there didn't seem to be any boiled eggs nestling among the usual contours down there; my buttocks had just about held their own in the battle of wills with the saddle. A quick flutter of the eyelashes – not a twinge, Mr LeMond. Having said all that, I usually find the time to take some of my clothes off before getting into bed, and don't often do so at 5.45 p.m.

Horribly disorientated, I woke up two hours later with my abdomen pleading noisily for rectification of a huge calorific deficit. The Ibis at Futuroscope could have been almost any-where, but taking belated stock of my immediate surroundings it occurred to me that I was now definitively in a French hotel. Balding flock wallpaper, knackered wooden shutters, carpet that exuded visual and olfactory evidence of having been licked by a dog rather than vacuumed, and under my aching neck an unyielding bolster pillow the size and weight of a drugged publican. Dopily I washed my shirt and shorts in the basin, then wrung them dry in the spare towel – an old pro's trick picked up from Paul Kimmage's book (how monstrous it seemed that, having flogged themselves half to death in the saddle, peloton riders were expected to relax by laundering their own filthy kit in a hotel bidet). Then, round-shouldered and espadrilled, I shuffled out to inspect the town that from the afternoon of 2 July to the following morning would be the focus of the sporting world's attention.

By being rather ugly and boring, Loudun offered the first suggestion that towns prepared to pay apparently large sums for brief glory as a 'ville d'étape' – one where a stage ended or began – were invariably hoping to rectify some sort of image problem. The threatened thunderstorm had come and gone during my slack-jawed coma, leaving the messy streets wet and empty; the only sign of life was a lot of bad-tempered shouting from a snooker hall under the scary hotel that I'd tried first and was delighted (not to say astonished) to be told was full. The *Rough Guide* could find no reason even to mention Loudun in the course of its 1,124 pages, and it wasn't hard to see why. From the trolleys upside-down in the pot-holed supermarket car park to the sombre ranks of dirty-windowed nineteenth-century terraces there was the drab, neglected air of a place where there was nothing to do and yet so much to be done.

A lot of the small towns I'd passed through that day had introduced their unique attractions beneath the road sign that welcomed you in: *Ouzilly – ses parcs, Lencloitre – son château.* Approaching Loudun the locals were getting desperate: *son camping* was the best one place could do; the next could only manage *son parking.* Loudun itself gave up altogether (though did proclaim to visitors that it had been twinned with a town in Burkino Faso, presumably because no one else would have it).

43

Outside a bar near the centre, however, I did see an ad for a modest casino wooing punters with the memorable boast *son craps*.

There were National Front posters on most of the many abandoned houses; the youth whose parents once occupied these places had presumably gone off to the Big Smoke, or at least the small puff that was Tours, 60 kilometres to the northeast. The few who remained now cruised mournfully about in sorrily customised, black-glassed old Renaults souped up by the traditional bucolic expedient of long-term exhaust neglect. Hordes of discarded blue flyers rain-glued to the pavement suggested that the place to go for club-style nightlife was Morton, which I later noticed was a tiny village over 20 kilometres away. Having perused the local estate-agent windows it wasn't hard to conclude that however tempting the possibility of trading your poky little London flat for a huge nineteenth-century château with turrets and woodland, you probably wouldn't want to do so if it meant having to do the weekly food shopping in Loudun.

Still, they were trying. After an aimless fifteen minutes of rather zombie-like, malnourished blundering, I eventually found myself in what must have been the old town, up on a slight hill, its narrow, meandering streets brightened with fountains and frantically scrubbed limestone. And wandering at random into a cellar crêperie, I pondered that though there isn't much to be said for being marooned in a dead-duck, dead-dull town, at least in a French one you get to eat well. Around me, even on a wet Tuesday night, shifty, sniggering kids were doing it en masse, clinking glasses of rosé and tossing their *salades vertes*, whereas in England they'd have been hanging dimly around a bench with a damp bag of chips, trying to think up a new way of melting stuff.

With the tolerance that the mean and hungry man experiences on finding himself presented with a large plate of cheap food, I set about a Bible-sized lasagne in a mood of rapprochement. The NF posters were old and faded. The Burkino Faso link imbued the

44

town with a sense of exotic mystery. The arrival of the Tour would resurrect Loudun's flagging fortunes and unite the dispirited populace; thinking about it, even my hotel had been getting ready for the big day, or anyway thrown all its old carpets out into the back garden. Brushing aside the deleterious effects of three thousand calories on an empty stomach and four glasses of red on an empty head, I even attempted to enquire of the unkind-looking waitress what the Tour meant to Loudun. She stared grimly as I floundered through my syntax, then delivered a wordless answer that was both inscrutable yet somehow eloquent: the bill.

On my unsteady way back, I found the hotel I should have stayed in, all burnished stonework and chandeliers. On going up to the porch to see what it would have cost – actually only three quid more than my rusty-bidet job – I incidentally learnt something else. There, photocopied from a local paper dated two weeks previously and taped to the window, was a detailed map of the stage route as it passed through the region. With the idiotic phrase 'beeeeeeg secret' looping around my brain, and soon trilling idiotically out of my pursed lips, I knelt down on the wet stone stairs for a closer look. After Loudun the Tour headed off northwest to Nantes; because this route quickly took the race out of the local département of Vienne, there were no details beyond the first few kilometres. But after trooping up to Brittany, it wound back through Tours four stages later, proceeding down to Limoges. The minutiae of this section were displayed in full, and as standing water soaked slowly through my trousers I avidly scribbled down the relevant village names on the front flap of my Michelin map: Chambray-les-Tours, Loches, Verneuil, Saint-Flovier, Azay-le-Ferron.

Still muttering darkly to myself, I set off towards my bed under an angry sky. Old tramp's bottoms to the press officers of France. What was wrong with these people? Why, I asked myself, could they not have told me what they told the Arse-end-of-Beyond Advertiser a fortnight earlier?

Sighing and blaspheming, I sheltered under a Peugeot garage canopy as the first spots of rain fell. It was 9.30, but a group of old fellers were still playing pétanque in a sliver of parkland up the road. Only when forked lightning split the sky and the thunder started booming against my chest like drum 'n' bass did they pack their boules into little briefcases and set off home, cursing foully into their Obelix moustaches. One stormed splashily into a huge, crippled house right opposite me, emerging two minutes later, amid harsh female laughter, wearing a parka and leading two silly little dogs. I'd now been under the canopy for twenty minutes and, galvanised by the presence of other life on the street, made a run for it. This was a mistake, and one that could not be fully undone by sheltering under a short tree next to the pétanque court. The storm was now a real brown-sky drainpipe-gusher, a tempest whose ratcheting fury soon shredded much of the vegetation from my arboreal umbrella. It was a bad time to be wearing espadrilles, particularly when I looked down and saw a small canine leg cocked over my feet.

Three

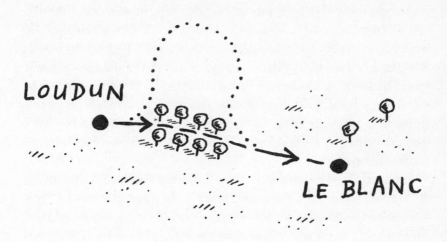

They say cheats never prosper, but whoever they are they can't have done much cycling in France. The first ever bike race was held in Paris in 1869 (won by an Englishman, James Moore, who I'm delighted to claim as my great-great-grandfather, even though he wasn't), and it didn't take long for sportsmanship to be superseded by gamesmanship. Bidons, then made of glass, were deliberately tossed over shoulders to puncture the tyres of following riders; fans were on hand with handfuls of tacks if that should fail. Riders stole all the ink from checkpoints so that their pursuers would be penalised for failing to sign on. The winner of the inaugural 1903 Tour, Maurice Garin, was disqualified after finishing first in the 1904 race when it emerged that he had employed the unimaginative but devastatingly effective measure of forgoing his bicycle in favour of a railway carriage during some of the longer stages. Indeed the next three finishers were also stripped of their honours, two of them for being towed uphill by cars trailing corks which they popped between their teeth. Itching powder in rivals' shorts, spiked drinks, altered road signs – it was all a bit *Wacky Races*.

Another popular trick was to saw through important parts of a rival's machine while he slept, something I'd been peripherally mindful of when asking the hotel proprietor to lock my bike in his garage. The early riders always took their bikes up to their hotel bedrooms, a measure recommended by Richard Hallett to combat theft rather than sabotage, but one I'd have felt much too peculiar both requesting ('Yes, we'll take the honeymoon suite') and experiencing ('Budge up, ZR, it's always me who gets to sleep in the oily patch').

I suppose it's becoming obvious that I am about to justify an act of mountainous deceit as being merely the carrying on of a long and proud tradition. Sitting alone at breakfast, pouching bread and jam and tapping my cleats on the cold, old tiles, I looked out at another grey day, a sky of clouds barrelling along on a potent westerly. Was I really going to head into the teeth of this dispiriting unpleasantness, hauling my panniers of wet espadrilles up to the coast of Brittany on a route I'd be making up as I went along, away from the sun and the Alps and everything else the Tour was about? Or was I about to do a Maurice Garin, sticking my bike on a train to Tours and rejoining the race four days on, where at least I'd be pedalling down roads I knew were the right ones?

Every time I pored over the *procycling* Tour map the same tempting thought had nagged me. Snip that irritating little loop off; make the route look more like the Grande Boucle it was supposed to be and less like a dropped shoelace. On the other hand, I'd be pruning 634 kilometres from the itinerary, and though this still left 3,000 kilometres, 634 was a lot whichever way you looked at it . . . A fold here, a tear there, and the *procycling* map was effectively doctored. Time for recriminations later. I had a train to catch.

In a sport riddled with chicanery, it's inevitable that the best cyclists are also the best cheats. Maurice Garin probably wouldn't have planned Operation Choo-Choo in a tourist-information office two hours before the stage started, and so probably wouldn't have found himself being told: 'Zere is no train for . . . passagers. Only is for, uh, marchandises, oui?' Sigh. I looked at the map: it was an 80 kilometre ride to Descartes, where I could rejoin the route of stage seven. Accepting this as a form of penance (and one whose blow was softened by the realisation that if the weather persisted I'd be pushed there by a hefty tailwind), I made a slight fainting sound, then remembered the other reason for my presence in the office.

'The Tour is important for Loudun?'

The woman at the counter had reacted to my entrance as if she'd been locked up there since 1974, and was indeed dressed accordingly. Once the initial wide-eyed alarm had receded, she spoke with the nervous deliberation of someone hearing their own voice for the first time. 'Yes . . . zis ze, uh . . . first time Loudun is ville d'étape.' Was it to boost tourism? 'Non. No. Uh . . . Loudun is une ville bicyclette.' It is? With a start I realised I had not encountered a single rival cyclist – not even an old bloke in a beret with a pig in his panniers – since setting off. 'Ze maire is, uh, passionné du vélo.' Was he around today? Non. Did the town have to pay for the privilege? Oui. How much? Enormement. Would the teams be staying overnight here? Non. Poitiers. Only sree hotels ici à Loudun. (Tell me about it, love.)

Sent on my way with a shy but genuine 'Bon courage', I followed her directions to the finish line for stage two and the start line for stage three, the only parts of the route granted to Loudun's tourist officials by the fickle guardians of the Beeg Secret. The Place du Portail Chaussée, the stage three start line, was studiously unassuming: a silent, open thoroughfare bordered by a whitewashed billiard hall (une ville snooker, more like), a petrol station and a driving school in whose window plastic toy cars shared a dusty cardboard roundabout with many dead insects. Now I understood why Loudun looked the way it did: the ruler-straight roads that converged there from far afield suggested it had made its name as a transport hub back in the Napoleonic days, and all that late-nineteenth-century architecture showed the railway age had given it another boost. When the autoroutes came and the railway went, Loudun was suddenly surplus to requirements.

Picturing this scene thronged with cosmopolitan crowds, commentators and sporting superstars required not so much a mental leap as a triple jump. The night-before's finish straight, the service road for a half-built industrial estate round the back of the (hawk, spit) station, was a barely more credible stage for the world's biggest annual sporting event. The Avenue de Ouagadougou (clearly named either after something Burkino Fasan or the leftover letters at the end of a Scrabble game) had the sole benefit of linear uniformity, though even this was compromised by a huge sweeping turn about 500 metres from the end. Even I could see this causing problems for the sprinters, whose boisterous competitiveness makes a flat stage's final kilometre powerfully reminiscent of the film *Rollerball*.

But on the way out of town, hitting the dead-straight road to Richelieu with the wind behind me, I realised Loudun fitted perfectly into the whole ethos of the Tour de France. It was an ideal counterpoint to Futuroscope's mirrored-glass ultra-modernism, the other side of the franc. The idea that an ugly duckling could be a swan for a day was touchingly romantic, and it was a credit to the people of Loudun and their passionné mayor that they had invested so much to make this dream come true. I just hoped that when it did they'd all have woken up.

I'm sorry to go on about the wind, but it really did make me very happy to coast at such nonchalant speed across the flat fields of green wheat, the rustling sheaves all bending with me towards Richelieu. Men in berets smoking on huge log piles; dogs with their paws up on a tractor dashboard; a literally steaming barrow of ordure: if it hadn't been for the lorries this could have been the inaugural 1903 Tour.

Probably because I'd been more concerned with monitoring my physical condition, I hadn't really noticed the traffic before. It had certainly become obvious that French drivers treat cyclists as fellow road-users, indicating as they overtook and pulling respectfully right over to the other side of the road while doing so. There was never any of the impatient revving of engines, no I'm-bigger-than-you cutting up or jeers of the 'Get off and milk it, you dozy twat' variety that make cycling in Britain such a high-octane experience.

But despite their best intentions, the huge articulated vehicles that are a universal feature of the French landscape couldn't help but scare your cleats off when they passed. First the huge bow-wave of air they displaced would shove you forcefully towards the gravelly verge; then, a powerful vacuum suck of slipstream pulled you violently back towards the centre of the road. It was horrible. I'd read that, as a boy, Bernard Hinault used to train by racing lorries up hills, and remembering this as a sixteen-wheeler buffeted me into the fag packets and roadkill I realised he must have been even madder than he looked.

Richelieu was splendid, a proper walled town with moats and gates and a beautifully proportioned square. The whole lot was built by the famously horrid cardinal, bane of Porthos, D'Artagnan and Oliver Reed and one of history's moustache-twirling baddies. There were plenty of Tabac le Cardinal-style reminders of this, though I'm not entirely sure he would have approved of the huge branch of Intermarché, a supermarket chain that oddly styles itself 'The Musketeers' (check out their 'all-for-one' offers).

It was, in fact, a bit of a seventeenth-century day. A majestic classical façade facing the N10 at Les Ormes, fronting nothing, as deceitful as a film set; huge timber-beamed marketplaces reinvented as pétanque courts in almost every village. Pedalling over the first old Tour graffiti – fading emulsioned exhortations to French favourites Jalabert and Virenque, more general war cries of 'Vive le Tour!' – I breezed into Descartes, another Renaissance town with pyramid-roofed turrets (it changed its name from La Haye in honour of its most famous son, the man who thought and therefore was). Lunch was taken at an outside brasserie table, ZR locked to one of the many statues of the famous philosopher with his Sweet-style hairdo, both of us watching the farmers' wives putter home in their odd little two-stroke microcars, baguettes poking up over the passenger seat. Understanding that Loudun had been an aberration, I thought how lucky the French were to be able to take all this history and grandeur for granted. In almost any other country Richelieu and Descartes would have been sightseeing meccas; in a land spoiled for choice they were also-rans. The *Rough Guide* had nothing to say about either.

Lunch could be considered the highlight of the day and by far the most important meal, and that afternoon I patented the formula. The breadbasket was emptied before the patron arrived to take my order, invariably the plat du jour (in this instance a plate-overhanging ham omelette) with a side order of French-fried carbohydrates and a salad. Even on a tepid, windy day like this, fluid was ingested with reckless lust: half a litre of Badoit, and another, then a Coke to satisfy what was to become a habitual craving for sugar. More bread. Pudding where applicable (which is to say, when included as part of the menu deal). I'd been yawning almost uncontrollably for most of the previous twenty-four waking hours, which reminded me of the importance of double espresso as part of a balanced cycling diet.

Odd as it may seem, caffeine is on the International Cycling Union's list of controlled substances: a limit of six cups a day is apparently the rough guideline. All riders, even Chris Boardman, start a race day with two big coffees; Paul Kimmage, nodding off in the saddle during a debilitating stage of the Tour of Italy, had to shove up a caffeine suppository to keep going (that was bad enough, but you should have seen his face when the Coffeemate and sugar lumps went in). I had a picture of Eddy Merckx in one of my issues of *procycling* that was to become something of an iconic image for me in times of crisis. Flat out on a dressing-room bench, still wearing half his crap-splattered kit, one sock off, one sock on, mouth gaping limply, dead to the world: it was all you ever needed to know about the absurd physical demands of the sport. Just thinking about it made me want a coffee. And a lift home.

With a slightly embarrassed cough we move on to the 'Fluids – Other' section. I hadn't thought of alcohol as a performance-enhancing drug – to my knowledge, strip Cluedo has yet to be ratified by the International Olympic Committee – but it was quickly becoming apparent that, in cycling, anything that makes the world seem a better place (or anyway a different place) has got to have something going for it. In the early Tours it was by no means uncommon to watch riders stopping to down a huge bottle of wine, and in my 1973 Tour of Italy video I'd seen domestiques carrying bottles of lager up to the front runners. Bernard Hinault used to get his bidon filled with champagne before the last climb of the day, and when he quit the Renault team it was over an argument with his team boss about how much wine he was allowed at dinner. At the fateful foot of Ventoux, Tom Simpson joined a crowd of other riders on a bar-raid: he necked a cognac, which can't have done wonders for an amphetamine-jittered constitution; one of the French riders sank two glasses of red wine.

Anyway, there we are. The prospect of dining in French restaurants without drinking wine was too beastly to contemplate, and now I had an excuse (we'll just gloss over Tom for the moment). I drank a quarter-litre of wine that day; the next it was up to half, and so it remained every lunchtime thenceforth.

Always rosé, though, which I don't actually like very much but somehow seemed less tawdry. You don't see tramps on benches with their teeth stained pink by years of rosé abuse.

'Combien de kilomètres?'

I looked up from the bill – ludicrously small for such a parade of comestibles – to see a well-presented old gent who looked like a character from *Jean de Florette* dressed up for market day.

'Combien de kilomètres par jour?' he asked again, tilting his head at ZR. 'Deux cents? Cent cinquante?'

A Frenchman who thought I looked capable of doing 200 kilometres a day? I was overwhelmed. 'Cent trente,' I replied with a humbled smile, even though this almost randomly selected figure was clearly at the very limit of my capabilities.

'Oh, c'est bien, c'est bien,' he said sympathetically, and I knew then I would be morally obliged to do it.

I finally saw some cyclists as I left town, four of them in their fifties, pedalling towards me in big helmets, rear-view mirrors on their handlebars. Those, the panniers and the scoutmaster shorts smacked of a certain Englishness, a suggestion confirmed as the words 'Bob's off to do a recce' were blown towards me as they passed. I was still wearing my own baggy overshorts, but suddenly I knew they wouldn't be making another appearance. Looking at myself in shop windows I'd seen one of the more outlandish combinations from those children's books where you make hilarious figures by matching different heads to torsos and legs. I was stuck with the Seventies pot-holer helmet – the incident on Kew Bridge was sure to be repeated soon – but the knobbly-kneed molester legwear was bound for the bin. Old Jean de Florette had taken me seriously; maybe it was time I did so myself.

The rivers were bulging with the night-before's rain, filling bridges to the tops of their arches and brimming château moats. I was always awestruck by the procession of imposing castles glowering out over the fields from almost every hillside – the

54

surprise wasn't that there'd been a revolution, but that they'd waited until 1789 to have it. Nowadays, of course, there's nothing the French like better than a bit of high-profile direct action, and over the years the Tour has seen it all. The second Tour in 1904 was almost the last: as well as the endemic dishonesty of the competitors, crowd trouble got utterly out of hand. Mobs hid in lonely forests, assisting their own local favourites by leaping out to batter rival racers with clubs. Unruly spectators had to be dispersed by firing revolvers in the air, and that was when they were in a good mood. After a rider from Nîmes was disqualified for slipstreaming a car as the race approached his home town, 2,000 of his supporters fought a pitched battle with police and Tour officials. Later stages had to be rerouted after farmers expressed more obscure grievances by the time-honoured French tradition of blocking the road with machinery and produce. 'The Tour is finished,' proclaimed its founder, Henri Desgrange, dramatically, 'driven out of control by blind passion, by violence and filthy suspicion.' But however noble this speech, Desgrange was ultimately a businessman. He had conceived the Tour purely to sell more copies of his sports daily, *L'Auto Vélo*, and with circulation up by 300 per cent he quickly changed his mind.

Crowds are better behaved these days – a slightly mad old man punched Eddy Merckx in the stomach as he rode up the Puy-de-Dôme in 1975, and every year some ass with a compact zoom knocks a rider off his bike in the quest for a close-up – but for everyone else connected with the Tour it's a case of plus ça change. In 1966 riders protested against the introduction of dope tests by getting off their bikes just after the start of a stage and chanting 'Merde!' in unison for five minutes – not the most spell-binding exhibit in France's extensive museum of mob rhetoric, perhaps, but effective nonetheless: the positive sample that had incited the shit-shouting was mysteriously mislaid. (One wonders how the triumphant protestors felt after Simpson's death in the following Tour.) In 1998 they were at it again, sitting down in the road to protest about police searching their rooms for drugs. Three teams abandoned the Tour; the remaining riders tore their race numbers off and idled at strolling pace to the stage finish.

In 1968 it was the journalists' turn, blocking the road to illustrate their displeasure after the Tour's boss accused them of trying to discredit the event, and if you think that's the sort of tactical decision you might expect during an argument over whose Pokémon cards are the shiniest, then what about the photographers, who refused to take any pictures for a day in 1987 because the corporate guests got their own hospitality tent and they didn't.

Then, of course, there are the protests from those with no connection to the race at all but who realise the publicity potential of making a big fuss at the world's largest sporting event. Rare is the stage that escapes: tubby Basque separatists in replica kits pedalling out of the crowd to accompany the leader over a mountain col; student pranksters lining cones in front of the speeding peloton. In 1985, a group of protesting shipyard workers made the mistake of standing across the road when Bernard Hinault was in the lead. Because it was only the Paris–Nice race, he let them off with a few right hooks. If it had been the Tour, somebody would have been eaten.

The most notable example of what I suppose could be called secondary picketing occurred during the 1982 Tour. After a four-year campaign to get on the route, the village of Fontaine-au-Piré had been rewarded with a stage finish: the smallest French community ever to be given this honour. The streets were re-tarmacked, houses painted, changing rooms built – all paid for by villagers working through the night producing souvenir banners and T-shirts to be sold across northern France. Over 50,000 brochures were handed out, and on the day a huge crowd thronged the tiny square in front of a town hall bedecked with the flags of every competing nation.

Regrettably, Fontaine-au-Piré had the misfortune to be 40

kilometres down the road from Denain, where a steelworks was threatened with closure. Consequences: riders halted by barricades; stage cancelled for first time in Tour history; mayor jumps into blast furnace.

My Dr-Livingstone-I-presume appointment with the Tour route came at Saint-Flovier, announcing itself with a virgin stretch of shiny black tarmac and freshly painted kerbs. I had the idea that I'd be able to follow this all the way to Paris like some yellow brick road, but ten yards out of the village it abruptly gave way to a signless crossroads which dispatched three wobbly lines of pot-holed gravel over the rolling hills. As I had by now wandered off the edge of Michelin map 232, with a good fifty blind kilometres before I got back on to 233 (I thought I'd forgotten the relevant 238, but it turned up two weeks later in the middle of a *procycling*), there was no choice but to turn back and – as a man, I utter these words in a tone normally reserved for descriptions of domestic pest infestation – ask for directions.

'Oh, oh, monsieur, je suis malade!'

The Babar headscarf was a clue, as was the exuberant application of rouge that was more bleu, but I had failed to detect either indicator of madness in deciding the substantial old dear waving from her balcony might be offering to point a lost soul towards Obterre. It was 3 p.m.; her theatrical wails ricocheted off the shutters down an empty street.

'Oh, monsieur! Ma poubelle!'

I'd dismounted at her initial exhortation, but now looked up at her gesticulations with a sense of foreboding. 'Poubelle', as my schoolboy French remembered it, was dustbin, but used in the context of disease suggested a euphemism whose full horror would only be revealed when she flung her heavily stained floral skirt up over her head.

Further extravagant sounds and signals presently made it clear she was in fact referring to her wheelie bin, but relief lasted only until I understood she wished me to carry this considerable and unsavoury object up the rickety fire escape that connected her balcony to the street. That her physical condition made her ill-suited to this task was beyond question, but as I tilted the bin backwards and prepared to shoulder it, I was abruptly struck in the temple by the carbon-fibre fist of hard reason. What possible purpose could this whole scheme serve, other than the satisfaction of a senile whim? I released my burden, stepped back into the street and fixed her with a businesslike look.

'Obterre?'

'Mais . . . ma poubelle! Je suis malade!'

Following some idiotic horsetrading, during which I had frequent recourse to sotto voce asides of the 'blubbery old loon' variety, a bin-relocation/directions exchange was eventually brokered. Fifteen minutes later, leaving a vapour trail of kitchen smells, I hammered into Obterre.

One of the nice things about the Tour de France is the way it seeks out obscure roads and villages, giving everyone and every-where the hope that their fifteen seconds of international fame will come. For places like Obterre, a fairly hopeless settlement where the only visible signs of entertainment were bullet holes in the road signs, the Tour offers a rare excuse for a long-overdue civic makeover. Two topless gardeners were stocking an enormous embankment with busy lizzies; when I asked if they were doing it for the Tour (OK, the tower), the one with the hairiest back sent me on my way with sarcastic snorts and a heavy-handed 'Non. C'est pour ma mère.' There were new zebra crossings, and the fresh pavement asphalt was an eye-watering red. Only the dogs hadn't cottoned on. I was beginning to despise rural canines for their persistently unsettling habit of bounding up to the borders of their property as I passed and discharging a furious volley of barks. Three of them ambushed me as I left Obterre, and wearily climbing back into the skin I'd just jumped out of I thought: Come 7 July and you'll have something to fucking bark about.

Rain threatened but never came, and with the odometer reading 129.3 kilometres I freewheeled down a considerable hill into le Blanc. Two laps of a great, long square bathed in late-afternoon sun, all shutters and mustard stonework, and I brought up the 130. I had kept my word to Jean de Florette, and discounting a slight hamstring twinge I felt good. The most I had ever cycled in a day and I almost wanted to keep going.

It's a general rule that hotels with their reception desk on the first floor are horrible, but I found the exception, run by a motherly type who scored big points by helping me stow ZR under her stairs, then lost them again by the multi-sensory appraisal of my presentability whose conclusion was that I should give her my details after I'd showered. Le Blanc had been une ville d'étape three years previously, she said, and as the Tour wasn't stopping here this time no one was getting very excited. For a reasonable-sized place such as le Blanc, a town whose many road connections regularly channelled the race through it, I supposed the Tour was as much a curse as it was a blessing for the smaller villages. There was the wearisome civic obligation to string up the bunting and deadhead the hanging baskets, and all for two minutes of Lycra whoosh.

A quick pre-shower biological inventory was generally reassuring. The hamstring twinge was much better once I'd Boardmaned my leg up on the cistern, and I was particularly pleased with my Savlon-slathered perineum, which, assuming – oooh! – that was it, emitted only the dull bruised sensation one might expect to feel a week after falling awkwardly at a tap factory. On the other hand, the front seam of those skin-clamping shorts left a terrible scar down each leg, as if I'd recently endured a pioneering double thigh transplant, and there was an itchy fungal patch on my right love handle. No one had warned me that all that cycling would put hairs on your stomach – one could only hope the back wasn't next – and the idiotic cyclists' tan, which I'd been secretly cultivating as a sort of initiation ritual, had come up bright pink instead of berry brown. If Barbie had given me a lift in her Jeep I'd have looked like a headless torso.

Still, strolling about the sun-burnished buildings in slightly dank espadrilles, I grandiosely reflected that these things happened to us giants of the road. As a road warrior, you've got to expect a few war wounds. Kids were buzzing round the square on their mopeds, and I smiled leniently at their doomed efforts to imbue these foolish machines with streetwise rawness by sticking their feet up on the frame and gunning the hedge-trimmer throttle. Where were all the cyclists? It was certainly easier to imagine the Tour streaking across the mighty River Creuse to le Blanc's witch-hat-towered château than fumbling around Loudun's light-industrial hinterland, but neither scenario seemed particularly convincing.

I found a pizza restaurant, where, sitting alone in the tiny covered courtyard, I spread Michelins across the wobbly table to savour my achievements. Pedalling across fold after fold of three maps, I'd covered 234 kilometres (almost 150 miles) in two days, only six less than I'd been advised to do in three. No matter that this was 20 kilometres less than the longest single day in the Tour itself, and even less matter that my average speed to date, 21.1 k.p.h., was just under half what they'd manage. Sipping my rosé, I decided I'd settle for that. After all, I was clearly far worse than twice as bad as any other sportsmen. Could I complete a round of golf in 140 strokes? I could not. Four-hundred-metre hurdles in two minutes? Not without a ladder, and a piggyback. I'd always had a plan to wear down the world's tennis greats by perfecting the art of dispatching an unending series of net-cord services, but that didn't really count. No, I was good at this and I was going to get better, I thought, celebrating my future glories by raising a huge quadrant of pizza Napoletana to my mouth.

It never made it that far. The smell, an apocalyptic marine rancidity, ensured I would not be summoning any of my other senses in dealing with the chef's creation, save a tiny glance at the bloated, newt-like anchovies that were unequivocally responsible.

Being British, I love complaining about foreign restaurants, but being both a hypocrite and a frightful coward I always endeavour to do so either to myself, or outside and round the corner. Looking back, I can see that electing to break this rule in a French pizzeria was an error, such establishments providing impressive scope for a counterattack pairing Gallic truculence with Italian unpredictability.

Stifling a dry retch, I shrouded the plate with my napkin in a reflex flick. This was all very sad. It was a Tuesday night, which in this area dictated that all other restaurants I'd passed had been closed. There were no other dining options, and if I didn't eat a great deal of food very soon parts of my body would start to fall off. By the time the bullied-looking waitress appeared, I had downed my carafe of rosé almost in one; she tentatively raised a corner of the napkin as if concerned it might conceal a dying seagull, and recoiled as if it had when the stench hit her. 'Les anchois?' she gagged. 'The anchovies,' I wanly concurred.

In bad English and worse French we agreed upon a replacement Margherita, but no sooner had she disappeared through the kitchen doors with the offending pizza at arm's length than out burst the chef. It was not a good time to notice his uncanny resemblance to the more experienced of the two 1950s Cuban boxers in that Bacardi ad.

His face gave away nothing, but as he approached my table I noticed that from the fat, oily fingers of his left hand dangled a fat, oily anchovy the colour of the outside of a cold hardboiled egg yolk. When he was standing far too close, the anchovy passed from left hand to right, and thence towards my face.

'Anchois!' he barked abruptly, before slowly licking each of his oiled left fingers with pornographic relish. I found myself unavoidably recalling the night in Transylvania's Hotel Dracula when, along one of the many dark corridors, Birna and I chanced upon the cook and two waiters exacting intricate physical retribution upon a Bulgarian lorry driver we had earlier overheard muttering a protest about his starter, which, like ours, consisted of a single beige vegetable apparently preserved in carbonated Bovril.

Such professional pride is of course what makes eating out in most European countries such an involving experience, or so I failed to philosophise as the pizza chef's pallid hostage began dripping on to my trousers.

'You no 'ave anchois in Angleterre?' he said, his smelly face so close to mine I could see the enormous pores on his nose expanding as the surrounding features broadened into the sort of lunatic smile that precedes the righting of gangland wrongs.

Look, you hideous gargoyle, I've got half an arsing cupboard of cock-buttocked anchovies at home, or at least I did have until Birna took the kids away for a week and I ended up living off the contents of all the obscure tins emptied on to Ryvita.

'Oui,' I said, stoutly refusing to concede any linguistic quarter.

He nodded slowly, then, bunching his fist around the hostage anchovy, began to pace the suddenly dungeon-like courtyard. There was an ancient, tack-studded door on one side propped shut with a broom and something started growling behind it.

'Five year I make pizza,' he blurted to the flagstones halfway through his second lap. 'Five year, and nobody say zis.' On his way back to the kitchen he stopped beside me, crammed the anchovy pulp into his glistening chops and wiped both hands on my tablecloth.

By the time the waitress appeared with a Margherita in her hands and a desperate beam on her face, I had already sketched out contingency plans for the chef's return. Pepper in the eyes, cruet set in the teeth – and if all else failed, levelling up the playing field by kicking over that broom to free the beast.

I knew of course that the substitute dish would have been

imaginatively adulterated, but seven breadsticks hadn't quite bridged my 130-kilometre hunger-gap, and so, pasty-faced with disgust, I slowly ingested it all. Bleak and tired, I was preparing to pay the waitress when I noticed, with a nauseating jolt of distress, that both pizzas had made their way on to the bill. It is difficult to express the almost uncontrollable anguish this discovery caused me. In the red corner, fear and inertia; in the blue corner, justice and self-respect. The blues won after extra time.

Struggling to conjure up the cocksure hauteur that had propelled me into le Blanc, I made my way to the till, encouraged to note that the main restaurant was now heavily populated. The waitress appeared with an I-thought-this-might-happen look, and voicelessly veered off to the kitchen. The chef started up as soon as he came out of the swing doors. 'Something bad, you doan pay. You no like something, you pay.'

It all got shrill very quickly. Still determined to keep the linguistic high ground, in an aggrieved adolescent quaver I pointed out in French that his pizza was both bad and naughty; he replied in English that I did not understand how an anchois is. I had counted out the exact Napoletana-less amount to the final shitty centime, and was preparing to fling this noisily on to his glass-topped counter when he raised both hands in a grotesque parody of appeasement and in a voice as greasily rancid as his ingredients said, 'I make you a present. You no like, you must pay – but is your first time in my town, so I make present.' Imagining a putrid gift-wrapped anchovy, I watched as he flicked a pen across the bill to delete the Napoletana. Having paid, I turned for the door; then, with two dozen sets of eyes boring into me, my brain suddenly delivered a present of its own: the French word for disgusting. 'Degeulasse!' I shrieked as I crossed the threshold.

I didn't think I'd slammed the glass door, but as I flopped up the street in my espadrilles – surely the last-choice footwear option for this type of confrontation – I heard an enraged bellow from behind. 'You break my restaurant, I telephone to ze police! Ze police!'

'Allez-y!' I screamed back, getting into my stride, then immediately blundering out of it again with a stream of Norman-accented Anglo-Saxon abuse of the 'wankeur' variety.

Back in my hotel room, I washed my shorts, socks and jersey in guilty triumph, tired but content. Was all this physical endeavour somehow causing a build-up of testosterone and adrenalin that suddenly overflowed into uncharacteristic aggression? Certainly all that virgin stomach hair paid tribute to some sort of shift in my body's chemistry. The restaurant incident had been a bit unsightly, but reconstructing it I had cause to be grateful. Unfortified by the hormones, I'd probably still be cravenly sitting there now, a broken man paralysed and ensnared by this smelly-fingered Svengali, a freak-show curiosity for the locals: 'Mister Anchois, le rosbif qui mange uniquement les poissons rancides.'

Four

There's always a lot of weather in the Tour de France. In the space of a single day the riders can be slushing about in half-melted tarmac and half-melted snow: the two images that were my default mental encapsulation of the race were Tom Simpson weaving deliriously off the road as the mercury hit 131°F and the hypothermic ghost of Stephen Roche juddering up through the icy mist of la Plagne. And then there's the rain.

The morning Savlon ritual always seemed like the prelude to some act of obscure ghastliness, and that day it was. Heading south towards Limoges I'd soon be in the bottom half of France, but you'd never have guessed it from the weather. The proprietress waved me off into a vapoury drizzle that above walking pace imparted the sensation of being sprayed in the face by one of those houseplant water-pumps on the mist setting. I stopped to put on my rain top when the weather gods turned the nozzle to squirt mode, and as the D975 ploughed its rural furrow between wheat fields and herds of sturdy Limousin cattle they got out the fire hose.

In seconds my helmet was pinging with the spasmodic tattoo of heavy rain; in minutes so was the inside of my skull. The scenery pulled down the shutters, and before long my blinking, slitted gaze had dropped to the wet road in front of me. It was then that I got the idea for a recreation I dubbed slug tennis, a name that adds a deceitful veneer of respectability to what I can only shamefully describe as the bisection of roadside arthropods beneath rotating rubber. In any case I soon stopped, though only after noticing that at speeds below about 15 k.p.h. my shins got splattered with orange stuff. When the rain redoubled its efforts – at la Trimouille, 20 kilometres down the road – I invoked the phrase traditionally applied to games of soldiers, flinging ZR against a bar-tabac window and running through the door.

Inside was a Rita Heyworth barmaid with brown-pencil eyebrows, along with the usual mid-morning clutch of we're-only-here-for-the-kir regulars. There was also a large tear-off-the-days calendar, which informed me that today was St Eric's Day. And, in bold numerals, that it was also my birthday.

In a way I was pleased that 18 May had crept up on me unnoticed: this was exactly the sort of important personal detail that a one-track-mind pro would have overlooked. With a little inward sigh I accepted I was now as old as the oldest Tour de France winner, and ordered a treble espresso.

'Eh, Jacques – le Tour est arrivé!'

I still have no idea how even the tiniest communities each manage to support at least one bar-tabac without some sort of regional subsidy, but I'm very glad they do. Maybe the solution to the decline of Britain's rural pubs is to encourage more farmers to start drinking at 8.30 a.m.

Anyway, perhaps because bar-tabacs are almost by definition the domain of lonely people looking for company, I never failed to attract a circle of admirers. I suppose it was like being chatted up. Conversations of the what's-a-nice-boy-like-you variety were instantly struck up, and I quickly established that (a) the Tour had last passed through la Trimouille thirty-three years ago; (b) it was a pity Michel from the garage wasn't here, because he had a load of pictures from back then; and (c) if you want to win the heart of a wet English cyclist, try combing the breakfast remnants from your moustache and smelling slightly less of sick.

Somebody made a joke about me winning; somebody else delivered a series of hand signals that suggested the road to Limoges was either very up-and-down or menaced by the Loch Ness monster, and with the sun breaking through I left happy. Over the fields: hello there, cows; top of the morning, Mr Magpie; shut the fuck up, dog . . . For the first time, the problem was not fatigue or fear, but boredom. Presently I found myself moronically transfixed by my knees as they cranked out the kilometres: hairy red left knee, hairy red right knee, left knee, right knee, left, right, left . . . Why *do* cyclists shave their legs? . . . Aerodynamics, I suppose . . . Wonder at what point in their career they decide to start doing it . . . Does someone take you aside and say, look, son, you've got something special, but if you're going to be serious let's get the Bic out on those calves . . . What if you shaved them, and then realised you were actually rubbish after all? . . . Like Michael Hardaker on that scout-troop cross-country run when his dad rubbed all that Vaseline into his legs on the start line . . . In fact, what the naked arse was *that* all about? . . . Oh, there's a leaf stuck in my spokes . . . there it is again . . . there . . . there . . . there . . . gone now . . . And . . . *drrr-thwick* . . . what's that *drrr-thwick* noise?

It was awful the way the brain gradually homed in on the most inane and infuriating minutiae. At least it wasn't just me. Even proper cyclists find that when their minds start wandering they're too tired to reel them back in. Louison Bobet, Tour winner three times on the trot from 1953, was prone to debilitating peripheral obsessions: a spot of oil on his tyre, a spare tube wrapped in the wrong colour paper. And who cannot sympathise with Paul Kimmage, his chances in a 1989 Tour time trial destroyed by Paul McCartney's *My Brave Face*, played over the Tannoy on the start line and then spooled endlessly around his tortured brain for every one of the following 73 kilometres?

Drrr-thwick . . . That noise – and I can hardly bear to think about it even now – was eventually traced to a slight mis-alignment of chain vis-à-vis front dérailleur, overlaid with a synthetic swish as my left heel grazed against the pannier during each pedal revolution. Neither should have been difficult to rectify, but fiddling randomly with hex keys and screwdrivers always made both slightly worse, though not as seriously as the wit's-end kick that generally rounded off each roadside mechanical session.

Drrr-thwick, drrr-thwick . . . I'm not sure exactly when I realised that something more grandiose was going wrong inside my head, but it might have been when I went through a village called La Grande Mothe and started scanning the bracken for giant antennae. Feeling curiously hollow, I noticed everything seemed to be happening in slow motion, most notably my progress. I stopped, and for the first time since Kew Bridge I remembered too late to twist my foot out of the cleats: the fall into the damp bracken was so gentle and painless it was like watching it happen to someone else. Exhibiting a gormless confusion that would have done Stan Laurel proud, I sat on my wet arse and wondered what was going on. Stomach funny, head light, hands . . . two. One, two. Two hands. Must be . . . must . . . oh yeah: the vitamins.

Later, of course, I deduced that all the talk of 'vitamin shots' was either a direct euphemism for illegal performance-enhancing drugs, or a means of persuading reluctant riders to jab hypodermics into their bottoms. The big leap isn't what you stick in the syringe, it's the act of injecting yourself with it: once you've shot up B12, it's only a small step to steroids or amphetamines. Certainly Paul Kimmage realised this, sweating with shame as he lost his hypodermic virginity to an iron and vitamins jab.

But at the time I'd taken the apparently crucial role of vitamins at face value, filling an old sunglasses case with Sanatogen, along with extra tablets of C and B12 which someone had said the body flushed out quickly, and a handful of cod-liver oil tablets which I somehow thought might lubricate my joints. Having forgotten to take them that morning, I fuzzily withdrew the box and ferried a succession of tablets to my mouth with the wincing deliberation of someone performing long division at high altitude.

All better now, I thought, flobbing riboflavin into the muddy verge and pedalling off. But of course it wasn't. Passing through a hilltop copse, I turned towards the source of an attention-attracting cough: a fat man met my gaze, smiled distantly and neatly exposed himself. I'm almost certain he was a bona fide human entity, but the experience was enough to start up the bad thoughts again, and within ten minutes I'd fallen off for a second time and heard the taunting whisper, 'Shave them, Saint Eric, shave them.'

I was having a bonk.

Cyclists burn up 9,000 calories a day, roughly four times what the average shiftless 36-year-old needs to sustain himself for twenty-four hours of domestic pottering. Eat, eat, eat, I'd been told, but due to the awkward logistics of in-the-saddle refuelling I'd hoped I could get away with shovelling in the kilojoules at breakfast, lunch and supper. This was an error. Pros start nibbling their Fig Newtons after the first hour, and thenceforth maintain a steady intake of nourishment to avoid bonking, the term unhappily applied to the moment when the fuel reserves run out and the body starts eating itself. Sugar is sucked out of the blood, and a traumatic sense of delirious exhaustion sets in. Tunnel vision, seeing stars, Eddy Merckx up to his wheel rims in tar and not understanding why he's being overtaken – the Tour de France is a bad trip by any definition, and never more so than when you're bonking.

From then on I'd know to tide myself over until lunch with the half-dozen croissants I'd smuggle into my panniers from the breakfast buffet, or the trio of pains au chocolat washed down with a Coke for elevenses outside a village boulangerie. That day, with all the shops shut for lunch, it was a question of finding a restaurant before mythical beasts started popping their heads out of my bar-bag. I remember eating some sort of cheesy vealy thing in a restaurant full of plastic flowers and sons treating their mothers, but even now, looking at the map, I can only narrow its location down to le Dorat, Bellac or somewhere in the 12 kilometres between the two.

It is relevant to point out at this stage that I was lost. The itinerary I'd copied down at Loudun had ended at la Trimouille, and though the bar-boys there had been certain the route to Limoges (where the stage ended) was a straightforward D675/N147 job, I was sceptical. Because the Tour requires roads to be closed for hours, the organisers, where there's an option, generally choose quiet back routes. But as I swooped insanely out of Bellac towards the foot of a long, wet hill, the road broadened into a dual carriageway and I was suddenly engulfed in camions. The countryside was almost English – crisp, green and rolling as promised – but then so was the traffic. I'd become used to having the road to myself, but now I was harried and buffeted in an uncomfortably familiar fashion. A Peugeot estate with half a dozen bikes on the roof went past with a wave and a blast of the horn, the first of many drive-by hootings that were well-meant but nerve-shredding; the N147 began to undulate alarmingly about its horizontal axis and all I had to look at was roadkill: slugs, obviously, but also the odd weasel, badger, coq au van and hedgehogs a-go-go (or rather a-gone-gone).

With my shoulders rolling from side to side and every part of my body from the tops of my feet to my wrists in some measure of discomfort, I *drrr-thwicked* into an abandoned picnic-area and fell flat on my back, oblivious to the under-arse pine cones, the rain and the fact that crapping by the roadside is a widely enjoyed French pastime. Yawning massively, I blinked up at the dripping fir trees before drowning out the HGVs with a bellowed chorus of 'Happy Birthday'. The tomato/monkey/zoo version.

It was very difficult to believe that the Tour riders were expected to do Tours–Limoges in one day. A single hill seemed to slog on for a lifetime; the previous afternoon's incident with the mad binwoman of Obterre was like a recorded childhood memory, yet the pros would have taken only three hours to bridge Obterre and Limoges. I kept thinking about the riders who weren't sprinters or climbers, managing to win races on determination and stamina alone. 'Hard men' they were called, almost officially, and if you could bully your bike and body more brutally than most you might even aspire to the ultimate accolade of 'super-hard man'.

The last haul to Limoges was one for the super-hard men, a lot more ups and a few more downs, though they might have skipped the bonus round of squatting under the porch of an abandoned hovel waiting for the rain to shut up.

I can't think of many cities that don't look worse in a down-pour, except maybe Atlantis, but by any reckoning Limoges was unappealing. 'Not a city that calls for a long stay' was the *Rough Guide*'s tart assessment, and squeaking and splashing through the rush-hour it was easy to see why. Limoges was one of those places bodged together out of a job lot of leftover drab suburbs, with the sort of city centre you passed straight through without noticing. The china that made the town famous is no longer authentically produced – the kaolin mines were exhausted long ago – though this didn't stop a succession of souvenir shops displaying racks of plates garishly decorated by graduates of the Weeping Pierrot school.

Without wishing to extrapolate too much from my limited

contact with them, I have to report that the people of Limoges came up rather short on the awareness front. Keen to find the route of tomorrow's stage, south to Villeneuve-sur-Lot, I popped into a bike shop to catch fifteen minutes of *The Vacant Proprietor*, and the over-staffed and under-customered tourist office seemed profoundly sceptical of the concept of buildings with bedrooms and restaurants that tourists could stay in.

I did find a hotel in the end, up a loathsome wet trunk road whose gradient confirmed the unlikely truth that, flying in the face of conventional civil-defence wisdom, Limoges's founding fathers had opted to locate their town in a huge hole in the ground. The Hôtel Belvedere was named after its attractive view of many lanes of Toulouse-bound traffic, but the restaurant looked respectable enough – at least until I'd sunk a birthday bottle of fine wine and begun to do slightly fatuous things with the little 'Boeuf Limousin' flag that had been speared into my steak. By the time the crème caramel arrived I was waving it happily at an elderly Dutch-sounding diner at the next table.

Cointreau number two coincided with the arrival of half a dozen middle-aged and moustached men, who greeted the room with slight nods and a 'Bonsoir, m'sieurs, dames'. This extravagant display of respect, coupled with their whispered but earnest gastronomic discussions – agonising over vintages, asking the waitress if the goat's cheese was local – led me to wonder fuzzily if they weren't a party of retired Tour pros on a reconnaissance mission, a sort of warm-up brigade of sporting ambassadors. Only after I completed the painful ascent to my room – why did I keep ending up in the flaming attic? – did I find the truth, looking out of the window to see a phalanx of France Télécom vans in the hotel car park. Phone engineers with social grace and epicurean connoisseurship – it was enough to make you forgive an entire nation of spiteful press officers and tourist-board nellies. Providing that you had then gone to bed without watching telly.

Tuning into a late-night documentary about the Ariane rocket launch in French Guiana, my first thought was the recollection that there had been talk of staging the 2000 Tour prologue on the French Caribbean island of Guadeloupe, a 13,000-kilometre round trip for a 20-minute bike ride. Though this was cancelled on logistical grounds, the fact that it was seriously considered served as a reminder of how colonial France remains – imagine the FA Cup final being staged in the Falklands – as well as showing the evident relish with which the nation markets the Tour as an international showcase of France's global importance. Along the roads I'd seen regular reminders of French bitterness at the triumph of English in the battle of the world languages, advertising campaigns with English slogans – 'APPLE – THINK DIFFERENT' – followed by a little asterisk pointing to the indignant, sour-faced translation at the bottom of the billboard: 'Pensez différemment'. Even a sizeable proportion of graffiti is in English, or something like it. Putting ZR to bed in the hotel garage I'd encountered 'Fuck off the system' and 'Your face, your ass – what is the different?'

France had lost the war, but, as the rocket documentary reminded me, was still fighting rearguard actions in far-flung theatres. My memory of the Ariane programme is of rockets toppling over on launch gantries, U-turning into the sea or spectacularly showering a rainforest with small, hot pieces of titanium after eleven seconds of flight. In this I was at odds with the programme-makers, who chose to overlook the previous farces, and indeed the contribution of other nations to what is a European project, while compiling a trumpetingly propagandist account of France's technological majesty.

It was particularly interesting to note how local protestors – understandably reluctant to risk their shanty towns being incinerated by the now-traditional mid-air apocalypse – were portrayed as brainless Luddites to be cowed into submission by mooring a couple of huge destroyers just out from the beach.

When the control-room whitecoats finally pressed the button, the booming soundtrack was an orchestral celebration of the victory of progress over ignorance, the First World over the Third, France über alles. It was like watching a James Bond denouement in which Blofeldt wins: the digital countdown gets to zero, the skies above the secret jungle hideaway are pierced by a streak of smoking silver, a hundred brainwashed technicians rise from their monitors in synchronised triumph.

Inspired partly by this quest for technical perfection and partly by my own torrid battles against gravity, I was becoming mildly obsessed with reducing my burden. Toothpaste consumption had trebled, extruded cavalierly on to brush with a wristy squirt; my hangover that morning was treated with a paracetamol overdose; complimentary toiletries were left on hotel-bathroom shelves with a thwarted sigh. I knew all this was silly – a single discarded copy of *procycling* would have had far more concrete significance – but it at least made me feel I was doing something. Just as well, because my invented itinerary, almost due south on the D704, flung me directly up a monstrous incline that went on until lunchtime. I'll say this for it, though: I didn't have a hangover by the time I got to the top.

The landscape was too green, and there was generally too much of it. In Britain, close-packed herds of livestock nibble the grass right down to the quick; it was odd to see, through my drizzle-slitted gaze, a couple of cows marooned in a field the size of Heathrow Airport, surrounded by so much waist-high pasture that they didn't know where to start. And the wildlife hadn't quite adapted to the intensive nature of twenty-first-century life either, strutting gaily out of the damp fields into the path of heavy-goods vehicles. It is a surprising truth that whereas even a plump hedgehog bestows only a compact visceral legacy on the tarmac, your average skinny weasel really lets rip. I know this because one of the latter, carelessly permitting thirty-two tons of mobile machinery to compress it at speed, ejected a sizeable gobbet of gizzards that flew across the dotted white line and struck my front wheel, to be distributed piecemeal via the revolving spokes to my shoe uppers and, less acceptably, my bare shins. I did manage to eat some lunch, but somehow the usual bacchanalian intensity wasn't there.

Cleating myself wearily back into ZR – a process that was beginning to hold all the physical and mental appeal of self-crucifixion – I was passed by two old chaps on immaculate road bikes, gleaming pro-team jerseys pulled tight over their paunches. All their supplies were in little backpacks; they glanced with disdain at my panniers before swishing away up the D704. I knew that two riders relaying – taking it in turns to bear the brunt of the wind resistance at the front – could go at least 20 per cent faster than a lone cyclist, but being at least 40 per cent younger and 100 per cent less French I rashly decided to give chase.

Interestingly, it wasn't the ups that did for me, but the downs. The D704 was on a roll, and every time I got near enough to read the old blokes' sponsors' logos at the brow of a hill, they'd lean and glide and swoop nose-to-tail down the other side, leaving me to flail distantly about the wet carriageway, convulsing over the pot-holes. Whenever I tried to raise my belaboured behind from the saddle the weight of the panniers threatened to pull us all over, and above about 35 k.p.h. the wind rushing through my ears eerily replicated the sound of a motor vehicle nosing up to my rear wheel. The answer to all these problems was to grip the handlebars so tightly that the whole of my upper body would be in spasm by the time I got to the bottom. It also seemed slightly unfair that though none of us had mudguards, mine was the only jersey splattered from coccyx to nape with a healthy covering of road slurry.

When the muscles of the arse became an issue – and frankly it was about time – I pulled over, just as one of my conquerors turned to deliver what even at 200 yards was clearly a triumphant smirk. In half an hour of buttock-punching, hamstring-yanking, chest-broiling pursuit I had boosted my average speed for the day from a pedestrian 18.9 k.p.h. to a . . . oh, to a pedestrian 19.1 k.p.h.

I tried to rationalise the depressing implications of these statistics by tackling hills in a new way. The key, I decided, was to stop at the top of each and award myself a treat: a sip of water, a blow of the nose, a slow-motion cleated fall into the wet brambles. It worked until the rain reached pause-discouraging levels, and with my average speed (or 'AVS', as the stop-looking-at-me-like-that odometer would have it) stubbornly static I gave up and dropped back.

One hundred and one kilometres into my day I got to Montignac, saw a sign saying 'Alight here for the Lascaux caves' and decided that would do. I suppose Montignac has only prospered due to its proximity to the famous palaeolithic hunters' paintings, but it seemed a lovely place in its own right: timber-framed medieval houses with lopsided balconies overlooking a big river, a splendid pyramid-roofed, ashlar-colonnaded Napoleonic town hall and a venerable thirteenth-century hospital housing a clueless tourist office ('Le Tour? Oui, er . . . par ici, et après . . . Périgueux? Brive?' – both improbably located). I imagine Montignac must be completely overrun in high season – in the estate agents' windows all the details were in English – but on a belatedly sunny mid-May evening I had the place more or less to myself.

Just up the main drag from the tourist office I found a lovely hotel run by a lovely Mrs Robinson proprietress – white capri pants, snakeskin loafers – who ran her establishment exactly as my family would if they ran a hotel: lovely old Victorian wallpaper and high-back velvet thrones in the bedrooms; ceiling-mould and hairy plugholes in the bathrooms. Another feature of the latter was a deeply disturbing lavatory, the watery base of its bowl containing a waste-disposal grinder guarded by two rubber-starfish sphincters. It took me five minutes to find the flush button, and when I pressed it a large pink pill was mysteriously ejected by the starfishes with such force that it flew into the bath. It could have been worse. Pedal all day and there's only the tiniest residual evidence of those 9,000 calories.

I had a slow beer by the river, opening out the maps and watching some sort of swallowy bird swooping down to skim the ripples. On to Michelin 235 – an exciting moment, as this one, subtitled Midi-Pyrénées, revealed that I was unequivocally in the south of France. On the other hand, I was becoming progressively more weary every evening. Having spent all day looking like – and in fact being – an imbecilic two-wheeled tourist, I normally made at least some effort at camouflage in the evenings, buying the local paper and pretending to read it, nodding and tutting at the TV news in bars. That night, though, I simply couldn't be arsed, stumbling listlessly around Montignac with an armful of badly folded maps, in skin-tight black rain leggings, white socks and black espadrilles, like a Bolshoi reject.

I was so tired, in fact, that halfway through the second of three splendid courses of Périgord cooking at the hotel, my head sagged limply towards the riot of linen, crystal and electroplated nickel silver. Mrs Robinson's husband roused me with a gentle cough and a sorbet; Jesus, I thought, jerking upright with an equine splutter: asleep at the table at 8 p.m., and there were still 2,300 kilometres to go.

'Excusez-moi,' he began shyly, after I had dabbed away a gossamer thread of chin drool, 'votre nom – vous êtes apparenté à l'ancien James Bond, Roger Moore?'

'Oui – il est mon père,' I said, a little flatly, as during my visits to France over the years I had been asked this question perhaps forty times.

'Votre père!'

He was so excited I didn't have the heart, or indeed the vocabulary, to explain that I had been making an unimaginative joke. As I trooped out through the empty dining room, past the trompe l'oeil murals and marbled panelling, I saw the Robinsons peering at me excitedly from the door that led to the kitchen. This may explain why they forgot to charge me for dinner, though not why I didn't point this out to them. I really am very sorry.

I went up to the Lascaux caves the next morning, in predictable rain, and trooped round a very cold recreation of the world's oldest art gallery. The originals were sealed up in 1963 after it was noted that visitors' breath was turning the ancient horses green, and having spent an hour in there with a couple of dozen skunk-mouthed French OAPs I can understand why. What's really interesting about Lascaux isn't so much the paintings – the whole reproduction scam rather takes the gloss off that – as the fact that they weren't discovered until 1940, by four boys looking for their dog. It was a mark of rural France's vast emptiness that such a huge place should be used by hundreds of generations of prehistoric hunters, then lost again until halfway through the twentieth century. The guide accidentally locked us in – one old man started crying when we realised it wasn't a joke – and by the time we were released five minutes later I'd started wondering whether we'd be discovered in 17,000 years by four dogs looking for their boy. And then get breathed on and go green.

Tour riders, of course, never really get to do much sightseeing. Paul Kimmage sourly recalls how sickening it was to be cheered through purgatory by lolly-waving sunbathers, people so patently on holiday when he was so patently not. After a day in the Alps during the 1984 Tour Laurent Fignon told reporters he had climbed like a tourist, going on to critically compare the view from each peak; but then again, with only three stages left and an unassailable nine-minute lead, he could afford to.

Bugger the rain. The poppies were still out, but were now all wet and limp. More slug tennis, more hills, more rain – fewer restaurants. Foaming sweat into my airtight rainwear like a nobbled racehorse, I bonked alongside the Vézère river and down through lofty pine forests to the banks of the Dordogne. They liked their rivers big down here: to my addled, sugar-free brain the Dordogne looked as broad as the Nile, and the bridge I crossed to Siorac seemed like the gateway to another world. But don't knock the bonk – in many ways it was. The sun abruptly burst through, the clouds scurried away over Siorac's severe-looking château to the horizon and in four minutes I was getting a waitress to tilt the water off an outside table to make way for my pizza. Sorry: pizzas.

It was indeed a day of two halves. With a hefty wind behind me I gradually picked up speed and maintained it so effectively that I only realised in the evening that the road had been slightly uphill most of the way. Momentum is all, I said sagely to myself, feeling road-wise and fresh-legged as for an hour I whished along at 33 k.p.h. Before lunch I'd been wondering how the pros kept going all day, but now I didn't want to stop. Waiting at a level crossing I heard the words 'Astone Veelah' leaking through an open bar door and remembered that the FA Cup final was today, in fact now; but I had bigger sporting fish to catch, to fry, to eat.

When I finally did stop it was to strip off portentously my rainwear and long johns: by morning he is a mild-mannered transvestite ballerina, but in the afternoon he becomes . . . Super-hardman. As I slipped on the Oakleys and remounted, there was a dash of colour and another immaculate weekend-biker grandpa passed me. Right. One on one. *Mano a mano*, or anyway old mano.

The pannier/heel *thwick* was constant but my front dérailleur was now issuing an extended and prodigiously amplified *drrrrrrrr* against the chain, so loud that I didn't dare attack Gramps too closely in case he heard me coming. Only when he began to labour on the occasional inclines, up in the saddle, his gleaming silver machine swaying extravagantly beneath him, did I put the hammer down (and how I'd been waiting to use that most brutal of cycling clichés). I got him under a railway bridge and, though

I could hear him clicking down a few gears to get the revs up, when I looked back after two minutes he was miles back. I'd left him a broken man.

I'm slightly aware that this is sounding rather unedifying, maybe just two steps away from a solvent-fuelled knock-down-Ginger session at the sheltered-housing estate, but at the time I felt only a rich glow of exultation. And there was more to come – just up the road another team-jersey johnny was out for a spin; younger, this one, perhaps in his early forties, and though he was clearly giving it some I left him for dead without even turning round.

Green-lined scenic stretches; valleys of death where cement factories covered every abandoned butcher's and baker's in a layer of beige powder – it was all the same to me. I had the bit between my teeth and I didn't want to spit it out. Then, speeding into Fumel – a decaying industrial town about as nice as it sounds – I almost collided with a group of green-and-white Crédit Agricole jerseys pedalling silkily towards me. Crédit Agricole was Chris Boardman's team, and hang on, didn't that guy at the front have a big nose . . .

'Hey, Chris!'

No one turned round, which was just as well as afterwards I wondered what I would have said.

'Hey, Chris! I just want to say that . . . that I really love your stretching exercises – you know, the ones I forget to do every morning and evening. Yeah, those old cat stretches, eh? Yeah. Hang on, don't go – my gears are a bit fucked up and I wondered if . . .'

Still, it was an omen of sorts, even though I subsequently learnt that as he'd already withdrawn from the Tour it almost certainly wasn't him. I'd been planning to stop at Villeneuve, but feeling good (and having read that it was a dump) I decided to plough on the extra 30 kilometres to Agen, where the stage would start the next day. Two Mars Bars at Saint-Sylvestre-sur-Lot, a litre of grape juice just over the river at Penne and I was off again, up a horrendous incline out of town and over the warm fields.

I knew by now that any place with *haut* in its name was to be avoided on gradient grounds, but there was no getting round Hautefage and during its ascent I did hit a patch of rather poor form. But it was nothing that couldn't be undone by lying flat out in an orchard for half an hour, helmet still on, flies crawling over my face unimpeded by even the most half-hearted swat. When the road sloped down to the Tarn and Garonne, the pair of fluvial fatties that run through Agen, things picked up again. I was topping 40 k.p.h. when I weaved perilously through a snapshot of chaotic distress: a teenage girl watching in frenzied grief as a farmer boot-prodded a roadside cat that hadn't looked both ways when his tractor went by.

Naturally it all caught up with me as I creaked into Agen's unpromising wino-ridden suburbs, jelly-legged and suddenly irritable. Motorists were dawdling up a slightly Harlem-esque main drag, on a loud and messy, hot Saturday night, and only after a lot of weaving and tutting and manual obscenity did I manage to pilot my way to an Ibis hotel. There are times when you want a hotel to be an experience, when you want to play a glittering cameo role in the proprietor's life and vice versa, and there are times when you really don't want any of that. All I wanted was a lavatory that didn't look like it might disembowel me, a basin that didn't fill up with next door's old bathwater, and a breakfast buffet I could empty into my pockets without the worry that in doing so I'd be sending the boss's kids off to school on empty stomachs.

Having said that, the Agen Ibis was located in an uncharacteristically active quarter, all garbage stench, mopeds ridden down the pavement and 7-year-olds on the fourth floor throwing down front-door keys to their barefooted friends in the street. The New Zealand couple I met while locking up my bike in the basement car park seemed rather shell-shocked.

'Aren't you worried, cycling about on your own around here?' asked the concerned wife as I hoisted my belongings towards the stair door leading up to reception.

'I think I can look after myself,' I said, fatigue stretching my words out into a vainglorious drawl, one whose effect was compromised when I pushed against the door and was completely unable to shift it. 'Bloody panniers,' I mumbled cravenly as the husband came over and levered it open with one hairy hand.

Refuelling outside a studenty bar-restaurant while a middle-aged blues band entertained an audience comprised largely of their own small children, I could feel the day's 151 kilometres wafting slowly out of my body like a heat haze. As the shopkeeper who'd Mars-Barred me up in Saint-Sylvestre had said, the cycling conditions that afternoon had been perfect: not too hot, not too wet, a tailwind and generally benign gradients. It was slightly deflating to think that despite all this I hadn't quite managed 100 miles, though I felt better when I looked through the *Rough Guide* travel section and worked out that the equivalent train journey took 105 minutes. Overlooking the dilatory nature of French local railways, I was sure I could make this man-against-locomotive showdown sound impressive when I got home, particularly once I'd rounded it up to two and a half hours.

Five

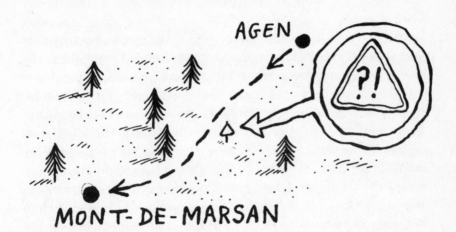

AGEN

MONT-DE-MARSAN

Leaving Agen's listless, jerry-built skyline in my dusty wake, I headed west across the rivers and motorways and into a slightly scorched landscape that bore little relation to the damp, tossed-salad lushness I'd been accustomed to. Yesterday the fields had been lined with tentative seedlings; today it was all wizened-looking crops ready for harvest, the rippled air thick with the smell of onions and dried slurry.

It was a Sunday, and for the first time I found myself moving among big groups of club cyclists, though not in anger. That morning offered the first suggestions that the malaise blighting French cycling may be traced to the neglect of competitive training in favour of poncing about in new-season jerseys affecting a look of extravagant ennui. Much has been made of the ability of top riders to shield their pain and fatigue beneath poker faces (and wraparound shades); the club-class poseurs had borrowed the expression (and the shades) while cutting out the irksome physical labour it was intended to conceal. And they were so snotty: having sneeringly assessed my outmoded jersey in a way that made me feel I'd turned up at a school disco wearing my aunt's gardening smock, they turned their heads with a dismissive tut.

I'd tried the Tour de France press office again that morning, and after an exchange of sighs and, no doubt, beastly gurns and hand-over-mouthpiece imprecations I had extruded the reluctant concession that the complete and precise itinerary would be made available to tiresome foreign irrelevances in two days' time. Looking again at the *procycling* map, I saw that the stage from Agen to Dax shifted west across France in a series of down-left steps; transposing these on to the Michelin directed me towards an enormous vacant slab of green, nothing but marshes, forested hunting reserves and firing ranges. As well as being wonderfully flat, this provisional route had the additional benefit of avoiding the nearby town of Condom, where I would be certain to encounter the sorriest sort of sniggering Britons.

You take the high road, and I'll take the low road, and I'll definitely be in Paris afore ye, I thought as the poppies and abandoned hotels petered out and the D665 plumb-lined through the parallel pines. Breathing in hot Badedas vapour, and trying not to notice that the wind was turning to face me, I ground on, bored as Belgium. Increasingly abstract speculations wandered into my mind. How long would it take me to cut down one of those pines with a screwdriver? Would I kill that blackbird and eat it raw for £20,000? A deer leapt out in front of a deer-warning sign, somehow arranging its spindly limbs into a precise replication of the complicated prance depicted, and for some considerable time I found myself internally debating how it was that these animals managed to survive for even twenty-four hours without snapping at least one of their silly legs off.

The forest thinned, but not the sense of isolation. I didn't know whether the Tour would pass this way, but if it did it was going to be too late for most of the towns. A tree grew from a church roof, a Monsieur Hulot Renault Dauphine crouched in a state of advanced decomposition on a forecourt, waiting for a fill-up that the oxidised-skeleton pumps weren't about to deliver. In some villages, two-thirds of the houses were roofless wrecks. Even the cartographers had given up: Bousses was down as Boussé, gradient chevrons and scenic-route green borders were bandied about at random.

The road began to blend seamlessly into the undergrowth, its surface defiled with horrid, scabrous pockmarks that were uncomfortable to both arse and eye. 'Chaussée déformée' warned the road signs superfluously. The French were good at this. If they spent even 2 per cent of their budget for warning you about carriageway deterioration on actually doing something about it, France would have the best roads in Europe. And it wasn't just the infuriating frequency with which they stuck up the triangled exclamation marks, it was the wilful obscurities they enamelled beneath them. The *bandes rugueuses* and *accotements dénivellés*, the *affaissements* and *aspersions* – all spawned more fears than they laid to rest. Even the few I managed to translate conjured improbable scenarios, the 'impractical surface' that suggested whimsical experimentation with brass or feathers, the dark conspiracies implied by 'holes in formation'.

I stayed in a town called Mont-de-Marsan. It wasn't very nice. I ate chips in the street. I found a room in a big hotel with long corridors and no people and a fat man on the front desk who licked his lips a lot and wrote my name in a big empty book. There were no shops but lots of bars with men who stared when you walked past, and lots more men standing on bridges over big rivers looking like they wanted to jump in. I got a bit scared and went back to my hotel. In the middle of the night I woke up and realised I was in Room 101 and couldn't get back to sleep.

Six

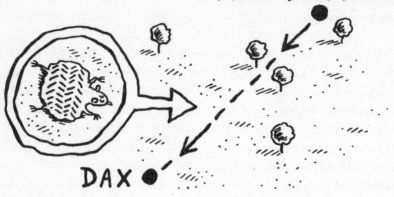

Eurosport was on in the breakfast room and there was Axel Merckx, Eddy junior, winning a stage of the Tour of Italy. This was the first time I'd seen real cyclists since I'd been doing some real cycling, and I found myself intently scanning the peloton for tips on technique. But there was no secret. They just pedalled really fast, and the man who pedalled the fastest won. Merckx senior, congratulating Axel on the line, was clearly still on race rations, eating for eight hours in the saddle – Fast Eddy had lost an 's'. The man they once called Cannibal looked about as man-eating as the owner of a small but prosperous chain of carpet warehouses.

I could talk. I was regularly sticking away enough fuel for 250 kilometres but doing only half that: I might be the fittest I'd ever been in my life, but I was also the fattest. The Pyrenees loomed and no amount of liberal toothpaste use would offer gravitational compensation for the nascent spare inner-tube ruching up above my shorts.

Mont-de-Marsan had been a profoundly horrid place, and I was so eager to leave it that I didn't notice until it was too late that the N124 marked on my – oh, seventeen-year-old – map had been supplanted by a 110 k.p.h. expressway. Parped reproaches informed me that my presence on this many-laned drag strip was inappropriate; lorries took especial pleasure in buffeting me into the calf-slashing tall grass that lined the hard shoulder. It was a long way to the next turn-off, and by the time I got there an already keen connoisseurship of roadside debris had been broadened still further.

We're all familiar with the bits of glass, rubber and animals that line major thoroughfares, and I could have contributed a thoughtful foreword to *Chrome Alone: The Lost Hubcaps of France*, but it was intriguing to note the range of objects that motorists discard voluntarily. Why all these hundred-yard lengths of cassette tape?

'Gérard, we love Johnny Halliday, right?'
'Everyone loves Johnny. Go, Johnny!'
'Yeah. Go! But I was thinking – why *is* that?'
'Well, because he's a global pop-rock legend who just happens to be French, that's why.'
'Even though no one else in the world has heard of him.'
'Well, yeah.'
'And even though he looks like a chain-smoking old tramp in mascara.'
'Yeah. But you know: go, Johnny!'
'Right. I mean, I really love Johnny too, but the thing is, all of his music is just so utterly, utterly abysmal, that I was wondering if we could carry on doing the whole love bit while at the same time throwing all his tapes out of the window.'
'Fair enough. We'll do it when we stop to crap in the next lay-by.'

I cut down to Dax on stretches of the old N124, through moribund villages that must have cheered the day the expressway took the traffic away but now looked like they were missing the noise and excitement. For much of the way I kept pace with a postwoman in a little yellow van: the dogs always gave her a welcoming pant as she ambled up their front paths, then flung themselves in spittled rage at their chain-link fences when they saw me.

The journey to Dax was a mere 60 kilometres – I should warn you that I'm about to start saying 'k' instead of kilometres – and I got there before lunch. Though by most standards unassuming, it was considerably less dead than Mont-de-Marsan, a place I'd erased from my mind so successfully that when the shopkeeper I asked for directions enquired where I'd come from that day I had to get the map out to remind myself.

Dax had a slightly flyblown, Mexican air, with plenty of scabby whitewash and hot dust, but there were a couple of breezy, palm-lined squares, a well-tended maze of pedestrianised shopping streets and the inevitable big river, this time bordered by a bank of enormously flash spa hotels. The most enormous and flashest was a dazzling art-deco palace unashamedly labelled SPLENDIDE, which was good news for me because, as I appear not to have mentioned I had booked myself in here before leaving England. This was the first of my stops under Simon's reward scheme, and though I'd arrived a couple of days early, due to the now-notorious excision of the Brittany Loop, the room I'd reserved was free.

Can't say the receptionist seemed overjoyed, however. Wheeling ZR across the Splendide's lobby, an echoingly regal Grand Central Station job, I'd felt somewhat out of place amongst the old men in dressing gowns perusing brass-and-glass cases full of expensive leather accessories and hampers of foie gras. The garage was 'not correct' for bicycles, she said, flashing tell-me-about-it peripheral smiles at passing guests as if to say:

Don't worry, we'll have this sweaty buffoon out of your way soon.

'That's OK. I'll just take it up to my room,' I said, raising the stakes with a wide-eyed beam.

'Non! No – I . . .'

'This bicycle,' I said, patting ZR's sweaty saddle with exaggerated respect, 'is worth 24,000 US dollars.'

The receptionist glanced down at the muddy panniers, then looked me straight in the eye and smiled with marked coldness. But she said nothing, perhaps knowing that the spectacle of laboriously levering my bike upright to fit it alongside me in the tiny lift would offer ample recompense.

My room was intensely exciting, a symphony of restored art-deco glass and mahogany, everything authentic except the whopping great telly and the groin-soaking turbo tap in the bathroom basin. And it was also immense, big enough to cycle round, though this didn't stop it feeling very odd to have the bike in there with me. Propped up against the mirrored wardrobe, it stared accusingly from every angle, even glinting in the dark when I went to the loo in the night. And, because the Tour de France press office fucked up and/or lied – difficult to accept, I know, but bear with me – there would be two nights for it to glint through before I could get my faxed itinerary and be off.

Still, it could have been worse. The room was just £40 a night – an absurd bargain – and a rest day before the (eeeek!) Pyrenees could only be good. After a pleasant interlude making alien faces in the wide-angled make-up mirror, I walked out into a lethargically hot afternoon and somehow ended up talking Tour at the town hall.

Turning up unannounced at a public office in France and requesting an instant meeting must be right up there with alchemy in the long-shot stakes, and I was still in shock when Eric, a nice young man in the *service de communication*, tapped a Marlboro Light on his desk and asked what he could do for me. Well! After five minutes I had learned that Dax had paid the

Société du Tour de France one million francs to be a ville d'étape; that doing so was considered an important investment for the town's national and international profile in terms of both commerce and tourism; that the civic celebrations would include music, dancing and bicycle-shaped flower-beds.

If my French or Eric's English had been better I might have learned more, but it was a start. In fact, as I was bundled into the office of his boss Isobel, I was rather wishing it had been an end. Isobel spoke no English, wore Heinrich Himmler glasses and had a Mini-Me secretary sitting beside her. 'Cinq petites secondes,' she barked, glancing flamboyantly at her watch, but it seemed like vingt grandes minutes before I managed to think of something to say, and that was asking if she liked bicycles.

Wisely ignoring this imbecility, Isobel slickly engaged human press-release mode. I tried my best to keep up. Dax had last been a ville d'étape in 1959 (possibly), was only a small town of 20,000 (possibly), and the arrival of the Tour would be a night for citizens to resemble each other and shoot cat-skins (possibly not). She also gave me rather a start by insisting that one of the main objectives was to lure old people here for 'termalisme'. This sounded uncommonly like a frank synonym for euthanasia, and my concerns for all those old dears playing bridge in the Splendide lobby were only laid to rest the next day when I saw the word, complete with silent 'H', emblazoned outside a health spa.

Eric rescued me with a slightly apologetic smile and saw me off with a 'Bon courage'. That was good, but what I really craved was a 'chapeau'. *Chapeau!* – hats off! – was the traditional roadside hosanna for those who had achieved the memorable: Merckx on a 130-kilometre solo attack in the mountains during his first Tour, Roche coming up through the mist at la Plagne. Wandering the soporific early-evening streets in search of food I withdrew my odometer, which I'd unclipped from ZR in order to gloat over. In seven days in the saddle I'd gone from wet north to banana-palm south, covering 808.4 kilometres; risible by Tour standards, but more than many pros aim to do in a week's training. And my top speed, 61 k.p.h., was the fastest I had ever travelled under my own steam, probably even including that youthful encounter with the 577 Crew on Ealing Common. Beginning to feel quite important, I strode into a pizzeria.

My previous experience of such establishments should have taught me some sort of lesson, but I can't be too hard on myself for failing to predict that my tormentors that evening would not be inexpertly preserved fish, but a trio of animatronic harlequins. There were three of them by the door, each the size of a 5-year-old child, and as they ushered me through the lobby area with jerky genuflections and Lurex sieg-heils I chortled merrily at what seemed the kitschest encounter of my life to date.

This was a response I had cause to regret as soon as I was seated at a table just behind them. It was then that I noticed the noise: ominously familiar, yet strangely changed. *Drrrr-thweeek . . . Drrrr-thweeek . . .* For a time I thought I could at least control the situation by working out which machine was responsible: the gold one, forever beating its brow in reproach for some unknown transgression; the red one, its outstretched left hand juddering uncertainly about as if passing a verdict of mediocrity; the silver one with the Queen Bess ruff, scything out a tune on an absent double-bass . . . But by the time the goateed waiter glided up it was already too late. My fillings seemed to be melting; there was something wrong with my spine.

Distantly aware that such a request would usually invite heavy sedation and the removal of belt and shoelaces, I nonetheless heard myself ask for the little golden men to be deactivated. The waiter's empathetic nodded wince said: If you think you've got it bad, try working here. But then he shrugged, looked bleak and in a voice racked with helpless frustration said, 'Le patron . . .'

Le patron what? 'Le patron spent his childhood trapped in a robot's body.' 'Le patron had a vision in which three metal boys came to Dax bearing the Ruff of Christ.' 'Le patron is in love with the one in red, but she's married to the gold one and won't leave him, so old silver's there to keep an eye on the pair of them.'

There was an argument for returning with my bicycle, wedging le patron's tie in the chain and pedalling off at speed, and this argument became more compelling when I noticed that all the tables were rhombus-shaped. What was wrong with the man? One could only imagine the Cinzano-raddled reasoning by which such features were thought to lure potential diners.

'Fancy a pizza tonight, Brigitte?'
'Nice idea, Serge. What about Benito's?'
'Well, I dunno – the food's good, but look at his furniture and you'll be hard pressed to find a single oblique angle.'
'Fair point. Dax Romana?'
'I dunno – the pitwheel in their cross-section model of a colliery hasn't revolved in *months*. *And* they keep their anchovies in the fridge.'

The waiter offered me a more distant table, but I knew that a whispered *drrr-thweeek* would play even worse tricks on a shot cerebral cortex, and he understood immediately when I said I would have to leave.

On the way home, chip-stuffed pitta bread in still-trembling hand, I began to fear for myself. For some days now I had become mildly obsessed with Eddy Merckx's explanation of what made a great champion: that while it was possible to assess a cyclist's physical capabilities, 'there are no laws that govern the will'. Suddenly I understood exactly what he meant. Clocking up the 'k's and bullying myself into physical condition, I'd slightly missed the point. The Tour was about mental strength, telling your brain to shut up when it started screaming at you to stop, to control physical suffering as if it was just a schmaltzy emotion, like crying in *Tarka the Otter*. I couldn't imagine Eddy driven to the dizzy brink of mania by three squeaky dolls. The mountains are coming,

I thought. My legs might cope, but will my will? My will won't.

There were two rest days in the 2000 Tour, one after the Pyrenees and the other just before the end of the Alps. Playing a rest-day joker before the mountains even started seemed a bit feeble, but then it wasn't my fault. All I could do was conduct myself in an appropriately professional manner, which, after reading Paul Kimmage's account of Tour rest days, required me to sleep a lot, wash shorts in the bidet and go for a quick spin on the bike to stop my legs from stiffening up. The first two kept me occupied until 6 p.m., whereupon I pedalled off for a ride-thru McDonald's, picking up a couple of lagers from a Leader Price store on the way home after seeing two sun-wizened winos exchanging crafty, incredulous smiles as they emerged with armfuls of bargain beer.

The alarmingly high alcoholic content of these ales helped tide me through an evening of French television, one whose prime-time content was dominated by toe-curling studio jamborees reminiscent of *Noel's House Party*. Then the phone rang. It was reception saying they had a fax for me from the Société du Tour de France.

The last day before the mountains is, for the élite riders, the end of the beginning; for the rest, it's the beginning of the end. When snow crops up on the horizon their sights shift from stage wins to survival, languishing up hairpins behind the guy who's worked out exactly how much they've got in hand before the broom wagon sweeps them up or they're excluded on time differential (anyone finishing a slow mountain stage in a time 4 per cent greater than the winner's is kicked out).

The receptionist had refused to confirm or deny that Tour riders would be staying in the Splendide ('I regret it is a secret,' she said; 'Any particular size?' was my unanswered counter query), but it seemed more than probable. I imagined them, like me, lying awake in the night and feeling they were about to go into battle after a week of phoney war. ZR's cleat-chipped crossbar glinted tauntingly by the mirror: this was what he had been built for, this was his time. D'you fancy a bit, son, he sneered; d'you fancy a bit of the tall stuff, eh, a bit of the old thin air?

Of course, in some ways it didn't make much difference to me: my agenda had been about survival from the start. If I hadn't made the mistake of looking through those endless faxed tables I probably would have been fine. But deprived of data for so long, I pored over them. Each stage was broken down in kilometre-by-kilometre detail, with every village, sprint and feeding station. Oh, and the climbs. Every eminence above a certain height is graded by an arcane formula, fourth category being the easiest, all the way up to the fearsome firsts, and beyond that the HCs: the hors catégories, off the scale, beyond the pale. These were the legends, from Mont Ventoux to the col d'Izoard, hairpin-stacked horrors where the Tour was won and lost. There were seven in all, and the next day's stage from Dax to Lourdes-Hautacam had two of them.

But worse than all this was the speed. There were three times listed alongside each climb and village, giving the riders' ETA at three different average rates of progress. On some of the flat stages, the most cautious prediction was that they would barrel along at 40 k.p.h. all day, with 44 k.p.h. the most optimistic. Tomorrow's stage was estimated to be the second slowest, but even then the organisers couldn't see the riders letting their average speed drop below 31 k.p.h. On a flat road, 31 k.p.h. seems fast. At that speed the wind noise deafens and your hair is blown right back. You're really travelling. If a red squirrel ran out in front of you it would be a dead squirrel. The concept of maintaining such a speed while ascending some of the highest roads in Europe was an outrage against logic.

I don't think I slept at all. At about 5 a.m. I filled the bath and lay for an hour up to my ears in Bond-girl foam. The breakfast-telly weatherman shouted out something about 28 degrees in the

Pyrenees, and when I finally wound up the electric shutters everything was already all hot terracotta and azure. Merciless sun and mountains – you wait all week for an unreasonable physical challenge, and then two come along at once.

I'd ordered breakfast in bed as a treat; 'Bon appetit,' said the chambermaid, but looking at all those little pots of jam I felt sick. The off-to-battle panic punched me in the guts again, and I had a strong desire to crock myself by knocking steaming hot chocolate into my lap, like the Somme soldiers shooting themselves in the foot as the order came to go over the top. After forty-four hours of virtual inactivity, my buttocks and legs still pulsed with discomfort. How could I have whined about those lovely flat forests?

Negotiating ZR through a sea of tables laid for some grand buffet reception, a Leslie Phillips chap with a waxed 'tache and cravat sidled over with a camp leer.

'Le Tour de France?'

I tried to look a bit less like leftover guacamole. After my stuttering explanation, he stood back, saluted theatrically and barked, 'Aux montagnes, Anglais!'

Seven

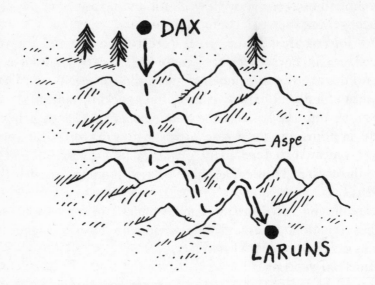

In a sporting world where the adjective 'professional' is often a euphemism for cynicism and naked commercial greed, there is no sport more professional than road-race cycling. Riders have always been willing to throw away certain victory if the price is right, often holding muttered in-the-saddle auctions to sell their services in assisting a breakaway. Most smaller races are shams, their results fixed in advance by an unsightly round of horse trading.

And the Tour de France itself can claim no noble Corinthian origins, having been founded purely to promote a sports daily; when the yellow jersey was introduced in 1919 it was to emphasise that *L'Auto Vélo* was printed on paper of that colour. Bike companies had been splashing their names across riders' chests even before that, and in 1957 the sponsorship expanded to include anything from ice-cream to beer. Soon it went a step further. I still found it hilarious that the names on the riders' jerseys – at least, the main names – were those not of the team's sponsors so much as their actual owners. In his prime, Eddy Merckx had flogged himself to the brink of collapse for the sake respectively of Faema, a manufacturer of coffee percolators, and Italy's leading speciality butcher, Molteni. At the end he was riding for C&A, which no doubt explains his early retirement. I guess I'd give it some oomph for a nice espresso-maker, and the thought of a plate of sliced salami might give you something to aim at when the bonk came knocking, but you just can't imagine Eddy grinding up the Casse Deserte under a merciless sun, driven onwards by the terrible, soul-swallowing prospect of a world without slacks.

Fans have always sought to emulate their heroes. You've got your replica bike and your replica jersey: all you need now is your replica amoral rapacity. This is where the *caravane publicitaire* comes in. The faxed itinerary plotted the progress of this brashly commercial vanguard as it sped along the route 30 kilometres ahead of the riders, and standing astride ZR on the Boulevard Saint-Pierre, starting point of stage ten, I pondered the scenes of grasping hysteria that would accompany it.

Channel 4 always breaks up its on-the-road coverage with behind-the-scenes reports, and a staple of these is the 'day in the life of a Tour follower'. I must have seen half a dozen of these over the years, but the one that really stuck in my mind focused on a Belgian couple holding a long, hot roadside vigil on some uninspiringly flat stage.

Mr Belgium, emulating his many surrounding peers, settled down at a folding table to consume pastis with a gusto that belied the hour. If he got to bellow aniseed-spittled encouragement into a hero's hot face it would have been a good day; if he remembered having done so, even better. But his wife was working to a different agenda. All morning Mrs Belgium had toiled morosely in the motorhome, assembling sandwiches for her unsteady husband and generally defining the adjective long-suffering; then there was a distant volley of silly musical horns and as a sort of Mexican cheer spread slowly up the road she rushed to the tarmac, clapping her hands, slapping her haunches and constructing facial expressions consistent with a triple jumper psyching himself up at the start of his final run-up: the free crap is coming.

A motorised tub of potted meat; four fibreglass racehorses frozen in mid-gallop on the roof of a Citroën; a mobile oversized gas bottle; a two-stroke globe with leering Michelin men strung round its equator; a coffee cup on wheels. Some of these vehicles and all the others were manned, in addition to the driver, by a couple of weary blondes hurling complimentary merchandise into the crowd, and the ugly feeding frenzy that occupied the next minutes of footage showed Channel 4 viewers the unacceptable face of audience participation.

Dazed and craven, Mr Belgium beat an early retreat. Blundering haphazardly from the scrum clutching an armful of swag, his sagging features fell further as he laid it out on the camping table: junk-mail brochures for car insurance or cubic zirconium jewellery, vouchers entitling him to bugger-all off his next packet of cack. What had happened to the packets of sweets and key rings, the cycling caps and yellow food-bags, the sachets of coffee and Camembert portions and sausages and windscreen sunshields? He didn't know, but having watched the truth emerge through Channel 4's all-seeing eye we did: everything, absolutely everything of any value had been caught, scooped, plucked or snatched by the darting form of Mrs Belgium. One moment she was diving full stretch to grab a packet of first-aid plasters from in front of an old man's cupped hands; the next she was screaming in the face of the Michelin blonde as if that promotional bottle opener was her birthright. Everything had her name on it. Through a forest of beseeching hands it was hers alone that came away clutching a France Télécom baseball cap; when a neighbouring Dane took a flying videotape in the guts and went down, there she was, snatching it from his side like a battlefield corpse-robber.

She was the star but there were some glittering cameo performances. A sockless loafer stomped proprietorially on a mini frisbee; a woman with a face like a spat-out toffee held a small child up to the cheesemobile, screaming 'Pour mes enfants!' in the manner of a Balkan beggar. Some sort of moped-based Norse god of the sea chugged past dispensing small items of unpromising aspect wrapped in cellophane; a man in aviator Ray-Bans scooped one up and yelled, 'Saucisson – magnifique!' Children were dispatched into the road on insane crap-catching missions, plucking caps and biros from the small gaps between vehicles. As the last biro-hurling bath-tub puttered laboriously away through the pines and the crowds, Mrs Belgium puffed out her cheeks, aimed a rearwards nod at her mountain of merchandise and announced to the camera, 'Une bonne récolte.' A good harvest. I mean, I appreciate a cascade of free crap as much as – no, much, much more than – the next man, but it takes a special sort of front-line foolhardiness to mix it with the Mrs Belgiums. It ain't what you get, it's the way that you get it.

The Tour riders were to leave Dax at 10.45 a.m., setting off an hour and three quarters after the publicity caravan. I gave myself a 25-minute head start and settled down into a rhythm appropriate for the considerable heat: slow enough to maintain on a slight hill, fast enough to get a breeze down the unzipped front of my humid jersey.

As the roads got narrower and the villages smaller, so the Tour preparations seemed to gather impetus. At Habas, three separate gangs were doing flower-beds, road markings and telegraph-pole creosoting; every tiny hamlet seemed to imagine they wouldn't be taken seriously without at least one mini roundabout.

It got hotter and quieter. There were no châteaux around here, and the farmhouses looked meaty and squat, like old forts; every barn was fronted by a huge chicken-wire cage of corn cobs, propped up on stilts to keep it out of the reach of the few rodents whose corpses were not festering by the roadside. Whole valleys reeked of smoked and smoking Bayonne ham. A rider in the crimson strip of Saeco careered towards me from a rippled horizon and shot past, a medley of loud respiration, sweat beads and nurtured machinery. There were signs for Pamplona, and then, biting into the heavens miles above the churches that wallowed up to their towers in heat haze, there they were. Some soft and round, with jolly Friesian snow patches, others shredding the sky with frightful grey claws: the Pyrenees.

Sobered, I got drunk. Lunch was taken in a fly-filled bar in the company of a loud road-gang who'd been resurfacing the Tour tarmac, all red wine, red faces, scratch cards and cap sleeves. There was no menu: the barman simply came over and filled the table before me with a huge aluminium tureen full of broth, a plate of black-pudding slices and a big jug of wine. 'Ah – le dopage!' guffawed the barman, sticking to the accepted script for all witnesses to my bidon-refilling routine. As I topped up water with Leader Price grape juice, he bent towards me with mock disapproval and sighed, 'Et voilà – l'EPO.' I laughed as much as I could. I didn't want EPO. I wanted GTi.

It was real fuck-this heat by now, a dogs-in-the-fountain afternoon that drawled out for a siesta. Detecting an odd slushy pulping sound as I approached my first official climb, the Côte de Barcus, I looked down and saw my front wheel almost up to its rim in melted tarmac.

It didn't help that I had no idea how much had been in that jug, except that it was slightly too much. They say that pride comes before a fall, but in my experience it's far more likely to be wine. Forgetting to decleat I keeled over into a ditch alongside the temporary traffic lights erected by the road gang, and when I wobbled up to the next roundabout the fingerposts were a sozzled, illegible mass of obscure consonants that raised grander doubts concerning my sobriety. Presently I understood I had entered Basque country, a region whose fragile linguistic tradition is these days bolstered by bilingual road signs emphasising a perverse fondness for 'k's, 'z's and 'x's. I never heard anyone speaking Basque, except on telly, but the heavily accented French was almost unintelligible. For two days I had to deal with people who greeted me with a 'bon-jewer' that sounded like a Yorkshireman reading from a phrasebook.

The Côte de Barcus was a coiling category – three ascent through Teletubbyland: meadows that were too green, sky that was too blue, cows that were too dun. It was bad, but not that bad. I reached the village of Barcus in third-bottom gear, hot but happy. In commentatorspeak, Moore was never in serious trouble on the first climb of the day. The regrettable truth is that such statements are almost inevitably followed by a huge, Pyrenean-sized but.

It had been a lovely, gentle ride along the Aspe valley to the village of Escot. The looming terror of the mountains had somehow been shielded from me by foothills and foliage, and with 110k up for the day I should by rights have looked for a hotel. But it was only 5.30 p.m., and the idea of tackling all the stage's big climbs the next day in one fell swoop (with more of the fell and less of the swoop) seemed overambitious. The col de Marie-Blanque was a category one, but on the Michelin map the road over it didn't flail about like a dying snake. The *hors catégorie* monsters went up to 1,800 metres; at just over a grand the Marie-Blanque couldn't be, or anyway shouldn't be, a ridge too far.

There were several large ifs to go with the aforementioned but. If I had troubled my imperial brain with the old-money translation, I would have realised I was departing at clocking-off time towards a formidable eminence as tall as Snowdon. If I had read Graeme Fife's *Tour de France* I would have found the Marie-Blanque described as 'a killer in disguise'. If I had spent a little more time looking at the map I would have noted that while the road was reasonably straight, it was also decorated not with a single, nor a double, but to you sir with the waxen death mask a *treble* gradient chevron.

I heard my first cowbells as I filled both bidons with cool water from an almost painfully charming dolphin-head fountain by the turn-off to Marie-Blanque. There was a shaded bench by the fountain, and sitting down with the full force of post-wine drought suddenly upon me I laid the groundwork for the most serious if. If I hadn't drunk two litres of chilled water.

One corner out of Escot and the peaks suddenly leapt out above me with a genuinely startling visual boo: great slabs of rock poking out from rainforest greenery, some of them so sheer that I couldn't crane my neck far enough to see the tops. A trio of thermal-topped riders swished towards me round a curve at enormous speed, wheel to wheel, leaning steeply into the corner. Ignoring the implications of their velocity and attire I plodded on, click-clicking down into gear twenty-four past the roofless shepherds' huts.

For some time the only sounds were ZR's click-clicks and *drrr-thwicks*, echoing tinnily off the granite walls. Soon, however, my ugly respirations became rather more dominant. The gradient didn't seem ridiculous, with none of the batteries of hairpin bends I'd been led to expect, but I seemed to be finding it hard to maintain the revs. Rhythm, I knew, was crucial, and while my heart was playing techno my legs were struggling to keep time with Mantovani. In contradiction of the modern maxim, there was pain but no gain. Click-click-click and I was in bottom gear, twenty-seven, with no more shots in the locker if the incline steepened, which of course it did just round the corner.

Tour riders have any number of terms to describe what was happening to me, and try as I might to resist I found them all parading funereally through my mind. I was going backwards, I was cooked. Grovelling, that was another. Dying. I had cracked. The sweat stung my eyes before being sluiced away down grimace lines that would show up tomorrow like long, white fencing scars on my otherwise broiled face.

There were names painted all over the road now, French, Spanish and even the odd outbreak of Cyrillic, and every one of them seemed a rebuke. I imagined people racing each other – *racing each other* – up this slope, fans shouting their names as they jockeyed and jostled and jumped on the pedals to speed away.

When your body is very hot and you make it very cold, bad things happen: cramps, essentially, affecting all parts of the musculature. Two litres, I learned later, is what some Tour riders restrict themselves to for an entire day. 'Driest is fastest,' said five-times Tour winner Jacques Anquetil. Pierre Brambilla, in 1947 the winner of the King of the Mountains competition for the Tour's top climber, guzzled cold water from a fountain during the scorched 1948 race and retired in agonies 10 kilometres further on. The day that Tour ended he buried his bike in the garden and never raced again.

My legs felt wizened and pickled, my arms bruised and tremulous. Filling my lungs was like hyperventilating next to a faulty incinerator, yet the fire in my chest could not melt the heavy, iced spasm into which my innards had frozen. I coughed up iron and vinegar and flobbed it feebly on to my forearm.

But at the same time, none of this was the problem. I had seen people feeling worse than this and carrying on, 400-metre athletes throwing up in full flow on the home straight, marathon runners wobbling drunkenly into the stadium, any number of Tour cyclists on any number of Tour mountains. Even I had too, I remembered: stumbling agonisingly towards the line in the second-year 800-metre 'A' race of 1974 as Neil Gross gritted his heavily discoloured teeth in the lane alongside, the tears already welling up in my eyes as I realised I couldn't make my legs move any faster and this Krankie-faced gnome was going to beat me.

It was Eddy's will thing. Bernard Hinault had talked about 'the doubts which sometimes overwhelm the rider' and now I saw exactly what he meant. As soon as you think you can't, you won't. When the first defeatist thoughts sidled tentatively into the corridors of my mind, the forces of determination immediately collaborated and gave the invaders a rousing ticker-tape reception. If I could have seen the top of the col it might have made a difference, but when I looked fuzzily down at the odometer and saw I'd only done half of the climb's 10 kilometres there was no option. Like Paul Kimmage on the col du Télégraphe in the 1987 Tour, I was just looking for somewhere to abandon. Going so slowly that I had to time my uncleating manoeuvre carefully to avoid an unsightly fall, I clambered off ZR by a barrier that closed off the pass's upper reaches in winter. It would have helped if the scenery in this section had looked a little more savagely Alpine and a little less like Box Hill on a pleasant June weekend. Nettles, buttercups, slugs . . . and then an off-key bell tinkling somewhere above. Forget the tree line – I hadn't even made it past the bloody cow line.

In the state I was in, pushing was barely easier. In 1933, Percy Stannard was picked for the British team to ride in the world championship after winning the national trials – his first ever race – by shouldering his bike and running up the hills. How *dare* you, Stannard. Every five minutes I remounted, but it never lasted long. Once you get off you can't really get on again. Cars suddenly started descending towards me at regular intervals; every time I heard one coming I'd whip the map out of the bar-bag and pretend I'd stopped to plot my progress. At least there were no more cyclists.

I did manage to do the last half kilometre in the saddle, and even had the gall to set up a self-timer shot at the top, standing astride ZR by the altitude sign and peering through the low sun at the bleak but benign eminences around. And of course the descent paid scant justice to the horrors of the climb, containing long flat sections where horses with bleached Human League fringes wandered over the road and I had to pedal fairly hard to keep going. I'd Velcroed myself into the all-weather top in preparation for a chilly, windswept downhill swoop, but it never happened. I was the Englishman who went up a mountain and came down a hill.

Wheeling into the main square at Laruns I was bonking fairly seriously, an awful mental and physical vacuum that left me ill-prepared for my reception at the only open hotel. As I swayed dead-eyed among the outdoor diners finishing their sorbets in the last of the sun the youthful proprietress fixed me with a challenging look. The rooms were 285 francs, she said, and if I needed a garage for my vélo, eh bien, that would be an extra 30F. 'Pour un vélo?' She gave me a next-please look. I told her that in that case I'd take it up to my room. With a sneering shake of the head she swaggered complacently back indoors.

'Excuse me,' I yawled, in a weary, drunken slur that raised faces from many sorbets. 'Do you think you could come back and try doing that a bit more rudely?' It was gone eight by now, and getting cold down at the foot of the vast encirclement of enormous green peaks beneath which Laruns cowered. I should have been in an oxygen tent on a drip, not fighting for my consumer rights in the street. Slowly waving a snot-gloved hand in her general direction, I remounted and rolled away.

On the outskirts I'd seen a sign advertising a hotel memorably called Le Lorry a kilometre beyond Laruns. I won't pretend that this was a short kilometre, or that Le Lorry was open, or that I didn't return to my tormentress with my tail, and indeed my head, between my legs. It was like surrendering to an enemy general whose humiliating terms you had haughtily rejected an hour earlier. She demanded my passport and kept it; she stood in folded-arms silence as I struggled cravenly with the up-and-over garage doors; she lined up her staff to watch me drag my panniers laboriously up the 9-inch-wide staircase. On the other hand, by looking less like a shovel-faced Def Leppard groupie, I had the last laugh.

The room was unpleasant – tall, narrow and gloomy, like a Portakabin turned on end, with an ever-present cough muffling its way through the distant ceiling to impart the atmosphere of a TB sanatorium – but, however hungry, I wasn't about to leave it. Gathering together the squashed croissants and pliable chocolate squares that had made their home in my panniers' basements, I lay on the bed and ate the lot while watching the final moments of the European Cup Final.

You're not real sportsmen, I thought as Real Madrid jumped about on the victors' rostrum, you're just good at football. You don't go out and flog yourself half to death every day. Only when the Valencia squad filed vacantly past to pick up their losers' medals did I feel an empathy. These were the faces of men who had just faced the ultimate sporting challenge of their lives, and had failed.

Still, I pondered dimly, aware that I was about to fall asleep with my clothes on again but not caring, at least I get another go. I had lost the battle but not the war. That's the good thing about the Tour. Every day, every stage is a race within the race. There's always tomorrow.

Eight

When, in 1910, the Tour first got serious about mountains, it was to the Pyrenees that the organisers came. An official tried to drive up the Tourmalet – at 2,114 metres the highest point on the Tour's Pyrenean itinerary and mercifully avoided in 2000 – but got stuck in snow near the summit and had to abandon his vehicle. Some hours later he blundered hypothermically into a police station at the foot of the mountain, and after a touch-and-go convalescence dispatched the following telegraph to Tour HQ: 'TOURMALET PASSABLE FOR VEHICLES. NO SNOW.'

The first Pyrenean exercise that year, however, was the col d'Aubisque, 1,700 metres up a twisting track that even the Tour scouts had conceded was no more than a muddy mule path. Tackling such an obstacle on clodhopping butcher's bikes with no gears, carrying spare tyres looped round their shoulders and all necessary food and tools on their backs, was understandably a challenge. On race day, Tour officials waited anxiously at the summit; when at last a rider did appear, he ignored their queries – 'What's happened? Where are the others?' – looking straight through them with distant, haunted eyes. Half an hour later race leader Octave Lapize appeared, filthy, famished, fucked as flotsam, pushing his bike through the mud and mist. He slowly remounted, pedalled up to the official party, stuck his face straight in theirs and summoned his last reserves to scream, '*Assassins!*' It is relevant to point out here that the riders had set off at 3.30 a.m. – that's right – and still faced 200 kilometres before the stage finish.

On this basis, it wasn't ideal that my first task of the day was the Ascension of the Aubisque: 16.4 kilometres at an average gradient of 7.2 per cent, the fourth-longest hors catégorie climb in the 2000 Tour. I was still in a bad way – when I tried to say 'Merci' for my hot chocolate in the café next door, nothing came out – but at least the elements were being considerate, sheathing the mountains in thick cloud that wisped down past Le Lorry as I rounded the first hairpin. The Pyrenees retain a rough, pioneering ambience that the Alps have long since sold for a blank traveller's cheque. The End of the Earth and the Circle of Death are both here, craggy, treeless highlands roamed by shepherds in snowshoes rather than futures traders in Gore-Tex.

Cycling into Descartes on my second day, there had been a terrible moment when I became convinced that my credit card was back in Loudun: by the time I realised it wasn't, I had already resigned myself to a 90k roundtrip to retrieve it. Since then it had become something of a mid-morning ritual to wonder whether I'd go back if I'd left my cards at last night's hotel, a means of gauging my morale for the rest of the day. Naturally, the distance I was prepared to retrace had dropped steadily each stage, and as I hunched and panted through the grimy old spa hotels of Eaux-Bonnes, 6k and as many fat hairpins up the road from Laruns, I knew I had recorded the lowest score yet in the Credit Card Challenge. This was good in so far as I hadn't left my credit card in Laruns, but bad in so far as I now realised that I had in fact left my passport there. Feeling internally puréed, I stopped and sagged bonelessly over the handlebars. Then, starting bolt upright and with my features savagely distorted into a Hinault of rage, I barrelled furiously down the hairpins, a terrible oath-fest ricocheting off the terraced walls. Even now I can hardly bear to picture the proprietress's face as she handed the document over, but when I do, yes – there it is again: a little smile.

Anyway, I eventually made it as far as the ski resort of Gourette, 4k from the summit, before getting off to push. There were signs every kilometre detailing the average gradient for the stretch ahead: these were supposed to keep cyclists' spirits up, but when, having agonised through a couple of 8 per cents and a 9, I was told to prepare for a 10, I surrendered with a cracked and puny rasp of anguish. It hadn't helped to hear cars that had overtaken me changing messily down into first gear as they disappeared into the mist above and tackled an even more alarming hairpin.

I'd tried to do it properly: bananas in my back pocket, apple juice frothing unappealingly in my bidons, limbs slathered in Ibuleve pain-relief cream instead of suntan lotion. But it was no good. I was not a climber. One of the final unexplored avenues for sporting glory was closing before me, and what was now left to a man of 36? Golf, perhaps. Darts. Curling?

I did at least manage to ride the last 2k, in time to see the mountains do a gentle striptease as the mist lifted, exposing my shame to rocks as wet and silver and green as an evil pizza-chef's anchovy. 'Félicitations!' said the cyclo-tourist sign at the top; the cyclo-tourist himself said something else.

It was nippy up at 1,709 metres. Each of the hairs on my arm dangled a tiny crystal ball from its tip, a shimmering droplet of cloud. My legs were rather less picturesquely slathered and spattered in road mud. After donning rain top and leggings I set off down a tiny, pot-holed road that clung to the rim of a great, sheer rock bowl half-filled with mist. With my hands numbstruck to the bars I swished in and out of Napoleonic tunnels that aimed small, icy drip-falls into my face. Dirty tongues of snow probed out on to the road – yesterday that underwheel slappy-mash sound had been melted tar, today it was slush. I was almost relieved when the road suddenly levelled and rose for the 4k climb to the col du Soulor.

During my failed assault of the Aubisque I had enjoyed some success with a downwards flick of the ankle that somehow seemed to help propel the opposing leg through the debilitating ten-o'clock-to-midnight arc of the pedal revolution, and employing this weapon, along with the old stalwart hand-on-thigh push-down, I crested the Soulor at some speed. This carried me at incautious velocity down a circuitous descent, my sagging mouth whipped and pulled about by wind and G-force.

The descent of the Soulor ended Chris Boardman's Tour in 1997 (torn back muscle and damaged vertebrae), almost ruined Lance Armstrong's 2000 preparations (a 75-k.p.h. fall in training) and in 1951 caused perhaps the scariest spill in Tour history. Wim van Est, the first Dutchman ever to lead the race, skidded and went off the edge of a hairpin, landing 20 metres down on the only ledge above a vertical eternity. To retrieve him his team knotted all their spare tubes together and lowered them over the edge to make a rope; van Est was rescued but the tubes stretched so much that the entire team had to abandon the race.

With blanched old Tourisms flashing beneath my wheels – RICHARD JE T'AIME; FORZA PANTANI; VIRENQUE = EPO beneath a huge carriageway-spanning syringe – I hurtled into Aucun, where I late-lunched in a ski-hotel restaurant, ZR's steaming wheel-rims cooling off in the tackle room usually set aside for snowsuits and sledges. The appalling exertions of the climb and the nervous strain of the descent hit me in full as I sat there among the afternoon's last diners, prim and elderly holidaymakers on mountain-air constitutionals. Blundering dismally into such genteel establishments looking (and often behaving) like the sole survivor of a pot-holing tragedy had long since stopped bothering me. Again I could only watch as flies grubbed about in my mud-speckled armhair, and when my grapefruit appetiser inevitably squirted citric acid straight into both eyes I didn't even flinch.

Fumbling parts of some sort of cutlet into my unstable maw I got out the stage itinerary, even though I could now recite it by heart. Ahead from Aucun lay a run up the valley to Argelès-Gazost, followed by . . . drool wine into Lycra . . . followed by . . . grasp knife in right hand like screwdriver and jab listlessly at meat . . . followed by . . . oh, to big bad buggery and back, followed by the steepest hors catégorie climb in the race, a 12.9-kilometre, 8.5 per cent assault on the colossus referred to by the organisers as Lourdes–Hautacam.

There had been bad times before but, anvil-flattened by the doubts which sometimes overwhelm the rider, these were the worst. The people around me were on holiday, and for the first time I accepted that I was not. Hautacam lay at the tip of a tiny, dead-end road drawn by someone, or rather someone else, with a degenerative nervous disease. I'd have to go all the way up and then all the way down. Today. I looked up and caught the wary eye of the quiffed, bow-tied waiter, and thought: please, please take me in. I can wash dishes. I can make beds. I can walk about reception on stilts yodelling limericks. Maybe if I pretended I didn't have any money to pay the bill . . . Maybe if someone stole my bike . . .

Lowering my face to the rim of a double espresso for an aromatic facial sauna, I thought how typically ridiculous the organisers were to twin the mountain with Lourdes, which lay 33 kilometres up the valley. It was a geographical pairing to embarrass the most devious estate agent. 'Lourdes–Hautacam' – read like that, it now sounded like a choice. Take your pick. And so I did. Was I going to do Hautacam?

One of the most unfortunate things about being an unfit Englishman cycling long distances in France is the number of signs that yell 'PAIN' down every high street, and directing my acid-impaired gaze out of the window I saw a strident red neon example swaying ominously above a distant boulangerie in the cold wind. It wouldn't have taken much to convince me, and in the geo-spiritual circumstances this counted as divine intervention. No, I was not going to do Hautacam. The way I felt it might take a miracle to get me to Lourdes, but I didn't have a prayer of making a sermon on the mount.

Feeling the same sense of sordid elation I felt when getting off to push up the Marie-Blanque, I pedalled up the valley a different man. This was like walking out halfway through an impossible exam; soon, I knew, would come the long, slow mudslide into guilt and failure, but for now I was feeding off an instant rush of ecstasy. I glided serene and alone up the misty road to Lourdes, Christ on a bike.

The heavens opened as I rolled through Lourdes, but only metaphorically. A thousand neon souvenir shops selling plastic jerry cans of holy water and glow-in-the-dark Last Suppers; a million Pac-a-Mac pilgrims queuing outside McDonald's or nodding vacantly along to the unholy muzak hissing out of every bizarre bazaar – Lourdes is the Blackpool of Christianity, the world capital of kitsch. It has more hotels than any French city except Paris, and may be the only town on the planet that sees no problem in selling alabaster saints alongside postcards of splayed female hindquarters emblazoned with the slogan 'Ahh – don't you love the smell of nature?' And who could not marvel at the effrontery of calling your nodding-saint naffmart Au Sacré Coeur de Jésus, or your package-holiday outfit St Peter's Tours? Madonna knew just what she was doing when she named her daughter after this triumph of two-faced tack.

The 1,000k came up as I was halfway to Bagnères-de-Bigorre, the old spa town 22 kilometres east of Lourdes where stage eleven was to kick off. I developed a detailed hatred for these dead miles, the off-the-route transfer bits the riders would do in buses and team cars, but wincing at my Hautacam surrender I gritted my teeth into the wind-driven rain and ground on in a spirit of self-flagellatory penance. And thinking about it now there was something slightly unreal, slightly apparitional, about the black-jerseyed granddad who slid gently past me in a shotblasting downpour with a beatific 'Bonjour'. Nose to the handlebars and rain-reddened thighs furiously pushing the pedals, I could never reel him in. The harder I pressed, the further away he seemed, a relaxed, almost jaunty silhouette freewheeling nonchalantly across an iron-skied horizon. I topped 60 k.p.h. downhill, sending impressive curtains of spray up over the hedgerows and aquaplaning terrifyingly up to a rush-hour intersection, but it was hopeless.

Another ville d'étape, another knackered spa town. Deep in introspective decline, Bagnères-de-Bigorre displayed no discernible character and was clearly hoping the Tour would leave some of its charisma behind when it rushed off. Comprehensively rain marinaded, I wheeled ZR into a hotel and instantly found myself being addressed by a proprietress whose fondness for one-sided discourse far outweighed her dislike for mopping up brown water. For maybe fifteen minutes I stood there, shivering first internally and then with all the convulsive abandon of a cartoon character, trying to smile and nod as the road filth slowly sluiced down my body and puddled muddily around my ankles. The hotel trade, her son in Clapham, Ryanair – all were debated at length, along with an extended lecture on her experiences of the 'derme', which I hoped at the time was a skin complaint but have just realised referred to the Dome. In all this time my only contribution was 'Stansted Airport?', and when that emerged unsteadily through my vibrating teeth, she looked at me as if I'd just pointed out she was wearing too much make-up and snapped, 'Non, Luton.'

A miner's face greeted me in the mirror above the basin – white helmet-strap lines down otherwise black cheeks, eyes like Polos on a chocolate muffin. This, I noted with tired pride, was the most road-warrior-like I had looked yet, the closest approximation to another iconic picture in my *procycling* Merckx special, of Eddy during the 1972 Paris–Roubaix. Held on an invariably cold, wet day in April on a route specially selected to include as many cobbled streets as possible, Paris-Roubaix is known as the Hell of the North – the definitive race for super-hard men. And there was Eddy, leaning into an arc of wet cobbles at a speed sufficient to blur the Ford Capri parked in the background, gaze fixed calmly to the road in front, fingertips artistically poised on the bars, and the filth: running from the corners of his eyes and soggy-Allbran sideburns in sweaty black rivulets, goateed around his mouth and chin, caked so completely over both legs that where his shorts have ridden temporarily up his left thigh is a cheeky little band of pink that separates black mud from black cotton like a garter belt (well, you know – after ten days alone on the road I was getting my kicks where I could).

Why couldn't I align myself with a plucky but doomed underdog, a Chris Boardman or a Paul Kimmage? Or Raymond Poulidor, perennial Tour runner-up in the Sixties and Seventies, still coming second at the age of 40? (And if that wasn't dispiriting enough, the French public nicknamed him Poupou.) It has always been my misfortune to lionise winners. When everyone was moaning about the loathsome behaviour of 'Superbrat' McEnroe, I was fondly indulgent – here was a man who just really wanted to win. Bernard Hinault might have been barking mad, but having started on his autobiography I was beginning to feel a strange awe for that monstrous ego. 'It's said that a great victory doesn't really sink in until afterwards,' he writes on winning the world championship in 1980. 'Not in my case! I knew straight away what I'd done. *I had conquered everybody.*'

Today's Tours are often won by small margins, with the

overall winner maybe only taking one stage victory during the race, sometimes none. Not in Eddy's case! In 1970 he won eight stages, and hogged the King of the Mountains prize for himself. His contemporaries were outraged – the tradition then and now was to share these things out, let others have a slice. The Cannibal's response was a phrase he learned to say in five languages (I heard the Italian version on my 1973 Tour of Italy video): 'I am completely indifferent.' Not a great one as catch-phrases go, but imbued with a cold arrogance that I could only admire. And he was Belgian, for heaven's sake. How could a Belgian be so brutally determined, so merciless, so . . . successful.

Velcro had played an important role in my life for the last two months: with those little prickly pads affixing gloves, shoes, rain jacket and any number of baggage items, any careless exuberance while dressing led to the sort of Gordian limb entanglements you might expect during the latter stages of a one-man game of Twister. Undressing wasn't much better. Pulling off the Velcro strips on my gloves unleashed drying-dog mud sprays all over the scalloped nylon bedspread, and after I discovered that the insect repellent had leaked into my plastic bag of washing powder I decided that the best thing all round was simply to go fully dressed into the shower (a plastic booth in the corner of the room) and soap down my clothes. This worked a treat, at least until I started stripping them off for a kickabout rinse in the shower tray, grape-crusher style.

The temperature control was one of those safecracker jobs: tiny clockwise adjustment – JesusChrist-ow-bloodybollocks-owowow-I'm-on-fire; minute anticlockwise compensation – Hoooooooly-Mother-of-Merckx-who-turned-on-the-hail. I had just pulled off shorts and one sock when some body part made inadvertent but sturdy clockwise contact, and the extravagant flailing that ensued cruelly exposed the cubicle's inherent design flaw, namely its lack of roof. But we all make mistakes, and another one of mine was not locking the bedroom door.

Attracted perhaps by my attempt to encapsulate the works of Hieronymous Bosch in a single sound, and perhaps by her leaking ceiling, the proprietress had seen fit to enter my room at a moment which coincided unhappily with my wild, humid egress from the cubicle. The lesser of the two issues here was that her furnishings had been liberally hosed down; later I had to remake the entire bed with the rank reserve blankets in the wardrobe, and the lampshades were still steaming the next morning. But of greater immediate concern to both of us was my troubling presentation. One bare, sultana-toed foot alongside a wet beige sock, then nothing but flesh and water until the soap-frothed waistband of my jersey. I didn't know whether to be glad or sad when I looked down while grabbing for a towel and saw that the elemental rigours of the day had apparently inspired my genitals to eat themselves. On the plus side, the appalled mumble that trickled from her lips as she backed out of the room was the last sound she addressed to me.

The Pyrenees were over and I was aware that I had not acquitted myself very well. Unwilling to tackle at this stage the painful core issues of gumption and vigour, I looked for a less abstract solution. One of my principal encouragements on setting off from England had been that there was no knack to cycling, no skill I would have to master, but waking up in my damp bed with merciful sunlight spearing the perforations in the shutters to polka-dot the room I found myself wishing there was. Thinking about Eddy's delicate pianist's touch on the bars had me wondering if the key was relaxing my own brutal, desperate grasp; then again, maybe if I could somehow dump my panniers I'd be able to stand up in the saddle and so fly up the climbs. Another guest had propped his noble, unburdened road bike against mine in the stairwell, and giving it a tentative, light-fingered hoist as I saddled up was a potent reminder of how much extra weight I was carrying. At least I was now remembering to do Chris Boardman's stretches last thing at night and first in the morning, even if – as that day – doing so strained all my leg muscles to the point where they felt about to snap and whiplash up like roller blinds.

Bagnères-de-Bigorre looked a lot better in the sun. The tall mahogany doors of the restaurant where I'd eaten snails the night before (what was it with me and arthropods?) gleamed venerably, and the hills beyond – oh dear – looked laundered and crisp. A little group of farmers were protesting benignly in the square: 'The sheep is the lowest form of farm animal' read the banner, though I think on balance theirs was probably a pro- rather than an anti-sheep demonstration.

It never seemed right or fair to be bathed in the sweat of hard manual labour before 9.15 a.m., but from now on this would always be the way. Stage eleven was supposed to be a flat one, a day off for the riders after their Pyrenean rigours, but as the D938 curved up through the fields of hairy-eared barley I was soon in trouble. So much so that I somehow contrived to get lost, blundering straight on when the D938 turned left, then careering down a hill so enormous that by the time I eased up to the unfamiliar town of Tournay at its foot a quick look at map and itinerary confirmed I had just earned myself an 18-kilometre detour. No ordinary kilometres these, though: as with all detours these were special 'shag-battered bollock sodding' kilometres, which may only be tackled in a temper so foul that it is common to find oneself insulting adjacent livestock.

The Tournay Misjudgement sullied an exquisite morning: large birds soaring on thermals; a castle-studded horizon; crops shimmering like fibreglass filaments; cowbells and crickets; everything growing almost audibly. The same sort of hillsides that had been speckled with unidentifiably tiny green shoots only a week before near Limoges were now lushly striped with burgeoning fronds of maize. Soon, I knew, the first hairy sweet-corns would swell and grow in the heart of each shoot, rising up, ripening in the hot French sun, until the day came in late summer when the crop was ripe and ready to be harvested by me and my dad legging it over the fence on the way home from a family motoring holiday. We always arrived in Calais with a plundered bootful. I once had a nightmare that the Jolly Green Giant chased us all the way home.

And though cycling might be the national sport of France, from what I saw that day strimming runs it a close second. Every garden and field buzzed with Canutean attempts to hold back the green tide, to keep the undergrowth from overgrowing. I even saw a couple of leather-faced fellers with scythes, which was pleasingly traditional. Death must be dreading the day when they upgrade him with a strimmer.

I finally rejoined the route at Mauvezin, a hilltop town with a huge panorama of wooded hills. Descending the first of these, swishing through troughs of hot air and layers of tree-shaded chilled mist, I hit trouble at 55 k.p.h. – a huge cloud of fat midges. It was like the *USS Enterprise* going through an asteroid belt. With my face, neck and helmet being painfully paintballed I could only concentrate on keeping my mouth shut, having already discovered to my cost that the hawking expulsion of throat-lodged animal matter is an unwise procedure at speed. The necessary parting of the lips allows further objects a way in, and the ejection process inevitably results in decorating one's cheeks, chin and clothing with phlegm-embalmed corpses.

It was interesting how I had learned to assess a settlement's altitude from its name alone. Somewhere-sur-Something and Blah-du-Blah were always good news for the slothful cyclist, both implying a riverside location and consequently benign gradients; but well before I got to Saint-Bertrand-de-Comminges I knew it would consist of a big old monastery surrounded by narrow alleys atop a small, brown mountain.

A bit of creative orienteering convinced me that the route actually skirted round this picturesque but irksome obstacle, and in bullying sun I dined at its foot. Most establishments were keen to process my dining requests in double-quick time and dispatch me with evident relish; it was my misfortune that day to find myself patronising the exception to this rule. Sitting at the most prominent outside table was normally a winner – the staff would rush towards me with nervous, uncertain expressions that suggested a whispered kitchen debate on whether they should hand over a menu or offer me a small cash sum to leave – but that didn't work, and nor did thoughtfully peeling off my flash-fried ear-flesh. I suppose the complete absence of rival or potential diners to nauseate didn't help my case. I filled my bidons from a gurgling stone hydrant across the dusty dead-end street; I picked up a hot brochure from a neighbouring table and found it dedicated solely to the cult of the strimmer, or *débroussailleuse* as I saw it was more properly known to native defoliation enthusiasts. I'd got as far as the hard-core end-section where men in welder's helmets set about a rainforest with rotary-bladed beasts harnessed round their waists before a large waitress of disagreeable appearance reluctantly emerged.

A craven consumerist pigmy after the anchois incident, I didn't dare complain, and it was two long, hot hours after our introduction that I finally said goodbye to Saint-Bertrand. On a day when the riders were averaging 43 k.p.h. that meant a lot of lost 'k's, which on this particular day meant that I was going to be late. The town of Mane was 40 kilometres away, and I had only an hour to get there. I had an appointment, you see. In Mane, with a man.

I put the hammer down but it bounced back and smacked me in the teeth; a headwind and some bastard little climbs ensured I arrived in Mane half an hour late. There, sitting as promised outside the Café du Pont, was a man who looked a little like a synthesis of all the actors who have played Dr Who, with a blonde toddler on his knee.

'Tim?'

'Nick?'

With ZR lashed to his Citroën and 2-year-old Jane installed perilously between the back-seat pannier mountains we set off up a gently rising gorge, the occasional black snake swishing sinuously across the road. I'd been put on to Nick Flanagan by Simon O'Brien, a regular visitor to Pyrenean Pursuits, the cycling guesthouse Nick runs with his wife Jan. I couldn't quite get my head round the concept of a cycling guesthouse, and nor, in a charming way, could Nick. His clientele, as I understood it, were a blend of pros looking for a training base and cyclo-tourists looking for a drinking base; on arriving at his establishment, a cosy three-floor chalet outside the village of Biert, there was to be found no identifying sign other than a gate cleverly crafted from two old bikes. 'We're not really bothered with passing trade,' said Nick in Scouse tones mellowed by nine years in the Pyrenees. 'It's more a word-of-mouth thing.'

Nick hadn't come to the area known as the Ariège for the money. He'd arrived in 1991 with his new wife and an early-retirement pay-off; both keen cyclists, the guesthouse concept had seemed the ideal business/pleasure marriage, with the latter wearing the trousers in the partnership. 'You don't need much when you've got this,' he said, seating me on his patio with a beer and passing a careless hand across a backdrop of towering green peaks. An orchard, a field over the road running down to the excitable River Arac, additional acreage up the mountain: 'I haven't found half the land we own yet,' said Nick indulgently. As he talked of skiing in the winter and horse-riding in the summer, the lifestyle seemed blissfully enviable (at least to people who don't find such activities both scary and ridiculous), and though I'd have predicted dark glances at the school gates and con-spiratorial muttering in the supermarché, the locals had apparently been cheerfully welcoming. 'The Ariège isn't like the rest of the south of France: it's a poor area, kind of remote, off the tourist track, and the locals respect anyone with the courage to come here and try and make a fist of things.'

Introductions were effected to Jan, their 6-year-old son Dominic and a sympathetically maternal one-eyed dog slobbering over a very tolerant cat and her brood of kittens, followed by another beer, followed by a quick tour round an extensive collection of cycling memorabilia that included a photograph of the peloton sweeping past their front door in 1997 and a warm personal message from Chris Boardman. Finally Nick sighed in an enough-of-me way and said, 'So – the Aubisque, eh?'

During our telephone conversations Nick had been brought up to speed with my project, but as his eyes twinkled encouragingly at me I realised I might have glossed over certain issues, most notably my physical ineptitude and an associated propensity to cheat. A minute earlier, leafing through a book on the Tour's history that had been presented to Nick by the author, I had chanced upon the statement: 'I am a cyclist. I do not get off and walk.'

For an accurate précis of my not altogether admirable Pyrenean performance one would simply cut the negative word from the second of these sentences and paste it in the first, but somehow it seemed a shame to disappoint him so early in our acquaintance.

'Well,' I began, concocting an answer that dropped right on the boundary fence of the honesty ball-park, 'I paced myself.'

He gave me an understanding smile. 'Ah – saving yourself for Hautacam.'

It was supposed to come out as a helpless self-deprecatory snort, but somewhere between brain and mouth it evolved into a heroic sigh of painful recollection.

'Paced yourself again, yeah?'

'No – no, actually, no. No, I didn't. No.'

'Chapeau!' said Nick, raising his beer can, and with a single modest shrug the humble economies of truth were inflated to a huge and ugly edifice of deceit. I think I might even have rubbed my legs with a showy grimace. What had I done? This was certainly the most idiotic duplicity I had essayed since pretending to be Portuguese during a youthful confrontation with two London Transport ticket inspectors. I could hardly ask Nick to sort out my gears now.

Much to everyone's surprise another guest turned up at this point, a middle-aged Australian with a face like a jolly 1950s schoolboy, wheeling a hefty tourer weighed down with front and rear panniers and a tent. Rhys had found something on the Internet about Pyrenean Pursuits, and was stopping off halfway through an eight-week European odyssey. He was older than I am, and fatter, but had done 2,500 kilometres already at 100k a day, and camped every night except one. Rhys was instantly identifiable as a very nice chap, but statistics like these were intolerable. I smarted as Paul Kimmage had done when a bearded tourist lurched out of an Alpine crowd on his panniered tourer and pedalled up past him as the Irishman struggled desperately to keep the approaching broom wagon at bay. Humiliated, and humiliated by a tourist, 'a bloody Fred'.

'Any mountains?' I felt myself constrained to enquire.

'Tim here just did the Aubisque and Hautacam in one day,' chipped in Nick on cue. I nodded slowly and fixed a flinty yet mystical gaze on the mist now smudging out the peaks above.

'Nah, well, no really big ones,' said Rhys mildly. 'I shouldn't really be doing this at all – the doctors told me my back wasn't up to it, and my ankle joints never fused properly when I was a kid. The pain's pretty bad after the first hour. But I guess you know all about pain after yesterday!'

We drank beer until it rained, Jan retiring to put the kids to bed and hone the website that had attracted Rhys, Nick disappearing into the kitchen to do quite outstanding things with ducks and flageolet beans. Rhys and I sheltered in the bar/garage, watching the Tour of Italy on Eurosport and playing about with Nick's turbo trainer, a bike with its front wheel removed and the back one wedged between resistance rollers. It was good to exchange road tales, the fly-swallowing and the loose chippings, though my rigged coronation as King of the Mountains loomed shamefully over the conversation. Rhys knew nothing about bike racing but plenty about bikes, and every time he started talking about gear ratios I tutted gutturally in what was supposed to be a matey don't-let's-talk-shop fashion and dramatically changed the subject.

This tactic was additionally employed over dinner to probe the motives for Rhys's extended journey, which at his stage of life I was fairly hopeful would involve some unspeakable lifestyle apocalypse: the gay affair that forced a messy divorce, a border-hopping white-collar-crime spree. But no: he'd been a civil engineer with the same firm for fifteen years and like all Australians was therefore eligible for three months paid leave. His wife and teenage daughters were waiting back home, hoping Daddy got Europe and cycling out of his system before his ankles melted.

Bloated with confit de canard and vin de pays I lay awake for some time in my room, scanning the whitewashed ceiling for spiders, while out in the rain woodland creatures did shrill and ghastly things to one another. It was good to have proper pillows again after eleven nights spent with my head cricked painfully against the sort of thing you would expect Gladiators to hit each other with, but I still couldn't sleep. The day's revelations had been almost uniformly troubling. Why had Nick beaten a teenage Chris Boardman in a 25-mile time trial? How had Rhys hauled half a branch of Millets for 2,500 kilometres on unfused ankles? When would I stop lying?

I crept back downstairs when everyone was in bed to call Birna on Nick's payphone, and drunk and tired it had all come out in one long blurry sentence. There was an extended pause when I'd finished, understandable when you're woken up at midnight to hear your absent husband mumbling words like 'pain', 'lies', 'bonk' and 'Fred'. In the end I carried on myself. 'I can't do it I just can't do this and next it's Mont Ventoux where people die and then the Alps and I just can't I'm just not no I can't.'

It wasn't a very Eddy Merckx moment. Birna did all she could in the way of offering soothing platitudes, and when they elicited only mid-pubescent wordless whines she tried out a pull-yourself-together verbal cheek-slap. That worked better, but it was still gone 4 a.m. when I slammed Bernard Hinault's biography shut, flicked a weary V-sign at the yellow-jerseyed slaverer on the cover and switched off the light.

Nine

The rain had flattened the long grass like a stampeding herd of bulls, but the sun was out now and, pouring me the first of half a dozen glasses of orange juice, Nick suggested the three of us go for a mountain ride. Because this could not be allowed to happen, I went back to bed until I heard Rhys and Nick leave, then shambled wanly downstairs to look at the map. Nick's proposed circular route up to the col de Saraillé and back to Biert down the gorge involved a climb to 942 metres up a tiny road whose impressive collection of double-gradient chevrons guaranteed a rousing 'sod-that' verdict. Instead I sat on the patio, reading selections from the Flanagan cycling library and enjoying the experience of wearing only slightly foolish clothing during the hours of daylight. The sun made my mottled, waxy nose throb; under the table, the one-eyed dog leaked sympathetic milk over my espadrilles. I was ready to go back to bed when I found myself gradually absorbed by the story of Eugène Christophe.

Leading the 1913 Tour as it crosses the Pyrenees, Christophe is hurtling down the Tourmalet when his front forks snap, propelling him into a wall of scree. Tour rules dictate that riders must effect all repairs themselves (a situation that persisted until 1930), so Christophe dusts himself down, shoulders his stricken machine and somehow runs with it for 10 kilometres down what was then Europe's highest road (sorry: 'road'). Arriving bloody and exhausted at the village of Sainte-Mairie-de-Campan, he is followed silently into the local forge by Tour snoops keen to ensure no illicit aid is offered or received. Waving the blacksmith aside and perhaps hissing lengthy compound insults through his teeth, Christophe begins to hammer wearily at strips of glowing metal, and after two hot, hard hours has somehow fashioned himself a set of forks. As he prepares to set off, now four hours down and in last place, an official blocks his way. The handiwork may have been all his own, but in allowing the blacksmith's boy to pump the bellows Christophe has accepted indirect third-party help. Illegal assistance – a further ten-minute penalty.

I put the book down on the rain-spotted table, leant back in my slatted folding chair and looked up at the mountains. Then I went inside, withdrew a number of other titles and thumbed through their indices looking for Christophe, Eugène. The early years were bad enough. In 1910 he ploughed through snowdrifts in the Milan–San Remo race, an effort which earned him a month in hospital and two lost years of racing; in his comeback Tour, 1912, he actually finished with a lower overall time than the winner, but because that year the race was decided on an arcane points basis Eugène was placed second. And then it got worse.

Determined not to abandon the 1913 race after the rather trying bellows incident, he somehow claws his way back to finish seventh. The war then intervenes, but in the first race afterwards, 1919, Christophe soon finds himself the inaugural wearer of the new yellow jersey selected by the Tour organisers to distinguish the race leader. During the stage between Metz and Dunkirk, at

468k (what? *What?*) the second-longest in Tour history, race leader Christophe feels an ominous shudder and then a mighty wrench. He can't quite believe it, but it's the front forks again. By the time he sources a new pair from a bike factory he has lost over an hour and again it is too much to regain. He keeps trying until 1925, when, nineteen years after his first Tour and now aged 40, he enters his last, abandoning well before the finish.

I restocked the library and went into the bar. I'd hidden ZR behind a table here to minimise the risk of kit-comparison sessions during which the extent of my ignorance would be quickly exposed, but now extracted it. Propped against Nick's turbo trainer, without the panniers it looked lithe and poised. I thought of a picture of Eugène Christophe I'd just seen: flat cap, recklessly enormous ringmaster moustache, spare tyre wrapped round shoulders of fisherman's jersey, filthy legs planted on filthy cobbles. And, held by one hand on the saddle, the other on the bars, his bike. It reminded me a lot of my first bike, the hand-me-down Wayfarer: no gears, meaty iron tubing, sit-up-and-beg handlebars – and a big chrome bell. *A bell*. Ding-ding! Ding-ding! Leader of world's most gruelling sporting event coming through! Ding-ding-ding!

Suddenly I understood something important. Part of the Tour de France was about trying to get one over on your opponents: better tactics, better equipment, better drugs – a competitive advantage by any means necessary. I remembered a helicopter shot I'd seen of the Tour of Italy, with half a dozen riders sneaking a short-cut across a petrol-station forecourt while the rest of the peloton log-jammed slowly through the adjacent roundabout. Stuff like this, and the more epically blatant chicanery of the early years, had appealed to me, and in my own way I had already done it all. But beneath this professional cynicism, the Tour was still fundamentally about the amateur ideals of courage and noble suffering, and this was a Tour I hadn't yet entered. In any case, who were *my* opponents? Carefully selected old men aside, I was essentially competing against myself: the shiftless, irresolute schemer facing the rather more reticent lion-hearted incorruptible, the one who got on his bike instead of getting off it. Humbly thanking Eugène, I went upstairs, changed into my jersey and shorts, came back down, cleated myself into ZR and headed for the hills.

The D17 out of Massat was thin, steep and so quiet that dogs slept on it. With the sun working on the wet greenery you could smell photosynthesis going into overdrive: Jan had given up her vegetable plot after weeding it became a painting-the-Forth-Bridge job, and Nick said hillsides like this one were regularly buzzed by police helicopters looking for pot plantations. It was almost tropical up there. I nodded at a couple of ageing hippies on their corrugated veranda; three blokes pretending to fix a barn roof jeered, 'Eh – le Tour est arrivé!' as I rounded the hairpin alongside. The road dipped slightly, then pitched radically upwards, but even as it did so I became aware of an important fact: I was not slowing down. The D17 climbed through a dark arc of woodland and I climbed with it, looking down at my back wheel to note that I was only in gear twenty-four, three shy of the bottom of the barrel. The trees petered out and suddenly there it was, a yawning 360-degree panorama of perpendicular pastures and snow-veined granite that swept all the way across to Spain.

My heart felt like bursting, but not for the reason I had become accustomed to on reaching such altitudes. Reaching the brow of the col de Saraillé was a religious experience: I am healed; I can see; in conquering the savage beauty around me I have, in fact, become its creator. The climb had not been a calvary but a road to Damascus, one that had converted me to a self-believer. For the first time in over twenty years I raised both my hands from a set of handlebars and punched the blue sky.

On the loop back to Biert up the gorge I stopped at Castet-d'Aleu for a celebratory coffee at an excellent bar/shop, where an unbelievably old man presided over dark cabinets of pre-war preserves. Was it the lack of panniers, I wondered as I sat outside watching the traffic, or the additional rest, or the brevity of the day's 33-kilometre itinerary? Probably all three, but none of them played any part in the conclusion I arrived at during the course of a bitter, beetle-black coffee and what would have been a complimentary chocolate if the old man's old wife hadn't nicked it while I was in the loo. I had gone off that day to search for the hero inside myself, and somewhere up on the col de Saraillé I had found him. To return to Pyrenean Pursuits and be obliged to dismiss my climb in casual terms was a very hard thing to do.

On this basis, it was a shame that in the pitiable depths of my long, dark night of the soul I'd already committed myself to more cheating. Biert was a good 60k off the route of a stage which dead-ended at the unpromising town of Revel, from where the riders would take a plane transfer across Languedoc to Avignon (alight here for Mont Ventoux). Birna had not been required to use all of her powers of persuasion to convince me on the phone to bunk off the bit to Revel, and had even, as a call from her that morning revealed, booked me a hire car to drive myself from Toulouse airport to Avignon.

I would get to Toulouse by train, or rather I wouldn't, for as Nick established during an epic sequence of chair-bitingly contradictory telephonic encounters with assorted transport officials, of the three trains a day which would accept bicycles, an impressive seven were affected by wildcat strike action. Of the remaining five, six were redirected to Barcelona, though the front two carriages of the other four would proceed to Carcassonne, arriving eleven minutes before they had left. 'I'll drive you,' said Nick; I instantly protested at this further act of generosity, but not for very long.

We left the next morning, my body still processing a snails 'n' quails gourmet extravaganza that had made an additional mockery of Pyrenean Pursuits' 250F-a-night half-board tariff.

Rhys, now infected by the Zen-like inertia that apparently governs many an Ariègeois lifestyle, was planning to stay a few more days, cooling his heels and more particularly their adjacent ankles. A serendipitous phone call from Nick's next guest, an American called Mike, asking to be picked up at Toulouse airport, made me feel slightly better about his 200-kilometre roundtrip, and proved an additional boon when it became clear that the only hire-car available at the airport was the one Mike had just returned.

It was odd to be driving again, odd to ease down on the sort of pedal that effortlessly whooshed you up to idiotic velocity. Cleated to the bike I'd forgotten what it meant to be footloose and fancy-free, and it was good to remember. Hammering eastwards on the hot motorway I passed the pop-up medieval horizon of Carcassonne, deafeningly serenaded with the bygone sounds of Nostalgie FM, the station selected by Mike and, after a fruitless attempt at mastering the tuning procedure, tolerated in default by me. I'd read somewhere that French radio stations are obliged to broadcast 40 per cent of their music in the native language as part of the nation's campaign to prove that it is better than England, and the distressing Halliday-heavy consequences of this made themselves apparent as I flew up the fast lane. Still, the Nostalgie playlist devisers had found the odd grey-area loophole. 'Michelle, ma belle' and 'Chanson d'amour, ra-da-da-da-da' had both blared out of the speakers twice before I began the first of several late-afternoon laps of Avignon's city walls.

Avignon was my second pre-booked flash-hotel stopover, though given the modest scale of my achievements since Dax I barely felt I'd earned it. I eventually found the Mercure Palais des Papes near the famous half bridge, embedded in the man-made cliffs that shore up the Pope's palace. My plan had been to bugger about up and down the ochre boulevards and high-sided alleys, then early to bed for a prolonged toss/turn session mulling over the looming horrors of Ventoux, but this scheme was adapted somewhat by the revelation at reception that my single room had been upgraded to the rather larger one necessary to accommodate Birna and our three children. The party had arrived on the TGV an hour before and, as I presently discovered, were currently in situ.

I will leave you to imagine the emotional, high-pitched yelps of 'Daddy gone but Daddy here now!' as well as my children's own reactions. Birna explained that my unsettling telephonic performance had triggered much domestic concern, and I belatedly understood that all the car-hire booking and detailed enquiries into my itinerary were related to the planning of this half-term surprise. 'In fact, I'm completely OK now,' I said with an effort. 'I went up a big mountain yesterday without any problems at all.' Birna has an impressive armoury of level looks, and she treated me now to her most horizontal. 'Isn't that what you said to those men in the Pyrenees?'

My morale roller-coaster had been round a few loops and corkscrews since that terrible phone call, but I realised just how bad I must have sounded for Birna even to have considered marshalling three children aged 1 to 6 single-handed from London on the train. I-Spy had regressed into We-Punch well before the Channel, and after the sweets ran out at Lille Birna had been drawn inexorably into yet another prolonged search for our children's on/off switches, or at least volume controls. A snooty businesswoman had repeatedly demanded that 'the *calme* of the wagon to be respected', and though she abruptly relocated to the next carriage after a co-ordinated 'bouncing' incident outside Dijon, those final hours of onboard high jinks had been inevitably trying.

The presence of my family was joyous but utterly dislocating. Things I had become accustomed to – strewing all my road-ravaged clothing carelessly about the room, spending less than £400,000 an hour, performing Mr Boardman's Patent Stretches without rowdy hecklers, waking up in full daylight – were to become distant memories. Of course all of this was comfortably outweighed by the benefits of an Alpine support vehicle, loaded with panniers and cheerleaders, urging me up the mountains. Then watching in grim-faced, nauseated disillusion as I wheezed and swore and flobbed and fell and failed.

You really don't want to cycle up Mont Ventoux when it's hot. 28 May 2000 might not have been as fearsome as 13 July 1967, but even at 10 a.m. the dark green litter bins out in front of the Palais des Papes were sufficiently sun-grilled to make a small child squeal almost as loudly as the slightly smaller child he was trying to upend into one. I looked up at the cloudless sky and tried to regulate my breathing. Tom Simpson's fate wasn't one I aspired to, and no matter how large a shadow he would cast over the day ahead it wouldn't be large enough to keep me cool. My stomach fizzed with trepidation, but click-cleating back to the car park I at least detected that for the first morning in two weeks my legs didn't feel as if they'd been energetically headbutted all night by someone wearing a welder's helmet.

With my departure delayed by the amount of time it takes to manoeuvre three children past a merry-go-round, a Pokémon stall and a dead pigeon, the sun was already high when I returned to the hotel room to fill my bidons with the usual fly-friendly blend of grape juice and tap water. The plan had been for me to drive to Carpentras with ZR in the boot of the Twingo, then set off for the 149-kilometre stage to the Ventoux summit, where Birna and the kids would meet me in the distressingly dear Renault Espace we had hired. The issue here was that on past form I would require at least eight hours (including the non-negotiable long lunch) to do those 149 kilometres, and that was without taking the gradient factor into account.

As it was now midday, this schedule appeared an irksome one. Additionally keen to minimise the scope for hot death, I abruptly decided to sit out the worst of the sun by bunking off the preparatory meanderings. Driving beyond Carpentras to the village of Sault, I'd skip 89 kilometres and gird myself for a late-afternoon assault on the final 60k. This, after all, included most of the awful bits.

It was a sombre send-off. My 6-year-old son Kristjan had only recently been disabused of a misconception that I was competing among cycling's élite in the actual race; horribly crestfallen, he looked at me with the betrayed air of a child coming to terms with the fact – first suspected, perhaps, during those self-mutilating Swingball sessions – that his father might not be the world's most complete athlete. Untroubled by such concerns, his 2-year-old sister Valdis filled the lobby with gay chortles as I strode out of the lift in full Lycra. I can normally count on 4-year-old Lilja for an appropriate sense of theatre, and this was briefly supplied when she tugged at my shorts, looked up with wide eyes and pleaded, 'Don't go up the mountain, Daddy!' I hardly had the chance to ruffle her hair with a brave smile before she added, 'It's *really boring.*'

A long, broad hump of a hill, Le Mont Ventoux didn't in fact look that bad as I drove into the unremarkable town of Carpentras, half an hour southwest and 6,265 feet below its round, chalky summit. In a certain light, the topping of bare, bleached rocks is said to give the impression of a permanent layer of snow, but on a wincingly bright afternoon in late May, rising gently out of the cherry trees and lavender fields, Ventoux seemed benign, a big sandcastle recently washed over by the first wave of an encroaching tide.

Still, you couldn't miss it. Six thousand two hundred and sixty-five feet: hoist the Eiffel Tower on top of Canary Wharf, then stick the whole thing on Ben Nevis – let's face it, we've all wanted to – and you'd still be looking up at the summit. Ventoux isn't an Alp, nor whatever the single of Pyrenees is – it's just there on its own, looming up on almost every Provençal horizon, making its own weather, that squat, muscle-bound bulk spread across a fold and a half of my Michelin map like a whole mountain range in itself. The eye is drawn to it, and often the feet follow. Mountaineering was invented here: by conquering its summit in 1336, the poet and scholar Petrarch became the first man to climb a peak as an end in itself. Almost six hundred years later, future Prime Minister Edouard Daladier had a road built to the top, again for no practical purpose other than curiosity and a determination to tame nature.

On this basis, it is no surprise that the Tour de France should regularly make its way to that slightly lunar summit. Unspectacular as it might look from a distance, Ventoux is the most feared mountain in the Tour's considerable arsenal. 'It is not like other mountains' has been a common refrain among riders since the race first went up it in 1951.

And here I was, a pallid, flimsy tourist in nylon and Lycra sportswear, unsuccessfully trying to remember at what precise time this whole stupid scheme had seemed like a good idea. Striving to psych myself up, something I've never ever been able to do, I acknowledged that for the first time I was up against a legend of the Tour. By conquering Ventoux I could feel a direct affinity with some of the greatest names in sporting history. This would be like taking a penalty at Wembley or portentously bouncing a yellow Slazenger on the Centre Court baseline, only with better weather and a nice view. And if I took it easy, it couldn't be that hard, could it? *Sans* panniers, I'd breezed up the col de Saraillé. This was just a steeper, longer hill, I reasoned, and if I could cope with feeling slightly less breezy it could be mastered.

Regrettably, stage twelve, Carpentras–Ventoux, was by any standards beyond reason. A perfect exercise in agonising futility, it ended with a summit finish: up to the top, from A to B, then all the way back down to A in the team coach. The stage profile map was a horrible document. My 60 kilometres included the second-category col de Notre-Dame des Abeilles, a fourth-category hill and the merciless ascent of Ventoux, at 21k comfortably the most drawn-out hors catégorie climb in the Tour's itinerary.

Ventoux's notoriety was of course sealed in the 1967 Tour. You can blame the heat, you can blame the drugs, but the bottom line is that Le Mont Ventoux remains the only peak in the Tour's 97-year history to have caused a man's death through physical overexertion.

I'd bought a video of Tom Simpson's life, and watched it before I left. It was the ordinariness of his story that made its final chapter so desperately poignant. An inevitably humble upbringing in Durham and Nottingham as the youngest of six kids, the one who always had to win at Ludo; the borrowed bike that won him the first race with his local club at the age of 16, nicknamed Four-Stone Coppi in reference to his hollow-cheeked, beak-nosed similarity to the great Fausto, cycling's first superstar. The additionally inevitable 'happy-go-lucky' descriptions from those who always enjoyed a chat and a laff with Tom.

The cycling scrapbooks under the bed, the determination that had him writing to pros all over Europe for advice; winning a bronze at the 1956 Olympics then going off to Brittany with £100 in his pocket to turn pro; adapting to the people, language and food so successfully that when he met his future wife Helen a year later she thought he was French. Winning four of his first nine races and writing home to say he was earning big money. Almost grabbing the lead in his first Tour in 1960, aged 22. The first big victories – Bordeaux–Paris, Milan–San Remo – wearing the chequered-band Peugeot jersey like the one that now clung to my thumping chest. The big car, the holidays in Corsica. The home movies: skiing with his two young daughters, sleeping in a deck-chair, training on a bike on rollers. Mastering the hierarchy and tactics of road racing, and its accompanying PR duties: as the rest of the 1960 British Tour team fidget gormlessly in front of the Continental cameras, there's Tom grinning hugely with his sponsor's cap right in the lens. Contriving the media-friendly invention of Major Tom, a brollied and bowlered city gent whose sociological origins shared nothing with his own. Sofa-splitting living-room mayhem in Nottingham when Tom wins the 1965 World Championship in Spain; as the first Briton ever to do so, he's voted BBC Sports Personality of the Year. The autographed publicity shots in his world champion's jersey, a clean-cut young man with a cheeky, crooked grin. Major Tom playing the accordion with his gaping mouth frozen in lusty mid-chorus. The broken leg that cost him the next season, and coming into 1967 knowing that at age 30 this was probably his final chance to do well in the Tour and so underwrite a comfortable retirement.

Oh, Tom. I stocked up with raisins and dried apricots in Carpentras, and followed the Tour itinerary to Sault. The organisers were obviously being kind, contriving a route that bent away from Ventoux, tactfully shielding it from the riders' line of vision until the last possible moment. The sky was the colour of ZR, a deep, almost metallic blue, its intensity emphasised by occasional smoke-signal puffs of white cloud. Kids were ambling home for lunch along the flat, scrub-lined roads into empty towns shuttered up for the long afternoon.

It was an airless day, but in the harsh Provençal sun everything seemed unnaturally sharp: cherries gleaming like varnished holly berries, neon poppies lining dayglo lavender meadows. Up the col de Murs I overtook a stretched-out crocodile of steadily toiling cyclists, rocking slowly from side to side as they ground out each revolution. Everyone was taking it easy today.

Oh, Tom. Before the 1967 Tour started he'd marched into a Mercedes dealership in his adopted home town of Ghent and put a deposit on the flashest model, the one spinning slowly on the turntable. If he had a good Tour he'd pay off the balance: 'Got to have something to aim at,' he told his team-mates. He genuinely believed he could win, and though he hated heat, and during his previous experience of the mountain had built up a loathing for Ventoux – 'it's another world up there, the white rocks and the blinding sun' – he was still hugely confident.

He started the thirteenth stage seventh overall, kept at the front of the pack up to the foot of Ventoux and, in the bottom part of the climb, shaded in pine trees, set off after a pair who burst away from the leading group. The Alps were over; he'd been saying all week that if he could stay within three minutes of the leader for the final time-trial, this could be his year. To catch him, his team car had to pick its way carefully through a long line of suffering also-rans, and when they got to Tom, now out of the trees with the summit in sight, he was still up in sixth. 'But that was when we realised some difficulties were being experienced,' said his mechanic.

There was silent newsreel coverage of this on the video, and however terrible it was to see a man literally pushing himself beyond the limits of human endurance I found it grimly, horribly compelling. Weaving arthritically from one side of the road to the other, he labours forlornly to chase down two riders who have just passed; as they power sturdily away his bobbing head drops, he slows and almost wobbles off the left-hand side, a precipice of white rubble. The mechanic, Harry, shouts and prepares to leap out of the car but Tom rights himself, only to totter straight into the bleached scree on the right. Harry jumps out and undoes his toe clips – 'That's enough, Tom' – but it isn't, not for Tom, and from somewhere he summons anger – No, no, no, let's get on, let's go, do me straps, Harry – and though Harry doesn't say so this is where Tom rasps, 'Put me back on the bloody bike.' He hates the bike, but this is his job, and he's been world champion, and what will they think back on the sofa in Nottingham, and this is his final throw of the dice, one last effort to set up the rest of his life, keep his kids in matching snowsuits and his wife sitting pretty in that 280SL with electric windows.

It's make or break, and he breaks. Two hundred metres down the road the race passes under the 1 km-to-go banner, normally a vision of miraculous redemption for the riders but not this time for Tom. Two fat Frenchmen in vests have stopped him toppling over on to the hot tar and are guiding Tom to the side of the road, and though he's being held by two pairs of big arms he's still pedalling automatically. Harry has been standing up in the sunroof of the team car and now he vaults right through it and jumps down to the roadside. Tom's hands are locked to the bars and it takes some effort to prise them off, unclip his shoes and lie him down on those awful bare rocks. The last thing we see is his floppy torso, those shaven legs and Peugeot-emblazoned shorts, being crudely belaboured by the vest men, trying to shake some life back into him as Harry gives mouth-to-mouth. Then doctors, oxygen, helicopters and headlines.

Oh, Tom. I knew it wouldn't take much, and it didn't. Nostalgie FM was murmuring away in the background as I parked in Sault, a quiet cluster of spires and pantiles stuck up on a hill with glorious views available for anyone able to tear their gaze downwards from the hulking bulk of Ventoux. I killed the engine, and as the clear tones of Gilbert O'Sullivan tinkled melancholically out of the dashboard I felt the back of my neck fizz and the tips of my nostrils quiver. My soul had left the door open, and scarcely able to believe his good fortune after three decades of jeering, two-fingered rebuttal, Mr O'Sullivan strode gloriously in. I got a gloved hand over my cheeks before they became wet, then having snot-wiped them dry raised a tear-smeared gaze to the heavens above that bald, brown summit. It was better to get this out of the way now as I certainly wouldn't possess the wherewithal when I got up there. Ground control to Major Tom.

Ten

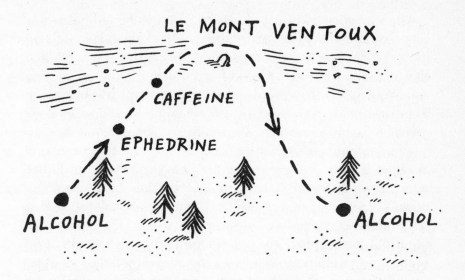

The trouble with cycling up mountains is that – panniers or, as today, no panniers – after about four minutes, as soon as that first metallic-tasting, lactic gasp rasps inward at the back of your throat, any thoughts of appreciating your surroundings, contemplating the Continental way of life or otherwise entertaining an appropriate holiday mentality have been booted out of your brain by an all-encompassing him-or-you struggle to the death with the force of gravity.

If I'd known this, of course, I might have made more of an effort to admire the view as I'd sat under a café awning in Sault, unenthusiastically ingesting two-thirds of a croque-monsieur, my usual half-litre of the old pink stuff and a Coke. A good few dozen cyclo-tourists take on Ventoux every day during the summer, and as I bounced and booted and bullied ZR's front wheel into its carbon-fibre lugholes a trio of large, ruddy Americans freewheeled slowly by in auspicious silence, their mashed-rainbow cycling jerseys clashing with everything and themselves. If *they* can make it, I thought . . . But then I realised they probably wouldn't.

The category two col du Notre-Dame des Abeilles was supposed to be only the warm-up act, but as I wound gingerly up its lazy, shadeless curves it soon became clear that it had fulfilled this role rather too well. Cresting it with sweat stinging my eyes and dripping hissily on to the scalded crossbar, I was beginning to feel a karmic payback for the terrible things I had done as a boy involving sunny afternoons, a magnifying glass and woodlice.

The summit took me by surprise; one second I was creaking along at a rate that permitted detailed perusal of the health warnings on discarded Gitanes packets, the next I was screaming down at terminal velocity, airborne fauna spattering my larynx; hot, thin tyres neatly bisecting an unwary lizard. A sudden blast of mistral snapped back the poplars, yanked the helmet chinstrap against my windpipe and buffeted me towards a family of hard-shoulder picnickers; the bellowed warnings were ripped from my mouth and dispatched so abruptly that I never heard them. A transient whiff of roadkill, a flash of vineyard, a fleeting, wobbly glance at the speedo – Jesus: 65 k.p.h. – and then I was easing into the Provençal plain, able at last to raise a glove to my nose and restore some element of facial respectability.

Maintaining the momentum, for an hour I was eating up the kilometres rather than choking on them. There was a fourth-category hill somewhere along the way but it came and went unnoticed, and I cruised with growing confidence into Bédoin, the town at the base of Ventoux, untroubled either by the parched associations of its name or the mobile donation unit in the main square emblazoned with a banner heralding the following morning's 'Day of Blood'. It was here that Tom had necked that fateful cognac, and I was just wondering under which of the bar awnings he'd pegged it when I became aware of an abrupt and painfully bone-shaking decline in ride quality.

There are few sights more instantly dispiriting than a wrinkled, folded, cellulite-dimpled, pancake-flat bicycle tyre, particularly when accompanied with a cortex-freezing epiphany that somewhere within the panniers one has so joyously hurled into a car boot lies the pump. I couldn't believe it. Over a thousand kilometres covered and I hadn't even had to put any air in the tyres up until then. And what made the scenario even more cat-swallowingly infuriating was that I'd remembered to stick all other repair accessories in my bar-bag – tyre levers, patches, glue, spare tube, even a shag-arsing square of emery board, for cock's sake.

It was while wondering whether to tackle this situation by biting random parts of the bicycle or gluing repair patches over my eyes and mouth that I looked to my right and saw a thin man in army shorts standing before a barn full of mountain bikes. In less than a minute he had cheerily repaired my tyre free of charge and sent me enigmatically on my way with a banana.

It seemed too good to be true, and after fifteen minutes of dusty maize fields and increasing gradient I found myself wondering whether it was. Things were starting to acquire a queasily ethereal air, a heat-haze sense of unreality. By now familiar with the early-warning signals of an impending bonk, as soon as I found myself struggling to remember which side of the road I was supposed to be on I transferred a couple of handfuls of hot dried apricots from jersey pocket to drooling chops, then exhausted my daily innuendo allowance by choking on the tyre man's banana. It didn't help. My slowly pistoning knees, focus of most of my head-hung visual attention, began to look blurred and distant; my skull pulsed and swelled to helmet-cracking proportions. I was already in twenty-seven but still pawed feebly at the gears, like an addicted laboratory rat clicking a deactivated cocaine button in its cage. And try as I might I could not banish a conviction that my increasingly ragged inhalations and exhalations had adopted the precise rhythm – and after a while the tune – of the theme to *The Wombles*.

Finally, just where the road got tired of faffing about and turned directly up towards the summit, I saw what could only be a fully-fledged mirage: a bulging wallet on the tarmac. As I blearily dismounted for further investigation, it suddenly darted off violently into the hot pine undergrowth. The sight of two chortling boys reeling the wallet towards them by the fishing line threaded through it briefly distilled dazed confusion to simple slapstick humiliation. But endeavouring to reciprocate the merriment, I felt my face twisting uncontrollably into a vicious, drunken sneer, and listened in helpless horror as a terrible, demonic growl leaked from that sagging mouth. Swaying slightly on my feet, I watched the boys scampering away in noisy panic through the fir cones and dimly contemplated a terrible truth. It wasn't the heat or the bonk or the chronic fatigue that had left both body and brain so incoherently mired. It was the drugs.

Every time a cyclist fails the 'naughty wee-wee' test, there is a frenzy of hand-wringing recrimination and a chorus of heartfelt pleas for the sport to return to its amateur ideals. 'It was never like this in the old days,' people say. And they're right: it was worse. I have before me an article from the July 2000 edition of *History Today* which reveals a sport riven with substance abuse almost from its inception; addicted, in fact, from birth. In 1896, Britain's Arthur Linton won the marathon Bordeaux–Paris race (the next Brit to do so was Tom Simpson) in record time. Two months later his exhausted body belatedly succumbed, and the obituary in *Cyclers' News* makes interesting reading for anyone who has compared the behaviour of people before and after an extended visit to the toilets in a Soho nightspot: 'I saw him at Tours, halfway through the race . . . he came in with glassy eyes and tottering limbs, and in a high state of nervous excitement. I then heard him swear – a very rare occurrence with him . . . At Orleans, Choppy [Linton's trainer] looked after a wreck – a corpse, as Choppy called him, yet he had sufficient energy, heart, pluck, call it what you will, to gain 18 minutes on the last 45 miles of hilly road.'

Call it what you will? OK, how about heroin, trimethyl and strychnine. 'Choppy' Warburton – and let's face it, that's a name to have any prosecution lawyer rubbing his hands – was later banned from English tracks, and there seems no doubt that he drugged Linton up to his walrus 'tache. Doping wasn't illegal and in the early days was barely covered up: cocaine flakes were dropped on to cyclists' tongues as they pedalled past, or drunk with coffee, or mixed with cocoa butter and rubbed into their legs. The Belgians went for ether-soaked sugar cubes, and the French dabbled with digitalis. Heroin and cocaine 'speedballs' were almost standard. And if you think strychnine is unlikely (it apparently has anaesthetic qualities in low doses), then contemplate the desperate frenzy of experimentation that led to some riders clearing their airways with a quick nip of nitro-glycerine.

In 1924, Henri Pélissier, the previous year's winner, abandoned the Tour in a huff after the organisers tried to penalise him for discarding a jersey in contravention of another of those mindlessly draconian stipulations. 'You have no idea what the Tour de France is,' he ranted at a journalist later that day. 'But do you want to see how we keep going?' In high strop Henri emptied a bag of bottles and ampoules out on to the table: 'Cocaine for the eyes; chloroform for the gums. You want to see the pills, too? Under the mud our flesh is as white as a sheet . . . our eyes are swimming, and every night we dance like St Vitus instead of sleeping.'

If this was a scandal, it quickly blew over. During the war, soldiers on all sides were given amphetamines – 72 million tablets in total – and after it cyclists were quick to see the value of a drug that stifled fatigue and pain under a mental blanket of aggression and stamina. Gino Bartali, winner in 1938 and 1948, died the week before I'd left and the obituaries had been unanimous: Bartali was very probably the last untainted champion. (History won't be too hard on him for the three daily cigarettes prescribed by his doctor to augment a dangerously low heart beat. Bartali's only other stimulant was 'faith in the Madonna'.)

His great rivalry with Fausto Coppi was underscored with a conviction that Coppi was doped; Gino searched Fausto's room for pills, and once drove 150 kilometres through the night to pick up a suspicious bidon he had seen his nemesis discard during a race. The subsequent analysis turned up nothing racier than bicarbonate of soda, but Coppi himself was later outstandingly candid on the issue. Interviewed on French radio near the end of his career, he casually remarked that all riders took *la bomba* (Italian road-slang for amphetamines) and that those who claimed otherwise knew nothing of the sport. Did Coppi himself succumb? 'Yes, when it was necessary.' And when was it necessary? 'Almost always.' Jacques Anquetil, five times Tour winner in the Sixties, was even more forthright. 'Only an imbecile imagines that a professional cyclist who rides 235 days a year can hold himself together without stimulants.' Coppi was Simpson's hero; Anquetil the leading rider of his era. Tom's choice wasn't whether to take speed, it was just how much and what brand.

In today's witch-hunt atmosphere such alarming frankness is unusual, but not unknown. 'Let's not be hypocrites. You just don't do that on fizzy mineral water and salad.' Hearing the Tour's rigours thus encapsulated by a spokesman for one of its chief sponsors, Crédit Lyonnais, I knew I was going to be in trouble. That was a month before I left, and anticipating that two decades of fetid sloth might not be undone by a couple of spinning sessions and the odd jog, I'd consequently spent some time covertly researching the Tour's extensive pharmacological hall of shame.

Up until the Seventies, the emphasis was on drugs that made you *believe* you were capable of great things; although, as Paul Kimmage states, it is still common to charge up with

144

amphetamines at local races without drug controls, the modern breed of naughty rider looks to more sophisticated medications which as well as being more difficult to detect actually *do* make him capable of great things. Human growth hormone (HGH) builds lean muscle and reduces body fat; the infamous EPO boosts the blood's capacity to carry oxygen and is said, in almost meaninglessly crass terms, to improve performance by 15 per cent.

That was the kind of stuff I wanted. I remember taking a doomed cat to the vet's and being sent away with a cancer-crusted X-ray, an apologetic smile and some mysterious pills that would make old Kurt 'feel better in himself' during the swansong of his ninth life. This, I supposed, was the effect of amphetamines, from simple ones such as alcohol to the more full-on pinprick-pupilled jaw-grinders of youth-culture lore: to make you 'feel better in yourself'. But this wasn't enough. I needed to *be* better *than* myself.

Three main drawbacks, none of them particularly surprising, soon suggested themselves. Supplies of EPO and HGH were almost impossible to track down, and ludicrously expensive if by some chance you managed to do so. Then there were the side effects. EPO thickened the blood, and when inexpertly administered did so to the point where the heart laboured to extrude the crimson slurry through its ventricles. A professional cyclist's heart beats at a slower rate than any other man's – often down to 30 beats a minute at rest when they're in full training – and herein lies the danger. In the early days of EPO misuse, half a dozen Dutch and Belgian cyclists went to bed and never got up, their soporific hearts clogged; when sleep was recognised as a danger period, EPO-takers started setting their alarms to go off twice a night so they could get up to exercise and get the old tickers ticking faster.

That sounded almost as bad as dying in your sleep; worse, in fact. So I just said no to EPO. As far as HGH goes, I need only point out that side effects include excessive growth of bones in the hands, feet and face, and that I just typed that sentence with my nose and chin.

It took a bit of homework to find my drug of choice, one that married a subtle psychological boost to a physiologically galvanising punt up the arse. Ephedrine has been around since ancient China, a herbal infusion that increased heart rate and therefore stamina. It was first synthesised in the Twenties, becoming popular as a treatment for asthma and hay fever, a drug that broadened the airways and so enhanced oxygen intake. These factors, coupled with the increased heart rate and stimulated release of pain-blocking neurotransmitters, inevitably – though rather belatedly – attracted sportsmen. By the Seventies it was a popular – and illegal – pick-me-up; when Maradona was thrown out of the 1994 World Cup, ephedrine was the drug he tested positive for (though not the one, I hoped, that inspired the now-notorious display of camera-eating mania).

Ephedrine; hay fever pills. It sounded good – innocuous yet effective. I can't remember where I copied the following quote from, but as my preparatory training petered forlornly away it had developed into a mantra: 'It is the unrealistic pressure to perform day after day that lies at the heart of the drugs issue, which is not an excuse for it, just an explanation of why it might happen.' It would happen. And here I was, striding up to the pharmacy counter of Sainsbury's to make it happen.

'Hay fever,' I said to the white-coated young chemist, following it with a sniff whose alarmingly theatrical quality caused her to look sharply up from her prescriptions. 'Drug-pills . . . *remedies*. Remedies for my hay fever.'

It was a bad start. She eyed me keenly, then glanced behind her at the relevant products. 'Which do you normally use?'

I'd been prepared for this. 'Over the years? The lot.' Then I gave a world-weary, guttural sigh intended to summarise a life blighted by flora-related nasal congestion.

She started to read out names from the shelf and I followed her sequence. 'Clarityn? Beconase? Piriton . . .?'

'Yep.' Feeling the need to drum up some authenticity, I carried on with the next product along. 'And Acumed.'

She swivelled. 'That's a pain-relief patch for rheumatic conditions.'

'No wonder it didn't work!'

Unwilling to brave the cold-eyed inquisitors of Boots – I once went in to buy some Calpol for my son's flu and came out red-faced and empty-handed, feeling like a thwarted solvent-abuser – I'd hoped a supermarket chemist would be a pushover. The wrongheadedness of this assumption was now apparent, and with a queue building up behind me I cut to the quick. Slowly.

'The doctor recommended ones with effer . . . effer-something,' I announced with demonstrably counterfeit vagueness.

'Ephedrine?' she replied carefully.

'. . . Yeah. That's the stuff.'

'And who is your doctor?'

Oh dear. There was some muttering from behind. 'I didn't say *my* doctor. I said *the* doctor. *A* doctor. My wife's father. Sort of like a doctor-in-law.'

Look, I felt like saying, I don't want to sell this to kids out of an ice-cream van or slip it in policewomen's drinks. I just want to cycle up some hills feeling better in myself.

'Are you allergic to hydroxybenzoic acid?'

'I wouldn't have thought so.'

'Any history of high-blood pressure?'

A confident shake of the head. This was getting better; I was going to get my drugs.

She raised her voice very slightly. 'Are you taking hypnotics or medication for depression?'

'Not yet.'

Tuts from the rear; tetchy superciliousness from ahead. The chemist turned, plucked at the shelf and reluctantly slid a packet of Haymine across the counter like a suspicious bookmaker handing over winnings.

I palmed them, smiled, then piped up, 'Oh yeah – and three packets of ProPlus.'

I'd actually dabbled with Haymine up the Aubisque, but with the panniers on, half a tab hadn't made any perceivable difference. This time it would be more systematic. (ProPlus, for anyone without experience of student last-minute revision practices, is a caffeine tablet with the lusty kick of a treble espresso.) I'd fumbled one Haymine tab into my sweat-mired gob halfway up that first col; just beyond Bédoin, when my speed slowed to single-digit kilometres an hour and the suddenly monstrous peak of Ventoux appeared fleetingly through the lavender, I'd topped this up with another two and a couple of ProPlus. Slapping myself much too hard on the cheek, I remounted and tried to forget all the stuff about not operating machinery if affected.

In every important respect I was in another world. A sign leered over at me from a side turning: *élevage des sangliers*. I'd read enough *Asterix* to know that *sanglier* was wild boar, but if *élève* was school pupil, then didn't *élevage* mean education? What the fuck kind of weird pig-teaching shit was going on down there? And the next sign didn't help: 'Patrick Troughton'. What? Patrick Troughton? The dead Doctor Who? This I had to see. I wobbled listlessly off down the indicated switchback path and found myself facing a modest warehouse emblazoned with a name that after running a finger beneath the letters and mouthing each in turn I eventually conceded might, in fact, be Parquets Traditionels.

The idea had been that the drugs would work together, turbo-charging my lungs, twin-sparking my heart, hot-wiring invincibility into my brain. But as the first painted names slipped slowly beneath my wheels and I forced myself up in the saddle like an old man rising from a disabled toilet there was a clashing bodily discord, a chemical castration. My heart seemed to have filled most of my upper half, throbbing through the forearms, flicking at the back of the throat, battering the inside of my skull with the frenzied irregular staccato of popping corn. I was breathing as if I'd just learned how to do it, and every time my legs pushed down on the pedals it was like pressing a huge bruise. I dropped back to the saddle and for the first time it started giving me grief, forcing me to shift about from buttock to bollock in a futile quest for perineal comfort.

Riders were now streaking down, a sickening swish of air-billowed clothing, a speeding fragment of a 'bonjour' or a 'hiya' caught by my hot ears. With bike and body rolling agonisingly from side to side I came up to a fat hairpin. There was something painted on it. In English. 'Hey – only 11k to go!' I'd been on the ring road of hysteria, and this propelled me up the main drag. Eleven fucking kilometres? *Eleven*? It had been 22 at Bédoin. When he was only halfway up, he was neither up nor down. Not just a body blow, a mighty rabbit punch in the perineum. I'll see your year in Provence and raise you a bloody lifetime. Why had that stupid good Samaritan been there to fix my puncture? If I'd yelled the chorus from 'Fame' or eaten my watch or hissed at him like a cornered stoat he'd have legged it straight back into his garage and I wouldn't have to be here now.

The revised arrangement with my family had been to meet at the summit at 7; it was now 6.15. I shouldn't, I couldn't, let them see me like this. As a great coal-sack of fatigue settled heavily down on the back of my neck I scrabbled a rigid claw into my bar-bag: one last Haymine, one last ProPlus. Cry God for Tommy, England and St George. I took my helmet off and immediately felt less mad; reeling my brain back in from the brink I taught myself to live with the jiving pine trees and paisley-haloed tunnel vision.

Tutting indulgently at the sundry distortions of reality around me, I got into a rhythm and began to make better progress, not quite redoubling my efforts perhaps but certainly requartering them. An incentive system was established, a series of little sticks and carrots: if I get to that next corner I'll lower my jersey neck-zip; if I get to the next I'll have a sip of fluid; if I don't get to the one after I'll grab a fistful of raisin slurry from my jersey pocket and cram it into my parched, protesting gullet.

Fascinatingly, it worked. As the road weaved relentlessly through the thinning spruce trees, a heavily cambered uphill slalom that just went on and on, I even caught the Americans, down to two now, a few pounds lighter no doubt but notably redder. There was no spare breath for gloating or greeting, but the one in front went with me as I nosed past, and for a ridiculous minute we were shoulder to shoulder, both feigning non-chalance. 'Marty,' pleaded his now distant colleague in a cracked rasp, and with a thwarted huff Marty dropped back.

The boarded-up café known as le Chalet-Reynard was mankind's final stand before the summit; a dead squirrel in the car park did for the animal kingdom, and the plants didn't last much longer. When the last sickly little Christmas trees gave up the ghost just round the corner, all that lay above me was a bald and soulless slagheap of concrete-coloured rubble, the road zigzagging crudely up to a drab, antenna-topped weather station as if drawn by a giant's clumsy finger. Four miles to climb 1,700 feet.

Ahead the tarmac was liberally decorated with heroes past and present, as if even the spectators knew that from here on in the riders would need all the help they could get. Soundbites from pre-Tour press conferences gone by tolled out in my still slightly fermented brain: 'There's nothing there . . . you can't breathe . . . it's like the moon.' I had been playing about with ZR's twenty-seven gears, but twenty-six of them were now irrelevant.

I'm still not sure why it hadn't occurred to me before, but it was only when I winced agonisingly round that first corner and suddenly found myself being punched backwards by a hurricane screaming rudely in my face that I deduced the name 'Ventoux' might in some way be connected to wind. The Windy Mountain. Though this in fact turned out to be completely wrong – the name actually derives from *vinturi*, Ligurian for mountain – I did learn later that Ventoux is the world's windiest place, the mistral having howled over its summit at a record 320 k.p.h. just a few months before Tom's last stand. Forehead pressed to the handle-bars, I somehow forced my unsteady legs to the next corner, where a huge gust suddenly shoved me in the back so violently that I all but freewheeled up to the one after.

The wind and gradient were one thing, which is to say two things, but in the light of Tom's Saharan demise I hadn't been prepared at all for this abrupt and appalling cold. Those great heaps of rock blocked off the setting sun, a sun whose rays I had been so desperate to shelter from before but now missed terribly, and with the chilled gale suddenly freeze-drying my sweaty limbs I was soon shivering uncontrollably. I hadn't seen a soul since le Chalet-Reynard, and when a sturdy-looking bloke wheeled way-wardly down towards me, eyes slitted, teeth gritted, hands off the bars and wedged for warmth into their opposing armpits, I understood why. This last stretch was inconceivably merciless, so much so that only the most brutally determined managed it.

Wincing along between the barber-striped snow-depth poles, I forced myself on, each turn of the pedals like a one-armed push-up. The Womble breathing was back, ragged and panicked, supercharged painfully down my throat by the deafening wind. Then, with all remaining physical and mental resolve galeforced out of me and final surrender imminent, I stole an upwards squint to my right and there it was, a modest gold-lettered slab of pale granite just above the road. The Simpson memorial. Tommy's stele.

With a final, draining wrench I yanked my right foot out of its pedal cleat, eased it to the tarmac and for maybe thirty seconds leant there, head on the bar-bag. Then I uncleated the left, dropped ZR where Tom's bike had been lain, and juddered coldly up to the stone. At its foot was a messy memorial mound of sun-bleached, weather-worn cycling detritus: old tyres; caps; a saddle; bidons weighted down with chalky lunar rubble; a PVC rain top, one sleeve knotted around a white stone, the other whiplashing furiously in the wind. On the slab itself was a bas-relief of a hunched cyclist, speeding gleefully down a mountain rather than languishing palely up, and the words:

A LA MÉMOIRE DE TOM SIMPSON
MÉDAILLÉ OLYMPIQUE, CHAMPION DU MONDE,
AMBASSADEUR SPORTIF BRITTANIQUE,
DÉCÉDÉ LE 13 JUILLET TOUR DE FRANCE 1967
SES AMIS ET CYCLISTES DE GRANDE BRETAGNE

Nothing but hard, loud wind and silent, bare rock above and below and all around: a wretched, lonely place to die, a godless, extraterrestrial wasteland. Tom's story was one of umpteen hindsight sadnesses, and one of them occurred to me now. 'It's a good rider who can ride himself into the ground.' That was Tom himself. And then I thought about Harry the mechanic's last words on the video: 'He destroyed himself – he had the ability to do that.'

I stumbled back down to ZR, cackhandedly slapped some heat back into my legs and remounted. But there was nothing left, not a single unburned calorie, not one watt of willpower. Nothing. My legs buckled at joints I never knew existed and I folded myself creakily off my bike and on to my back. For a moment ZR and I lay there side by side, my dead eyes trying to focus on the masts and aerials at the summit, a kilometre and a half up. Then, jarringly, a cheery volley of horn parps, juvenile shrieks and squeaks and the support vehicle/broom wagon had arrived. I had failed, and I had failed in front of my family. I had taken that penalty at Wembley and toe-poked it wanly at the keeper; the

Centre Court ballboys were still sniggering as yet another serve ballooned towards the Royal Box. Such was the drug cheat's comeuppance.

Seeing their taunting smirks wither into frowns of concern offered some succour. Lain across the front seats I gazed glassily up at the vanity mirror: raw and crevassed lips crowned by a nose the colour and consistency of an overripe fig; bridging both temples a Zorro mask of tears and dust. Unprotected by the helmet my sticky hair had been blasted by the elements into a viciously backcombed Strewelpeter. As Louison Bobet, first over the top in the 1955 Tour, said: 'A son at the summit of Mont Ventoux is not a sight to show his mother.'

Wedged obliquely between infants I was gently chauffeured to the top, but didn't feel I deserved to admire the sunset back-lighting the vineyards down to Avignon. Birna went out for a quick, lopsided walk and could hardly heave open the door when she got back. 'What's . . . there,' I muttered, sounding like Tom Waits on a Domestos bender.

'Wind. A couple of Fifties-ish barrack things and some police cars. Oh, and an advertising poster saying "Tampons pour cyclistes".'

On the wordless descent all I could think was how benign the gradient seemed from behind a windscreen, how feebly unde-manding. 'No mountain too high,' read one of the rain-smeared epitaphs beneath Tom's memorial, a phrase which in the circumstances didn't seem entirely appropriate for him but was abysmally inapt for me. Whatever strings had been attached to my conquest of the col de Saraillé, I'd just tripped over the lot.

Approaching le Chalet-Reynard I spied Marty round the next bend, bike in the gutter, hands on hips, remonstrating with his colleague, but – judging by the latter's doubled-over stance and slowly shaking head – wasting his time. My first foggy impulse was to ask Birna to pull over so I could sneak the bike out of the

boot and freewheel breezily down past him, but brittle fatigue
and a humbled sense of unworthiness prevented me. Or anyway
should have.

Eleven

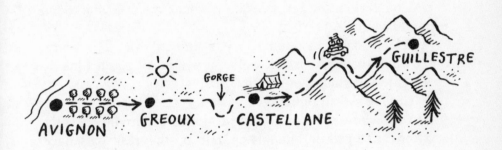

'Did you read any of this?'

Birna was studying the extensive 'patient information' leaflet supplied with my packet of Haymine; I was building up pain tolerance and mental resilience by showing the children how long I could hold my magma-hot mug of breakfast chocolate in both hands.

'That? No. I didn't think it was relevant for my . . . ow.'

I blew my ruby palms while she recited.

'"Take one tablet every twelve hours." How many did you have?'

'Two in six hours.' This sounded better than four in two. Birna read on.

'"Ephedrine Hydrochloride will reduce nasal congestion while counteracting some of the possible drowsiness that the antihistamine Chlorpheniramine may cause . . . you may also experience slight giddiness, rapid heartbeats and some weakness in the muscles."'

I looked down at the backs of my hands, idly picking at the stigmata-like hemispheres of scabby red flesh that had formed in the gloves' exposed ventilation area.

'"Alcohol will make any drowsiness worse; avoid alcohol when taking Haymine"'

Muscle weakness, giddiness, a half-litre of rosé. The drugs don't work, they just make it worse. It was looking as if I might have made a fearful ass of myself.

'Well . . . I feel all right now.'

And somehow I did. The flaccid, doped-up invalid absently hoisting an unsteady thumbs-up out of the rear passenger window at Avignon's late-night tarts bore no relation to the following morning's chirpy athlete looking forward to a long day in the saddle. I'd always been astonished at how Tour riders creaked up to death's door in the late afternoon, yet just a few hours later freewheeled gaily out of the starting gate. But here I was, a child on each knee, folding up the map with eager impatience.

It was a splendid day. Still marvelling at my new-found powers of recuperation, I agreed the usual late-afternoon rendezvous with my support crew and swished out of Avignon's hot claustrophobia, away from the Japanese tour groups and the pee-stained alleys, away from a juvenile populace who for two nights had competed with such diligent distinction at moped polo, played in the traditional Provençal fashion with beer bottles instead of mallets.

A warm wind whipped the café awnings as I emerged with a discreet whoop of liberation through the city walls at Porte Thiers, and – bless my frothing bidons – it was behind me. Mixing it cavalierly with every caravan and coach and camion blanc homme I pedalled slickly out of town at 40 k.p.h., muttering my own respectful commentary on Moore's smooth, effortless style as he pulls away from the peloton on this flat but sunburned thirteenth stage to the military town of Draguignan.

Fresh new tarmac shaded by poplars; garish cherry orchards edged by rustling, house-high bamboo groves; luminous vineyards with tiny, newborn grapes like bunches of broccoli. At Robion I even took the uphill, downwind sprint, standing up in the saddle along the dead-straight, tree-lined boulevard to pip a farmer dawdling along in his foolish microcar.

Like a thousand partisan spectators the wind pushed me up a fourth-category climb to the crest of the long, low Montagne du Luberon, from where tight, tall Italianate hill villages looked at each other across the plain. Nearly all were cute, Bonnieux the most painfully so just as long as you didn't mind the bijou art galleries and estate agents and Austrian number plates, and most particularly paying three quid for a can of Coke. A huge, lorry-licking descent into a granite canyon, all dead snakes and air brakes, then a ham baguette of reckless proportions by a fountain in Lourmarin, a knot of narrow streets that opened on to a sort of oversized village green backed by one of the haughtiest châteaux I'd yet seen.

The wind was getting slightly out of hand now, spinning rotary signs outside petrol stations into a deafening turbine frenzy, sending waiters across pétanque squares in pursuit of airborne parasols. But so what? It was behind me. A mistral in full howl plays havoc with the Tour: in 1969 it blasted straight into the riders at 70 k.p.h., persuading the organisers to let everyone hide behind their team cars, and two years later blew Eddy Merckx and 200 hangers-on into Marseilles so far ahead of schedule – 250 kilometres at an average speed of over 45 k.p.h. – that no one was there to greet them. By the time mayor Gaston Deferre turned up two hours later to present the prizes, Eddy and co. were in the shower back at their hotels; Deferre could have taken this humiliation badly, but being French he merely vowed that the Tour would return to Marseilles only over his dead body. (After twenty-seven consecutive visits up to 1971 the race next visited Marseilles in 1989, three years after Gaston's last gasp.)

More screaming fighter jets buzzing the barns, a bollock-bullying stretch of cobbles, three kids riding waywardly home from school on a moped – I flashed through villages, in and out of slow lives at glorious speed. At Pertuis, which I had only previously been aware of in an onomatopoeic context as the noise Snoopy makes when orally expelling an unloved foodstuff, I even managed to intimidate a trucker who drove me off the road. When I jumped up on to his footplate at the next set of lights, battered his window and described in detail some of the more surprising aspects of his lifestyle, he just did what I always do: stared straight ahead and clicked down the central-locking button with a discreet elbow.

I crossed the gaping river Durance at Mirabeau, the monstrous fluvial power that once sliced out the gorge around me now castrated by hydroelectric schemes and canals. At Saint-Paul-lez-Durance the Tour route veered away, perhaps to avoid doing what I now did – namely, cycling right through the middle of a nuclear-research complex the size of Berkshire. The French really are a bit funny about this sort of stuff. I still cannot quite believe that over 70 per cent of the nation's electricity is produced by nuclear power, nor that there is almost no opposition to this state of affairs. When their secret service blows up Greenpeace boats so that France can test its nuclear bombs in the Pacific, Parisians just snigger like Muttley. Mind you, it never pays to delve too deeply into French politics – flicking through the *Rough Guide* I discovered that two-thirds of the adult population are in favour of deporting legal immigrants who commit any crime or are unemployed for over a year.

I'd arranged to meet Birna at Vinon-sur-Verdon, and in homage to Eddy's break to Marseille I got there long before my reception committee. Four o'clock is always a good time to arrive in a small French town in summer: one minute everything's all scabby and dead and shuttered, then the shop-fronts all swing down or clank up and suddenly the streets are full of garish fruit and noisy housewives. It's like watching a chrysalis open.

Vinon wasn't exceptional, but sitting there in the tree-dappled shadows of the huge main square, Coke in one hand, Mars Bar in the other, I was happy. One hundred and twenty-two kilometres: Moore was back. I didn't even mind when the family turned up and Birna immediately announced that Vinon was a dump and that she'd found a nice place 10 kilometres up the road.

'Come on, Daddy,' said my 4-year-old, 'you can put your bicycle in the car and go asleep on my feet like yesterday.' But I wouldn't hear of it. Yesterday the bicycle had been a monstrous invention, an absurdly impractical device that I'd looked at with the same amused scorn normally reserved for Reliant Robins and the wearers of platform trainers. But not now. Now it was a superlative machine, the ultimate synthesis of form and function, a part of my body. I winked at my children, cleated up, put the hammer down and got to the Hôtel le Grand Jardin in Gréoux-les-Bains ten minutes before them.

Gréoux was the sort of slightly-past-sell-by spa town that could have done with a direct hit from the Tour rather than this year's near miss. Poodles and pearls, solitary Scrabble, Mills et Boon, a coach party of Lancastrians with noses like W. C. Fields – the arrival of our family halved the average age and doubled the decibels. When we volunteered to eat outside and so minimise the scope for Generation X scaring the frail diners into Generation-Ex, the uniformed waitress politely insisted on laying out the full silver service on our plastic pool table: thirty-five pronged and bladed instruments for the five of us, or seventy after Valdis knocked my Bloody Mary over the lot as the waitress aligned the final fish knife.

Alimentary malaise is the unacceptable face of cycling infirmity. Crossing the line with dried blood caked on your face or a winged arm pressed to the chest of a shredded jersey is heroic in a way that soiling your Savlon can never hope to be. Yet unsurprisingly, effective digestion is way down the body's priorities during a Tour, and many a cycling swan has crossed the line as an ugly duckling, his feathers all stuffy and brown in the most unfortunately literal fashion.

If I could pin down the exact moment when I realised I might not have made it as a professional cyclist it wasn't when I fell over at the Kew Bridge bus stop or cracked on the col de Marie-Blanque, it was when I read Paul Kimmage's account of the 184-kilometre tenth stage of the 1986 Tour. 'LeMond was in trouble today. He had a bout of diarrhoea. He rode by me with thirty kilometres to go . . . God, the smell was terrible. It was rolling down his legs.' Oh, no, no, no. Having the physical reserves to *ride by* people in that state, and the mental strength to deal with a scenario from the worst public-shame nightmare . . . it was beyond contemplation. And Greg LeMond went on to win the Tour that year.

Such were my thoughts as I'd lain awake in our restless dormitory, wondering if that noise was my stomach or two fat women mudwrestling on slowly deflating Spacehoppers. A certain reluctance at the breakfast buffet was inevitable, and by the time I'd pedalled into a Saharan headwind to rejoin the route at Ginasservis, I was in no position to speculate on the origins of its pleasingly odd name.

It was certainly the hottest day yet. My guts were percolating horribly and, though I knew I should be eating, the mere thought of the Dried Fruits of Ventoux was enough to spark off a parched retch. My warm-grape bidons were quickly but unenthusiastically drained, and all I thought about was their refrigerated replacements: beers, carbonated beverages, anything glistening with condensation.

Crossing the river at Aups (I did it again) I found myself recalling that the title sequences of both The Goodies and The Monkees featured cyclists pedalling at speed into extensive bodies of water. I couldn't get the thought out of mind, the delicious immersion, the baptismal sense of salvation from the hot highway to hell, the distant acceptance that having forgotten to twist out of the cleats I would quickly drown, but not caring because I would drown happy, hopefully before Mickey Dolenz tried to give me the kiss of life.

It's always a bad sign when I can't remember where I had lunch. No such problems, however, in recalling its constituents: beer, Badoit, Coke, Badoit, beer, and a 300-degree segment of uneaten pizza. Sitting vacantly in the restaurant garden with cold sweat dripping from my temples to dough-up the pizza flour on my shorts, I was gently approached by the concerned patron and his wife: 'Ça va, monsieur?' No. Not really. 'La Tour passe . . . passe . . .' I began automatically, but I didn't finish. A teenager was cycling at some speed up the considerable hill next to us, a compelling sight made more notable by his below-average limb quota. Spotting my Peugeot jersey he raised his one arm from the bars as he passed, accompanying it with a defiant yell: 'Vive le vélo!'

Having rushed away to do terrible things to le patron's vitreous enamel, I was clambering pallidly back on to ZR when he trotted over. 'Voilà,' he said, pressing a postcard of his establishment into my clammy hand. 'Pour vos amis.' I don't know why I did this – possibly it was a slightly delirious obsession with saving weight, more probably because the composition was dominated by a huge platter of glistening innards – but as he turned back I wearily flicked the card away.

I could never whistle with my thumb and forefinger, or catch a pile of coins dropped off a crooked elbow, or get the Pritt-Stick to adhere temporarily to the laboratory ceiling directly above the teacher's chair just before Mr Burrows came in, but the one juvenile pastime I mastered – though, thinking about it, I can also skim stones and blow up a telephone box – was the ability to propel a playing card at high speed over some distance by means of a wristy backhand flick. In defiance of my debilitated condition the postcard left my sweaty fingers already spinning fast, curving slightly up and around in a curtailed death-star arc before striking the retreating patron sharply between the shoulder blades. He yowled in distress and messily threw his hands in the air like a stuntman picked off by a sniper; then, pressing a hand to the point of contact, turned to survey me with confused horror. His lips were starting to jabber; soon sounds would come out of them, then questions, and because I didn't want to answer these I held up a traffic-policeman palm, saddled up and fled. It was the rudest thing I had ever done.

By announcing itself as 'home of the artillery' Draguignan hardly coos beguilingly at passing tourists, and though I only saw its ring-road hinterland, the usual bland, beige boxes stalked by Ronald McDonald and Monsieur Bricolage, the word 'unprepossessing' loomed large. In fairness, I was distracted. Despite the heavy traffic barging along my alimentary canal, I had once again allowed myself to be lured into competition, this time with a knees-out, boiler-suited mechanic on what I could only assume was his grandmother's bicycle.

It was an unedifying contest, particularly given my reluctance to share the work at the front. In Tour argot, I was wheel-sucking: toiling in his slipstream, letting a man on a rusty sit-up-and-beg do the sitting up while I took care of the begging. Winding it up round the cork-walled Gorge de Châteaudouble, he never looked round once, not even as he rumbled off down a side track, jabbed a forefinger at the road ahead and shouted out a rut-juddered 'Bonne chance!'

The road narrowed, carving into the sheer gorge walls, writhing round corners of sufficiently exaggerated radius to ease oncoming tourist coaches right into my path. Stage thirteen had finished in Draguignan and I'd continued seamlessly into stage fourteen, which by common consent was the most appalling, the sort of ludicrous itinerary that made substance abuse almost inevitable: 250k northwards into the cold heart of Alps, with two first-category climbs that were statistically more awful than some of the HCs, topped off with the notorious col d'Izoard whose poisoned, Martian summit stood over 1,000 feet above Ventoux.

Oh, and the second-category Côte de Canjuers which Knees-Out had presumably been indicating, an attritional, never-ending ascent of hot, red earth and unabundant scrub. The sun was still high and so, as far as I could tell on the rare occasions when I angled my gaze up from the softening tarmac, were the haze-topped peaks ahead. If those were the Alps, then these, I supposed, were their foothills. It should not have come as a surprise to discover that the Alps had very large feet.

This was a tourist route, all big gay Germans on big gay motorbikes and roof-racked British estate cars with painstakingly yellow-painted headlights. At least the Brits noticed me. Every other nationality has been brought up in a culture where pedalling some poxy bike up a cliff for no good reason is considered almost humdrum behaviour, but the looks I got from the occupants of right-hand-drive vehicles were very different: a sort of intrigued horror that had me running a hand over the top of my helmet to check for snagged roadkill.

Up through the wizened weeds I went, into an empty world of crumbled rock, one with ample disincentives to settlement even without the enormous military firing range the road now gingerly traversed. After inching pained but ecstatic over a crest, I freewheeled round the next corner to be confronted with the full horror of the term 'false summit'. This was an awful moment. Come friendly bombs and fall on me.

As a weary nod to Chris Boardman's training diktats, I'd been scribbling occasional contributions to a 'performance feedback' diary. His sample entries were along the lines 'a hard day, but never pushed into red' and 'sore, no stress'. Deciphering the diseased scrawl I penned at Comps-sur-Artuby, where my attempts at refuelling were once again confounded, this time by a restaurant sign stridently recommending 'Tripes et Daubes', I can just make out the words 'v. bilious/feeble'.

It's difficult to imagine that the one-man Fanta festival I held at Comps ameliorated this state of affairs, as evidenced by the shaming scenes enacted in a lay-by just beyond it. I'd somehow grovelled through 100 kilometres, but there were still 28 to go before the arranged rendezvous with my – hollow laugh – support vehicle. If the road had not immediately lowered itself into a mammoth descent that obviated pedalling for 16 of these I cannot imagine I would have made it.

Freewheeling past hill-topping castles, almost Arabian in their ochred bulk, I eased into the Grand Canyon du Verdon, an excitable river squeezed between granite flanks. The canyon is by common consent the most spectacular in Europe, but the incredible truth is that it wasn't discovered until 1905. It still amazed me that the caves of Lascaux had remained hidden for so long, but overlooking a 12-mile-long, half-mile-wide hole in the heart of the world's most densely populated continent is in a different league of geographical apathy. And less than fifty years later it was almost flooded for a hydroelectric scheme, one only abandoned when the money ran out: you can still see, and I did, the side tunnels they bored out in preparation. Then I saw a sign welcoming me to Castellane, and just beyond it a parked maroon Espace, and after 128 very different kilometres from those I'd breezed through the day before I had somehow made it.

Castellane was compact and noisy and overlooked by a tiny chapel stuck terrifyingly atop a towering rock: not so much standing guard over the town as hoping someone would catch it when it fell. The other point about Castellane was that it was full, complet, no vacancy, keine zimmer. 'Ascension Day,' said Birna, though at the time neither of us appreciated the hilarious incline-related irony. I lacked the wherewithal to participate in the so-you-think-you've-had-a-bad-day post mortem, nodding limply through the support crew's breathless catalogue of in-car vomit and vertigo. 'I wheel-sucked a mechanic,' was all I could whisper in reply.

I was all over the shop, but the Tour pros would just be setting their stalls out. There was a sprint scheduled at Castellane – *a sprint*. And then another 200 kilometres of mountains, with a combined tariff equivalent to cycling up and down the Empire State Building. Eleven times. I hated myself for dwelling on the looming awfulnesses, but at the same time couldn't help it. Tour riders at the end of the day don't really want to stop talking Tour – can't, in fact. They live and breathe the event more literally than competitors in any other sporting contest, and at the end of a day all they want to talk about is tomorrow.

I had a splendid photographic history of the Tour, and of the many hotel-room après-cycle snaps only two depicted what might be described as R and R (though each was a perfect cameo of national traits: the Italian Felice Gimondi autographing a blonde's thigh; Belgium's Eddy Merckx looking no less exhilarated as he turns over the four of clubs in a game of patience). The rest were all either winding down – a pin-pupilled Anquetil being forcefully massaged; Ottavio Bottecchia letting off a soda siphon into his aviator-goggled face; two Frenchmen being interviewed in the bath; Coppi with his feet in the bidet – or psyching up: Gino Bartali poring over tomorrow's maps; three Spaniards squinting myopically at the sports pages. No time or energy for the sort of endlessly inventive after-hours horseplay practised by Switzerland's Oscar Plattner: had the 1955 world sprint champion been a Tour rider, *procycling* might never have been able to reminisce on an endowment so extravagant that 'in the right circumstances he could accommodate seven budgerigars, provided the last stood on one leg'.

The only bed in town was within a cardboard-walled chalet at a campsite, which was fine with me but less of a hit with Birna. Apparently intrigued by our dual-format holiday transport, the crisply-shirted Portuguese proprietor drove over in his little golf buggy for a chat as we corralled the children up to our plywood veranda. I'd long since given up on impressing a Frenchman with my endeavours, but because Portugal has no real cycling tradition, and also because his English was accomplished enough to decode my feverish ramblings, he was soon engrossed. 'You do the whole, *en*tire race?' he asked, knitting his well-developed eyebrows in justifiable concern. I nodded gauntly, then indicating my fetid kit asked where I could get a laundrette token. 'No, no,' he said, and raising both hands by way of reproach insisted on laundering it all in his own machine. On any day this would have been a kindness, but I only appreciated its especial selflessness on that particular day just after he hummed away in his buggy. I'm so very sorry, sir.

I'd hardly describe it as my strongest suit in any circumstances, but in a campsite suffering in silence is never an option for the unwell. Our wobbling walls offered minimal sonic resistance to the traditional canvas lullaby of Teutonic snores, but I still cringe at the catastrophic voidances I shared with my fellow campers throughout that night. I could have suffered no greater shame if I'd strolled between the tents in broad daylight asking for a hand with my seventh budgie.

You may gather that I am not a good patient. Half my childhood was spent crawling round my mother's feet dismally moaning 'I think it's my spleen', and I made such a fuss about a teenage tummy ache that they took my appendix out to shut me up. (Mind you, the investigatory probings were by any standards rigorous. I'd like to meet the man who doesn't scream the glass out of the surgery windows when a greased-up doctor is in him up to his elbow. Actually, perhaps I wouldn't.) As dawn prodded at the curtains I was still writhing and groaning like an ankle-tapped Italian footballer, and with the roused children already holding a rowdy bedside vigil Birna blearily yawned that holiday tummy didn't normally last more than a day.

'Holiday tummy?' I creaked, trying to muster up some shrillness. 'This is a *serious digestive disorder*. I think . . .' and here

I was momentarily drowned out by an extended fizzing wheeze from somewhere within my knotted innards, 'I think it might be dysentery.' Kristjan looked at me with innocent concern; I placed a moist hand on his shoulder and rasped, 'Daddy has The Bloody Flux.'

I went through the motions, so to speak, tottering half-heartedly about with maps and gloves waiting for Birna to stop me. It didn't take her long. 'Don't tell me you're getting on that bike today.'

'Oh, OK then,' I said, slightly too quickly, staring at my flaking, hollow features in the mirror above the little kitchen sink. From Castellane the stage profile peaked and troughed like a frightened rodent's heartbeat, and there I was, French-fried, sun-dried, thin 'n' crispy. Swilling my bidons out I noticed that even my ears looked ill.

Birna watched this negligent operation with interest. 'Aren't you going to wash them up properly?'

'No point if I'm not cycling today.'

'What do you normally use?'

After the washing powder's insecticidal contamination, there had been only one all-purpose emulsifying surfactant in my life, used for laundering shorts, socks and jersey, cleansing bidons and – applied directly to a pilfered hotel flannel – to bring an occasional shine to ZR's filthy flanks. 'Wash 'n' Go,' I said.

'That isn't very good,' she replied, and it wasn't. Apart from anything else, whatever I poured into the bidons now came out tasting of perfumed paint. 'And when did you last boil them?'

When did I last . . . If this moment had been filmed, the camera would have careered towards me on rails as I slapped palms to cheeks in a wide-eyed, round-mouthed epiphany of painfully abrupt realisation. Nick and Jan had asked me that same question; had in fact offered to do it for me. 'Whenever we get a big party here, we always boil all the bidons once when they arrive and once before they leave.'

I just thought they were being . . . well, British. You know: fussy. Driven by a mindlessly slavish adherence to routine. You were supposed to pump your tyres and wipe your chain and brush the crap off your dérailleurs every night, but my progress didn't seem to have been adversely affected by not doing any of these things even once. In my book – and what a smelly little pamphlet that is – bidon-boiling was on a par with the checklists headed 'Preparing for a long journey' that they always put in car manuals, which you flick through while you're on a double-yellow waiting for your wife and kids to come back from Clark's, and then think, Jesus, I'm sitting here in a Volvo estate reading the owner's handbook while my children are having the width of their feet measured, which may mean that I am already one of Europe's dullest men, and if anyone thinks I'm now going to start inspecting wiper-blades and hosing loose chippings out of my wheel-arches every time we breach the M25 they've got another think coming.

But Birna is not British. Birna is, in fact, the answer to the riddle of what you get if you cross an Icelandic virologist with an Icelandic immunologist. The agenda of her life was forthright: the global eradication of filth. Tough on grime, tough on the causes of grime. Adopting a tone and rationale normally employed against children who don't wash their hands after going to the loo, she railed, 'You've been putting fruit juice and God knows what in those bottles, and they've been fermenting away in the sun all day mixed up with your saliva and . . .' Appalled at this toxicological scenario, the rant tailed off into a little quiver of revulsion.

I had imagined that my condition was stress-related, not so much mental as the physical strain of Herculean effort: I had made myself ill by trying too hard, pushing myself beyond the limit. 'He destroyed himself – he had the ability to do that.' Now I saw that it was none of these things. I was sick because I was dirty. I was a dirty boy.

I sent Kristjan into the campsite office to retrieve my laundered kit and with ZR dismantled in the boot we drove into the centre of Castellane. A day of campsite convalescence had been on the cards before I calculated that Birna and the family had to be back in five days, and that on current form the Alps would be occupying me for at least that length of time. A reluctance to attract public attention to my modest rate of progress had inspired me to spurn the support vehicle the day before, but in the ghostly light of the ensuing travails I wanted to see out the mountains with a back-up crew in close contact. A lost day was off the agenda, and cheating was back on it.

Before leaving Castellane, however, there was something I had to do. Birna pulled up outside a pharmacy, I clambered wanly out and hobbled in. Water purification tablets were what I wanted, though as I saw the silver-haired chemist listening in some alarm to my request for 'pills to sterilise myself' I clumsily effected additional explanations to ensure I didn't end up with a very different sort of medication. Henceforth, the content of my bidons would have all the zesty refreshment of a lusty swig from the municipal paddling pool, but at least I wouldn't die. It was awful to think that up Ventoux and the Alpine foothills – and, who knows, all through the Pyrenees – my bottles had been nurturing contagion, that with every parched sip I'd been slowly poisoning myself.

There'd been a chastening broom-wagon finality about stowing the bike in the boot. Today I'd be the one making rueful faces at cyclists from behind a windscreen, trying to gauge gradients, empathise with their labours and offer encouragement, but knowing that, whatever I did, to them I'd be just another gloating wanker in a car. We looped round the Lac de Castillon, its almost chemically turquoise surface dotted with pedalos, the surrounding hills all cedars and smooth granite, more Mediterranean than Alpine. The col d'Allos was the first proper Alp, a sprawl of off-season, shingle-roofed ski hotels at its base, the hairpins stacked up those Heidi-sided cowbell pastures. As the road twisted and rose we squeezed past the occasional cyclist, all pained, some traumatised, and one – a really very old man on a panniered tourer – engaged in such a rotary frenzy he looked as though he might spontaneously combust.

We'd just left him thrashing about in our wake when Birna stalled the car, yanked at the handbrake and in a voice destabilised with brittle fear formally renounced tenure of the driver's seat. 'That – there,' she quavered, waving an explanatory finger at the view as she roughly parted my knees and hunkered awkwardly into the passenger footwell. An altitude-related spiritual collapse had always been on the cards for Birna, and following her finger down to the distant valley floor I remembered that at 2,250 metres, this was the highest point of the Tour to date.

Perhaps due to medical jealousy, I must confess to a propensity for contracting sympathetic phobias from those around me. I was never troubled by spiders before that first infantile experience of my father's distinctive arachnid-encountering shriek, and now I can't go into the garden shed alone. Slasher movies were routinely dismissed with hilarity until a girlfriend dug her nails into my arm once too often during *Friday the 13th*; that night I ended up having to sleep on the floor next to my parents' bed, which is no place for any 20-year-old. And another unfortunate truth is that after years of intimate contact with Birna's vertigo, I have inevitably been infected with the disease. A milder form, perhaps, although you might not have said that if you'd seen the pair of us inching across Clifton Suspension Bridge on our hands and knees.

Plunging off mountain sides is a regularly indulged Tour pastime, but without the Pavlovian stimulus of Birna's keening wails I hadn't yet got the old height-fright on the bike. Now, positioning myself behind the wheel, I realised only a supreme effort would stop the hysteria spreading to the rear seat with wretched consequences for all, most particularly the old bloke who was wobbling back past us into a position where any get-me-outta-here flung-open nearside doors would neatly dispatch him to eternity.

A throat-stripping nursery-rhyme session drowned out the incoherent death preparations ululating up from the footwell and so carried us to the top, but the descent was worse, a lonely cliff-clinger with regular ominous gaps in the rusty railings. Birna finally raised her head above the dashboard at Barcelonette, one of those gravelly, moraine-slopped mountain-plateau towns that cry out for a covering of snow. Here we waited an eternity for the shopkeepers to arise wearily from a well-earned three-hour lunch nap, then devoured most of their wares by the frothing mud of a swollen glacial river up the road. This allowed plenty of scope for juvenile tomfoolery of the near-fatal variety, and not wanting to be left out I forgot to close the boot when we drove off, causing tennis balls, flip-flops and other loose pieces of holiday to bounce excitingly into the path of following traffic. The number of drivers returning to their native Italy – I realised later that the border was just a couple of miles to the right – ensured an expressive reception to the incident-packed retrieval of these items.

I felt better physically – the unwieldy baguette assemblage I wedged painfully down my gullet represented my first meaning-ful calories for twenty-four hours – but at the same time there was a bleak sadness. This peaked as we drove through the cheerily named village of La Condamine, where we gawped solemnly at haphazard ranks of what could only be prison cells hewn perilously high into the granite cliffs behind. Why is the French penal system so melodramatic? They were still sending people to Devil's Island after the war. And what could you possibly do to deserve being locked up in a mountain? I'd recently been struck by the related histrionics of their language, how you can never be sorry, only 'desolated', never bothered, only 'deranged'. We might think of 'yours sincerely' as archly pedantic, but how would you fancy signing off to your bank manager with 'I beg you to accept the expression of my distinguished sentiments'? I suppose it's all part of the overwrought romanticism that so endears the Tour to the nation's destiny-oscillators. (Actually, I found out later that they weren't prison cells at all, but old gun emplacements. But that's OK: this is known as the exception that proves the rule.)

Something caught my eye near the foot of the col de Vars. Propped against one of those 'Beware of enormous falling boulders' signs whose practical purpose always eludes me ('Attention: one of these might land on your car in a minute, and if it does, you are all going to die') was a deceased bicycle. I got out to inspect it. The tyres had rotted away, the saddle was a sprung skeleton and every spoke and crank and lever was lavishly ochred with flaking rust. I pulled it upright – an astonishing weight. As the family rushed out to commandeer the machine as chief prop in an extended session of madcap photography that would have graced any early Beatles film, I suddenly felt affronted by its presence. The col's first hairpin loomed around the corner, backed by a huge retaining wall professionally embellished with the word 'Hinault'. He flew up there fifteen years ago, said the dead bike, and a lot longer ago than that even I made it this far. And look at you, you old woman, pootling up the hills with your bike in the boot.

For 11 kilometres the road coiled uncertainly, back-tracking and switch-backing but always going upwards, a disorderly ascent through the trees and into a bare and rather messy wilderness of boulders, sheep crap and wind-whipped tussocks. At the unassuming summit – no wife-worrying precipices here – was a café. 'You can get a certificate there for cycling up,' read Birna from a guidebook as we wiped chocolate off our children's faces in a car park crowded with more of what was an apparently inexhaustible supply of gay German motorcyclists. I gave no audible response to this information. My necessarily curt entry in that day's training diary simply reads: 'The shame'.

You may have gathered by now that the Moore household economy is run very much according to the model sketched out by Jack Sprat and his wife, only with obsessive frugality in the role of lean-eater and the fat-consumption duties assumed by profligate recklessness – oh, and that serendipitous platter-licking denouement substituted with an endless series of ill-tempered debates. Hotel lobbies are the usual battlefield, and a good example of this genre was held in the reception area of Les Barnières, jewel in Guillestre's tourist-fleecing crown.

'Look,' said Birna, attempting to drum up some unlikely reinforcements from the starched-linen restaurant's bill of fare, 'they've got rosé wine from the slopes of Mont Ventoux.' I pulled the sort of face with which Oliver Hardy delivered his catchphrase. Birna persevered. 'It's the second cheapest on the menu.'

A small pause; a glance at the sunlit pool outside the window; a sigh of surrender. 'I'll unload the car.'

I was beginning to learn that the dolled-up pensioner is an integral feature of the Alpine summer, and the prominent ubiquity of the medical centre's telephone number throughout the establishment suggested that Les Barnières, to paraphrase Basil Fawlty, might more accurately have styled itself the Hotel for People with a Less Than Fifty Per Cent Chance of Making it Through the Night. Or, in my case, through the next day. But despite the unseemly griping, it was of course a splendid evening. I ponced about the pool in my cycling shorts, flaunting my ludicrous tidemark arm tan before an elderly audience more preoccupied with large-print fiction. The children dive-bombed and screeched; it was very much like the home-movie scenes of Tom Simpson's family Corsican holidays, only with a hairier-legged Daddy. I stuck away all my supper and half the kids', and afterwards sat out on our top-floor balcony beneath the chalet eaves, the glass-muffled carousing of infancy behind me and dotage beneath.

Draining the last pink mouthful of Côtes du Ventoux straight from the bottle I squinted at the darkness, tracing the black outlines of that formidable Gothic backdrop, those murderous granite claws scratching at the stars. 'Mon mari – avec son bicyclette,' Birna had joshed the fat wine waiter, or anyway the fat waiter who brought us our wine, pointing at the Giant of Provence's silhouette on the label. 'Ah oui,' he'd winked, in a rather silly way that indicated a forthcoming joke, 'et demain, l'Izoard!'

Was the concept of me even tackling such a mountain really so chortlingly improbable? Yes, so I had yet to make it up an HC or even a category one without pushing and, the one-off conquest of the col de Saraillé aside, my climbing experience could be encapsulated as one of hills, pills and bellyaches. But Simpson, Kimmage and Boardman had all implied that one's worst form often heralds the arrival of one's best, that after you've cracked one day it takes a much harder bonk to break you the next. Certainly I felt infinitely better, even allowing for the rosé-tinted spectacles. A small cluster of lights that I'd initially mistaken for a constellation winked off into blackness. A village? Up there? Jesus. But I'd have to go that high and higher tomorrow. Not much further up, the blinking red dot of a plane moved smoothly across the Alps. That was modern travel: rapid, painless, humdrum.

Being rather drunk, I found myself tapping into the Tour's spiritual root. A celebration of mankind's arduous history, of our forefathers' heroic efforts to triumph over adversity. The cavemen of Lascaux lanced bulls; we threw javelins. Spear-chucking was no longer a matter of life and death, assuming the stadium officials kept their eyes open, but somehow it seemed important to honour a time when it had been. And though the people of France could now hop on to trains or planes and zip across their nation in an hour, for their grandfathers this hadn't been an option. The bicycle was originally sold to rural France as 'the horse that needs no hay': a means of everyday transport, often the only one in what is still, by European standards, a large and empty land. Farmers would think nothing of pedalling huge distances over huge hills – or, rather, they probably thought plenty, but had no choice. What about that dead bike on the col de Vars? The Tour paid tribute to these men and the tough times they lived through, times when you might fall into an undiscovered gorge the size of Belgium and wait half a century to be found. We didn't have to do this shit any more, but watching 180 men in funny shorts forcing their punished bodies up hill and down dale gave us a vicarious taste of what we'd all have been doing in days now mercifully gone by.

In the middle of the night, I drifted gently out of a deep slumber with an inspiring warmth in my chest, a comforting glow that was soon spreading along my arms to caress the scorched flesh of my fingertips. This was it, I pondered dozily, the fire in my belly: this was what it felt like when the good form kicked in. Let the destiny-oscillation commence; I was ready now. Either that or a small girl had just peed all over me in her sleep.

Twelve

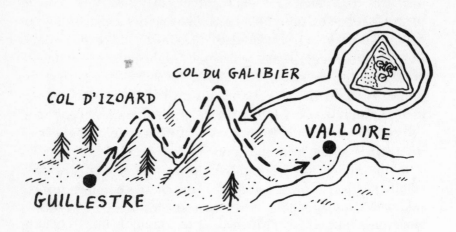

Vertigo 1, Dysentery 0. 'I really just can't,' announced Birna as I brushed croissant flakes off the maps. My support vehicle would not be following me up the Izoard, owing to the driver being a big girly weed. 'We'll take the valley road and meet you at Briançon. I'm sorry.'

She'd lost her sense of humour, and so had the Alps. Yesterday we'd passed through Les Prats and enjoyed distant views of the col d'Urine, but looking at the intestinal coils through which the route knotted and twisted for the next day and a half was a sombre experience. The Casse Deserte and Terre Rouge on the Izoard; a peak called Crève Tête – Punctured Head – en route to the Tour's penultimate hors catégorie climb, the col de la Madeleine. It was a cast list that spoke eloquently of the coming challenges, and what it said most clearly was, Don't fuck with us, bike-boy.

But the weather was glorious again, and because in both spiritual and alimentary terms I had nothing left to lose I rolled off into another blindingly bright Alpine day with a light heart and a sprightliness of bearing. Where before the sight of huge Flintstone boulders marooned at the foot of a mountain would have unsettled me, I now thought: I wish I'd seen that one fall. Fir trees leaned out from the gorge flanks, tilted at terrifyingly oblique angles towards the omnipotent torrent at the bottom but still clinging to life. 'No, no, we're all right,' they said to me. 'It looks bad, but you'd be surprised what you can get used to.' Indeed so. I kept my shades on through the dripping tunnels, oddly exhilarated as I negotiated them blind, and successfully stifled a retch of panic when the road forked, and there, neatly curtained by the vertical stone flanks around me, stood the preposterous 3,000-metre serrations of the Izoard's next-door neighbours.

Unable to take these seriously as sensible adversaries for a bloke on a bike, I fairly whistled up the straight but steepening D902 into Arvieux, last stop before the end of the earth. Here I refuelled sensibly: two Mars Bars with banana chasers from the village shop just as it closed for elevenses, then a gulp from a bidon which eloquently explained why chlorine has never caught on as a fruit-juice preservative. 'Il fait chaud,' remarked the shop-keeper, locking up as I swigged reluctantly on her threshold. 'Bon courage.'

This close, the really high stuff was hidden by foothills, which at least stopped me losing heart before the first hairpin. Even so, it was a brutal 4k up to that, a no-nonsense direct ascent through more scrappy, dandelioned pasture divided by the odd creaking chairlift. I'd noticed a lot of verge-side glints, and on dis-mounting to inspect the source I found myself examining one of several dozen foil pouches. Neither a condom nor a compli-mentary toiletry, 'Speedy Gel' was, or had been, a 'concentrated energy product'. The amateurs tackling the Izoard – wherever they'd got to today – did so to emulate their heroes, on look-alike bikes in look-alike strips; I supposed that by squeezing a covert sachet of glucose and amino acids into their mouths they somehow felt they were taking look-alike drugs. Oh, the shallow, deluded imbeciles, I thought, wondering where I could buy some from.

The road curled up and into the trees. It got steeper, which was bad, but cooler, which was good. I clicked into twenty-six and got on with it. The eye-stinging sweat came on tap, luring flies which could only be dispatched with energy-sapping flails, and there was a new *twurrrrr* counterpointing the *drrr-thwicks*, no doubt something to do with a screw that hadn't been there when I'd tried to adjust the dérailleurs that morning.

Soon I couldn't flob without following up with a drowning-man gasp as I tried to suck back that single missed breath. I desperately wanted to click down to twenty-seven but tried everything to avoid doing so, experimenting with the ankle flick that had carried me halfway up the Aubisque until my Achilles tendons sang, then hitting upon the brilliant scheme of going as slowly as possible without quite falling over. No one was going up but there were plenty now going down, and I was surprised to find I had the wherewithal to greet these in the accepted fashion: clicking up a couple of gears as you heard them approach, lifting three fingers in nonchalant greeting and attempting to bully that distraught grimace into a casual vista-surveying gaze.

Fifteen minutes later the casual gaze was beyond me; the best I could manage now was the ruby-faced preoccupation of a constipated toddler. But I was still holding it together when I gritted round a corner lined with parked cars and rolled up to the surface of Mars. The Casse Deserte: a devil's quarry of singed scree and rubble, a vulgar, lifeless panorama of rusted ballast. Behind me it was all chalets and Christmas trees; I had just crossed from the Sound of Music to the Sound of Silence.

Crouching by every other opened boot was a slightly old, slightly fat man assembling an immaculate bicycle, off to tame the Casse Deserte. From here the road surface was smooth and

178

fresh, a black beauty that swept down then across and finally weaved up through the stacks of rubble like a thread stitching the fragile mountain together. One of a pair of grey-haired chaps nodded in restrained comradely greeting as he locked up a Turin-registered Fiat estate and prepared to hoick a tanned leg over a polished silver crossbar; I nodded back and mimed a request for photographic assistance. The elder of the two, he soberly complied, capturing me as I solemnly surveyed the bleak backdrop, and we got into something approaching conversation.

'Torino?' I panted, and as he slowly nodded I detected an arresting resemblance, from the all-black strip to the well-groomed moustache and stringy, gnarled physique, to Lee Van Cleef in his role as The Bad. What made this particularly compelling was that his colleague, all shifty, stunted mania and overripe nose, paid alarming visual homage to whoever it was who played The Ugly.

I nodded as The Bad explained, in measured, baritone French that may have been worse than mine, that the Giro – the Tour of Italy – had crossed the Izoard just the day before (like the Tour, it regularly probes into neighbouring countries). He was here with his friend – this prompted a weasely wink from The Ugly – and together they'd watched the Giro sweat slowly past. Last night they'd slept in his car, and . . . 'Maintenant . . . maintenant . . .' He turned to face the toxic slopes behind, nodding slowly at them as he searched for a word to encompass their loathsome bleakness, and having failed to do so sank into a low chuckle.

'Fausto Coppi,' blurted The Ugly in an unexpectedly camp squeak. 'Gino Bartali,' murmured his friend, crossing his black chest and glancing up at an azure sky now mercifully dabbed with clouds. 'Tom Simpson,' I said, and never having done so in earnest crossed myself with such dramatic vigour that the undone jersey zip was snagged into the flesh of my craw just below the Adam's apple.

I've had a pretty good run with zips over the years, and

plucking tentatively at the trapped skin I accepted it could have been a lot worse. My brother once travelled home from Paris on a coach next to a young man wearing the ghostly mien of recent bereavement, and whose agonised under-coat lap probings implied virological fallout from a drunken indelicacy at the wake. Only when they stopped at Calais did he tug bleakly at my brother's arm and, with self-revulsion wobbling over his blanched features, silently raise the coat to reveal a complicated enmeshment of metal teeth and intimate flesh. A moment of complacency at the urinal was all it had taken to bring about this grisly spectacle, but what could my brother now do to remedy it? Following Princess Diana's death we are all aware of France's 'Good Samaritan' law that compels passers-by to assist at the scene of an accident. This, though, was long before that, so history should not be too hard on my brother for striding away up the aisle with a disgusted glare, having elected to interpret the situation as an obscure act of indecency, albeit one whose questionable erogenous dividends had left the perpetrator six budgies short of an Oscar Plattner.

My brother is a decent man who may still feel a lingering burden of guilt recalling this incident, but I am here to urge him to banish any such feelings. When he hears of the brief but intense masculine manipulation I endured in the back seat of that Fiat, and in particular of an exotic finale involving the carefree application of sun-melted butter, he can only have cause to rejoice at his course of action.

Still, when it's only your Adam's apple that's being greased up, a bond of sorts forms, and when lubricants had been dabbed away daintily – both appliers claimed to have worked in hospitals during their military service – we rolled off together across the orange crush, ZR and I sandwiched between The Bad and The Ugly. Down the slope, round the next corner – I was quite looking forward to seeing how I'd cope against them when the road started to rise again for the last, long haul to the top.

'Ecco là,' yelped The Ugly from behind; 'Ici!' boomed The Bad from in front. The Bad slowed and pulled over, I uncleated in confusion, stopped behind him and looked about in bewilderment. 'Here?'

'Si . . . 'ere. Voilà.'

I looked to the left; set high into a rock was a modest plaque. 'Coppi e Bobet,' said The Bad, paraphrasing the inscription that paid tribute to the two Fifties' legends and a monumental battle they had fought over here in 1951. 'In Giro,' piped The Ugly mischievously, 'no in Tour.' There was a long silence here, during which I began to get restless and The Bad began to cry. Out of the corner of my eye I saw the tear lodge in a crow's foot before running down a brown cheek, and The Ugly must have seen it too, because he clicked up the top of his bidon, raised it at the plaque and chirped, 'Fausto Coppi.' He then took a nip of what, judging by the alarmed exhalation he delivered following its ingestion, was probably not a soft drink; having been offered and having accepted a throat-torching memorial tot of my own, I can report that it was in fact the very hardest drink I have ever successfully swallowed. 'A la Tour,' I wheezed, commemorating once more the Tower. 'Al Giro,' reciprocated The Ugly, taking another formidable swig.

As pilgrimages go, theirs was a brief one. After an awkward wait I slung a leg over ZR, mumbled some attention-attracting sound and nodded queryingly up the mountain; The Ugly wrinkled his considerable nose and shimmied a hand in polite rejection. We shook hands, I dabbed a digit at my tender neck flesh with an awkward 'Grazie' and then, leaving them nodding and sighing in the cool shadow of the stele, gingerly proceeded. Onward and upwards.

This last stretch of plaited hairpins and scorched earth was where the Italian fans had gathered for yesterday's stage. Pink pages of the *Gazzetta dello Sport* flapped limply at the edge of the road, occasionally wedged under empty litre bottles of Moretti beer, the Tyrolean-hatted fat man on the label beaming at me through his stein-froth. They've never needed a Seventies revival in Italy: along with fare-dodging, drink-driving and sexual molestation, littering is just another in the nation's impressive roll-call of lingering period pastimes.

And if there's one thing they love as much as mess, it's filth. On-road Tour graffiti rarely ventures beyond the name of a favoured rider or team; a syringe labelled 'EPO' below a suspect racer is about as creative as it gets. But as I toiled up the dead bends, the smooth new asphalt ahead was decorated with complex artistic tableaux. Many of these were spoof road markings, perfectly composed 'give way' junction dashes neatly marked 'PANTANI – STOP', but most of them were not.

Simon O'Brien had been at Nick and Jan's place in the Pyrenees the night before the Tour passed their front door in 1997, and offered a stark warning of what can happen when you're out there in the dark with a paintbrush, how your intended ALLEZ CHRIS can find itself evolving into an EVERTON FOOTBALL CLUB or a FUCK THE MANCS. The Italians, however, sated these unseemly urges in a more appropriately artistic manner. Their preferred icon was the erect penis, sometimes as an incidental prop in a scene depicting unpopular riders eagerly fellating or sodomising one another, but more commonly as a stand-alone icon, a vast, scarlet-frenumed, wispy-scrotumed deity solemnly spanning both sides of the carriageway.

I'd just ridden across a testicle the size of a mini-roundabout when the road thrashed through one more hairpin, then straightened, then . . . what? *What? WHAT?* An obelisk, a souvenir stall, three dozen wandering motorists and bikers and red-faced cyclists and a 360-degree panorama . . . the summit, the second-highest point of the Tour. I hadn't just conquered the feared and mighty col d'Izoard, I'd pissed it. I couldn't understand how it had been so straightforward: was I getting better at cycling, or better at tolerating pain? The same thing, I suppose.

As sensations go, it was sensational. I was still beaming like a loon when I careered an hour ahead of schedule into Briançon, Europe's highest town, finally overtaking at a set of lights the caravan-towing Landcruiser I'd chased all the way down the Izoard. 'Capitale mondiale du vélo', trumpeted a billboard as I bounced and bumped along the pot-holed road through the old city walls; 'Let's talk mountains', said another, and I thought, yeah, OK, let's. It was Saturday lunchtime, and the sunny streets were lazily busy as I ate burger and chips outside a café in our appointed meeting place, the modestly fountained place de l'Europe. 'Ça va pas,' scolded the waiter genially as he brought me my Coke. 'Is hot température, the cyclistes not drink cold boissons . . .' here he clutched his ample belly '. . . is bad for l'estomac.' The last person who'd told me off for drinking iced beverages on a hot day – the grocer who'd sold me two bottles of Fanta at Comps-sur-Arby – had been lucky to escape without a bike-pump cappuccino enema, but the world was a very different place today. I nodded, shrugged, sipped and waited.

The support vehicle showed up twenty minutes early and its driver was astonished to find me there. 'Those mountains were *enormous*,' she said. 'It was bad enough driving under them. Have you found us a hotel yet?'

In the light of my previous exploits it had been assumed that one HC a day was the well-balanced way. But the rules had changed. The Tour riders, I recalled, would ride 249 kilometres from Draguignan – remember back that far? – to Briançon in a single day: even driving half of it I'd taken double that, and on this basis the least I could do was push on a bit further. 'I'll meet you in front of the town hall in Valloire at 6.30,' I said, having checked out the itinerary for stage fifteen, the penultimate day in the Alps. 'It's 50k up the road.'

'Well . . . all right. What's that on your neck?'

As she settled the children down to lunch – a verb that merits inverted commas if ever there was one – I rolled off into the crowds of shoppers, wondering if I should have told her that the only route to Valloire would involve me cycling, and her driving, over the second-highest road in Europe.

The haul up to the foot of the col du Galibier posed a severe threat to my enthusiasm. The col du Lautaret was a spirit-sapping, soul-slapping incline, 25 upward kilometres that were perpetually painful without quite being unbearable: in the words of Paul Kimmage, 'It's a long bastard.' There was a headwind and heavy traffic – the N91's passage between the 10,000-foot peaks on either side has been an important trans-Alpine route since Roman times – and though I did reel in and pass two fairly serious cyclists, an attempt to take on a third almost finished me off. A bloke with a close-cropped beard and a Giro-souvenir feeding bag slung over his shoulder, he had stared straight into my face after catching me, gauging my physical status as pros are taught to do, before jumping on his pedals with a vicious smirk. I rose to the bait – childish, perhaps, but then this was what real cyclists had to do – standing up in the saddle and pistoning my legs until every part of them seemed to glow with pain. I closed the gap to four coach lengths – easy enough to estimate in these road conditions – but couldn't get it down further, and entering the first tunnel I thought, well, I bet he hasn't done the bloody Izoard today, then issued the world's favourite impolite noise and backed off.

Motorcyclists were buying 'I climbed the Lautaret' T-shirts at the col-topping café; stifling an arrogant snort I wolfed down two bars of chocolate and an Orangina before heading off down a listless little road that prodded shyly towards a recklessly steepled ridge of snow-veined granite. 'One place you won't be cycling to . . .' was how the guidebooks chose to describe the 2,645-metre Galibier. Today was 3 June and I was surprised to learn from the waitress that the road over the top was usually snowed up for at least another two weeks. On any previous day the discovery that it had opened early would have been the excuse for anguished howls: betrayed by global warming.

The Galibier had undone hundreds of professional reputations, and it is still difficult to understand how I conquered it with such glorious nonchalance. The wind hit me on that first grassy, treeless flank, and when I entered the six o'clock shadows and lost the sun my breath started steaming furiously. But I never really slowed, never dropped out of twenty-six, even as the snow started to pile up at the roadside, gritted and muddy like ice-cream dropped on the beach. A kilometre from the top, negotiating a slushy brown stream that dribbled fitfully over the road, I came to the squat concrete cylinder of the monument to Henri Desgrange, founder of the Tour de France. I stopped, and with unaccustomed self-assertion flagged down a middle-aged couple in a Toyota. 'Un photo,' I ordered, pointing at ZR and Henri, and the balding husband nodded in cowed compliance. As he reversed to the edge of the road to make way for a minibus there was a horrid crack that echoed off the snowy rock behind; he had struck a boulder. 'C'est rien,' I said briskly, glancing at the negligible remains of his offside rear-light cluster. 'OK – mon photo.' He snapped me and drove quickly off without even inspecting the damage himself.

They'd stuck Henri here because it was his favourite mountain. Beside the Galibier, 'Giant of the Alps', the other cols, he remarked, were 'gnat's piss'. 'The ideal Tour,' he went on to remark, 'is one in which only one rider finishes.' I'd read that back home, and during some of my more epic sufferings had found the words recurring to me in a taunt that needed to be avenged. I thought of old Octave Lapize, creaking over the Aubisque and rasping '*Assassins!*' at the waiting officials; I thought of Paul Kimmage, squirming up the Galibier with the broom wagon almost up his arse in the agonised final minutes of his 1987 Tour; and then, I'm afraid, I went round the back of Henri's statue and anointed it more fulsomely than any gnat. He was one of them; I was beginning to feel like one of us. It was what the riders would have wanted.

That last kilometre was perhaps the steepest of my career as a cyclist, and it is possible that if I hadn't known it was only that far I would have given up. But I didn't. With an exultant grimace I rolled up to the wind-battered viewpoint, blithely wondering which of the pointy white bastards over there was Mont Blanc, and which of the grey-faced fuckers over there was the col de la Madeleine, tomorrow's 2,000-metre HC treat. I had covered 1,600 kilometres to reach this figurative and literal high point; two HCs conquered in an afternoon – it could only be, had better be, downhill from here on. 'Bravo,' said a voice, and a little Frenchman came up to share his reminiscences of a 1969 cycling weekend in the Benelux countries with a Dutchman who spoke no French, and as I smiled and nodded I began to understand how Alice Cooper must have felt when, while interviewing him some years ago, I proceeded to talk at length about the band I'd been in at school.

The descent was predictably fast and predictably bleak: grasping the brakes with numbed, unresponsive fingers through the slushy hairpins, slaloming madly between two lolloping beaver-like marmots, off home to their scree-piled treeless slag heap. At one point the icy, snowploughed detritus was piled into a corridor whose walls dwarfed me; it was like going down the Cresta run. Upside-down names flashed beneath my wheels: Virenque, Pantani, Riis; even the odd frost-preserved relic, the ghost of an Hinault here, a shadowy Roche there.

As the bends were pulled taut, unkinked into a straight, flat-out descent, there was no possibility of even stealing a sideways peek at the Scottish moorlands around me. The rushing wind swallowed up the sound of the thundering river alongside; I hit a cloud of flies by the first farm and came out the other side with one up each nostril and my sunglasses looking like a rally car's headlamps after a night stage around the Finnish lakes. As I topped 70 k.p.h. – getting on for 45 m.p.h. – the frame begin to bow and sing, or so it seemed, and I suddenly recalled that this morning my bicycle had been in many pieces, and that the person who had falteringly assembled these pieces was me.

I hit Valloire, very nearly literally, bang on 6.30, and found my support vehicle cruising its wide, desolate streets looking for the town hall. 'Thanks for telling me about that sodding mountain,' whispered the pale-faced driver as three junior assistants snuffled and snored behind her, before taking in my fly-flecked, frost-flayed features with a noise that combined awe with disgust. I removed my helmet, propped my shades up on my head and announced, 'I am an outstanding sportsman.'

Valloire was doing whatever the opposite of hibernating is, its five-floor chalets shuttered up waiting for the snow and the skiers. If we'd been here two days ago everything would have been closed; as it was, only one hotel was open: a trim, clean and rather spartan concrete chalet, all whitewash and window boxes, the kind of place you could imagine Hitler staying in.

In the bierkeller dining basement we had fondue, on reflection a poor choice for small children amply supplied with combustible table linen, and delicious local rosé – with a start I realised I had forgotten to drink at lunchtime, and desperately hoped this was not the reason for my enhanced performance. Then, with the children pinned under Teutonic eiderdowns as heavy as mattresses, we repaired to our balcony and watched a huge hare hopping about between the Volkswagens and geraniums in the hotel car park. The white-noise roar of Galibier meltwater seemed an oddly violent counterpoint to such a sleepy scene.

'Were they that big?' said a little, muffled voice as we came back in. 'The mountains you went up on your bicycle – were they as big as those?' I followed Kristjan's gaze up to the opposite peaks, silhouetted in the moonlight.

'Much, much bigger,' I said, because they had been.

'So are you all better now?'

I realised then that what I had done that day was the sort of thing that hitherto only other children's daddies had done, and by doing it I had joined some sort of élite club. 'I'm not just better,' I said in an assumed voice, 'I'm the best.'

It could have been worse. I almost said 'son'.

Thirteen

Paul Kimmage abandoned on the col du Télégraphe, early in the same misty stage that ended with the agonised heroics at la Plagne of his countryman Stephen Roche. In the morning, breezing gaily up the Télégraphe's modest slopes – not even a category four in this direction – I realised just how comprehensively bollocksed he must have been by that day's fearsome pace up the Galibier. Far more exhausting for me was the joint-juddering descent, 34 kilometres continuously downhill, from the dizzy top flap of the Alpen packet all the way down to the last squashed raisin at the bottom. I was going less than two-thirds as fast as the pros, but let me tell you now that if I drove a car like I rode that bike – at the ragged edge of the performance parameters of both man and machine – the passengers would be screaming to be let out after two minutes. I shot a tiny glance at the waterfall-veined, pine-wooded loveliness around me and as a result only accidentally missed a pot-hole the size of a punchbowl that would happily have killed me.

Soon after, something small and flappy got entwined in my leg hair – I really would have to address this issue soon – and I didn't dare slap at it until the road straightened into the Arc valley at Saint-Michel-de-Maurienne. When I dismounted for a pain au chocolat and a coffee, the underside of ZR's frame was littered with spoke-spattered fragments of thorax. Still juddering and shaken, I recalled that Bernard Hinault's obsession with aerodynamic posture had once led him to experiment descending with one hand on the bars and the other stretched out behind him, and picturing this immediately understood how important it was that I should never again read or say anything about this dangerous maniac.

There was a Sunday-morning club event of some sort being organised in the usual all-day siesta that entombs most Alpine towns in the summer, and as I was overtaken by cars with half a dozen bikes on their roofs I couldn't help wondering if one of the team bosses might lean over to the driver to yell, 'Hey – there's that guy who passed me going up the Lautaret: have his legs shaved and stick him in the first team.'

As soon as I thought that thought I knew I'd regret it, and it didn't take long. The col de la Madeleine didn't mess about: no Izoard or Galibier-style slow build-up, just a full-frontal assault from the valley floor. I'd noticed that some mountains seemed at one with their surroundings, overgrown green hills incorporated almost seamlessly into the pastures, but the peaks crowding the Madeleine were of the other sort: bare and alien rocks, huge flint hand axes flung petulantly into the earth at random angles.

It was another scorcher, and I was soon melting. The road was a slight shambles – white and thin as cotton thread on the map, frost-cracked and sunburnt in the flesh – but it rose to its challenge with admirable pluck, heading straight at the 2,000-metre summit with the minimum of dilatory hairpins: an 8 per cent gradient for 19.3 kilometres, steeper than Ventoux and almost as long. I'd averaged 34 k.p.h. from Valloire, but double-figure progress soon became a distant memory. Unsteady hands were fumbling regularly for the bidons; the first one had been sucked dry before the climb started, and the second only lasted me to the moribund village of Saint-François-Longchamp, last outpost before the top and the place where I'd rather ambitiously hoped to cadge a refill. But though necessity might be the mother of invention, it is also the grandfather of petty theft, and if people really must leave dozens of crates of Coca-Cola (ahhh!), Badoit (ooooh!) and Heineken (falalalala-la-la-la-la!) in the open back of an unattended pick-up truck in an area where the transient presence of thirsty British men might easily be predicted, then that's their lookout. As retribution goes, a slight dose of hiccups was a bit of a let-off.

Up the bikeless, lifeless last stretch, past shuttered-up shepherd shacks and broad green pistes, I struggled to keep the bad thoughts at bay. I'd been in twenty-seven almost all the way and sweat was being forced out of places with no previous history of perspiration, glistening on both forearms and bubbling out of my knees. The summit had none of the drama of the previous HCs – no monuments, no mist, just a boarded-up snack bar and a gravelly car park where half a dozen children were redistributing the last patches of granular slush to their parents' windscreens. But the view was nothing if not epic: what I proudly recognised as yesterday's peaks savaging the horizon to the south, and what I sincerely hoped weren't tomorrow's doing the same to the northeast.

The bonk was knocking at my door but as I laboriously focused on the plummeting stage profile I knew it didn't matter: the day's pedalling was all but done. The tin-roofed Savoyard villages I plunged through were a frail last bastion of Alpine life without tourism, those vast-planked hovels perching lowing livestock and wheelless Citroëns over the most fearful gorge yet. Sighing into the valley floor I purchased many inappropriate foodstuffs at a petrol station and ate them all on the forecourt; within the hour

I was rolling into Brides-les-Bains, our nominated afternoon meeting point.

Brides-les-Bains was another spa resort that had grown out of nothing when the railway arrived, then been slowly starved of tourists as cheap flights made foreign travel an affordable and more glamorous option. But, as proven by its perennial presence on the Tour route, it wasn't going down without a fight, and judging by the number of doddering jaywalkers dicing with vehicular euthanasia its efforts to reinvent itself as an OAPs' health-spa playground were clearly paying off. Regrettably, one aspect of this diligent pursuit of the grey franc was the systematic alienation of the pre-pubescent pound.

As Birna had discovered on the train to Avignon, genteel French society demands that children be seen but not heard. Because Lilja's default vocal response to any thwarted whim is of a pitch and volume that recalls a hospital surgery of the pre-anaesthetic age, we correctly anticipated ours might fall foul of this maxim. Even locking them in the car didn't work: hotel receptionists, detecting a muffled commotion, would contrive ever more ludicrous deterrents. Positioning themselves so as to conceal a well-stocked rack of keys, they would brazenly claim to be full; or not to have any cots or highchairs; or to own a 'beeg dergue' who might 'play too strong'.

In the end I parked the car half a mile from any hotel and stayed there with the children while Birna found us a room in a place with swan-neck taps and a slimmers' menu. The Ruth Ellis receptionist didn't look too pleased when the rest of us piled into her lobby, but of course she had nothing to worry about. It's not as if we peed in *both* saunas, or dive-bombed *every last* pensioner out of the swimming pool.

'This is *exactly* the kind of place where people go completely mad,' said Birna later, breathless after a hurried nocturnal outing to retrieve her eye-varnish or hair-liner or something from the car. Though I'd probably have opted for 'senile', there was something undeniably disturbing about Brides-les-Bains and not just because we had immediately dubbed it 'Brides in the Bath'. As well as the stroppily daunting scenery, we blamed the noise, that endless thrash of melted Alp roaring a final farewell to its birthplace as it headed off to the Mediterranean. No wonder there weren't any other children in town – with a watery lullaby like that they'd be in nappies until puberty. Just as well that most of the current residents were back in them.

Three weeks were up; the real racers would be rolling up the Champs-Elysées today. Because I was still a very long way from Paris, over breakfast I made the very easy decision not to proceed from Brides-les-Bains to Courchevel, the category-one eminence 20k up (and up and up) the road where stage fifteen ended and stage sixteen began. No, I would go straight back down the Isère valley, then straight up the next category one, swiftly followed by a not inconsiderable category two. 'I'm not doing those squiggly bits,' said Birna, following my finger up the map: the day before she had happily undertaken a 120k detour to avoid driving over the Madeleine. It was arranged that our two rather different itineraries should converge after 100k at the ritzy-sounding ski resort of la Clusaz.

You might arrive in Albertville not knowing that the town hosted the 1992 Winter Olympics, but there is not the tiniest chance of leaving with this ignorance intact. Its slightly Communist ambience of broad avenues and low-rise tower blocks is only enhanced by the number of enormous commemorative murals – peeling skiers slaloming down the side of a warehouse, a faded luge speeding along concrete embankments. Distant association with winter sports was no barrier: there was an Olympique tennis club and cycling centre, and even a hair-dresser's. I bought three pains au chocolat and a litre of Yoplait in a boulangerie with five linked pastry rings in the window, and click-clicking down, down, deeper and down, began the slow haul up to the col des Saisies.

You could tell they didn't get many cyclists round here. Car passengers were now looking curiously round at me as they passed, only partly because of the black-and-white-minstrel Yoplait mouth ring I discovered during my next confrontation with a mirror. And I'd become so accustomed to restaurant staff blithely pulling out a chair to accommodate my Savlon-steaming behind that it was a shock to be accorded the lunchtime reception my appearance deserved. Asking the waitress where the loo was, I saw the backs of a dozen grey heads quiver in sour disgust: 'Typical! Flies in his hair, yoghurt round his mouth . . . *and* he's got a bladder.' It wouldn't have been so bad – not quite – if the loo in question had not been one of those porcelain footprint jobs, the kind of sanitary fitting that makes it easier to understand why so many Frenchmen prefer the lay-by option. And when bladder-boy made the mistake of asking where the mustard was . . . well, you should have heard the roof-raising merriment as the waitress approached with a finger outstretched and slowly lowered this squat digit to the cruet set. Because . . . yes! The mustard was *already on the table*! Do you see?

Still, it was nice to bring some laughter into their lives. Though not as nice as it was to take seventy-one complimentary mints out of them.

The col des Saisies sported the most grandiose hairpins yet, huge lazy sweeps up a smooth bank of green dotted with immaculate chalets. Six-foot thistles and wild strawberries lined the road, but bad stuff was happening above: peaks disappearing into beige clouds; thunder rumbling off the opposite mountain sides. In the valley those big stacks of neatly hewn firewood by every garage were employed as faux-rural decorative features, but when the rain finally got me I'd reached the peasant zone where such things were very much for real.

When the storm caught up I sheltered in the porch of an ancient-planked barn, watching the cows graze on a 60-degree slope to my left, and looking down at the rainbow bridging the valley to my right. The road I'd turned off at the bottom was the back way to Mont Blanc, and in the humid mist the silhouetted mountains were lined up on all sides like ranks of stage scenery. The cars below were tiny mobile specks, and for the first time I was able to think: yes, I have just ascended an enormous vertical distance under my own steam without even trying. Viewed in this heroic light, it didn't seem appropriate to be cowering under a hovel, so out I went to be pebble-dashed and shot at by the elements, wondering if my tyres would save me from electrocution.

The road was steaming and so, quite literally, were my limbs, and through squinted eyes I entered a steep land where cows drank from old baths and proper milk churns were lined up by wood-shingled farmhouses. It felt like a different world, and the inhabitants clearly felt it deserved partial recognition as such. Tattered Savoy flags – they really should make them look less like the Swiss one – hung wetly by every barn, and SAVOIE LIBRE was daubed on bus shelters. And frankly, they can have it. If it was like this in June, I thought, what happens up here in bloody winter?

It stopped raining at la Saisie, and as the road broadened and levelled I rolled into a moribund concrete ski town – summer, Monday, 3 p.m.: dead to the power of three. Mankind's contribution to the beauty of this place was not altogether admirable, but nature was doing its best to atone: through the mist, peaks emerged distantly on all sides with ethereal sunlit haloes, lined up like an Alpine greatest-hits postcard.

It said something for my condition that I was beginning to dread the descents more than the climbs. Actually, reading that I recognise it as a terrible, terrible lie, but you get the point. Fear was beginning to challenge fatigue, and locking my wheels around the loose-chippinged curves into Fluvet I impregnated the thin air with deafening indelicacies in a language known to no man. Having squealed to a breathless halt down its (very) high street, I went into the only open shop in town and, finding all the

195

confectionery was behind the counter, found myself obliged to ask for 'A Snickers . . . ? Un Snickeur? Un Sniquet? Une Sniqueur?'

I made short work of this hard-won quarry, along with a half-litre of milk, as I wheeled ZR back past the dirty buildings. Remounting alongside the last, I spotted a young boy flamboyantly arching his back atop a low wall to its rear as he widdled gleefully into an unseen void. As he met my gaze with airy nonchalance I found myself contemplating perhaps the ugliest of the Tour's many ugly secrets.

I hope I am not alone in harbouring a mild obsession with the excretory habits of professional sportsmen. When a tennis or snooker player strides briskly out of the arena mid-match, as the commentator mumbles something about calls of nature I find myself curiously comforted: they might in most other ways be a different species, but here is evidence that at heart these champions are as human as you or I. Because Tour cyclists are not, however, they have to do things differently.

Until 1957 the unwritten rule in the Tour was that when a rider stopped to pee in the bushes, the rest freewheeled along, not taking ungentlemanly advantage by speeding away up the road. In that year, however, infuriated by the arrogance of Luxembourg's Charly Gaul, a small group did exactly that when the tiny Luxemburger pulled into the verge. 'No one takes the piss when I take a piss,' he may easily have said, because the next day he initiated the practice of widdling on the wing, pointing Percy at the pavement, baptising the bitumen. This could have earned him the nickname The Raining Champion or some unsavoury derivation of yellow jersey, but in France they preferred to call him 'Pee-Pee' (a shame his career didn't overlap with Raymond 'Poupou' Poulidor – what a hit they'd have been on the cabaret circuit).

Anyway, since Charly broke the taboo, mobile micturation has become the norm. The practice is even acknowledged in Tour regulations: you can whip it out wherever you want on the country roads, but there's a fine for anyone offloading processed Evian in a built-up area. I'd seen it more than once on the television coverage: a rider drops off the back of the pack, ideally on a straightish, emptyish stretch of road, then hoicks up the leg of his shorts and does what he can to direct things away from the bicycle. Obviously what you really want to avoid are the rapidly revolving spokes, and their impressive potential for fluid dispersion.

Sometimes, however, a rider may lack the opportunity or wherewithal for such an operation. In 1978 Michel Pollentier assured himself of an unwelcome place in Tour history with an astonishing two-act display of urinary recklessness. Leading the race up the formidable climb of Alpe d'Huez, *in extremis* he voids himself directly into his gusset; having won the stage he is required to give a sample but has nothing left to offer. These unappealing details are already tarnishing a heroic achievement, but as he slips off the victory rostrum to hesitant applause after an unusually restrained embrace from the podium blondes there is worse to come. Pollentier has also taken an illegal stimulant, and with the dope-testers making their way up to his hotel he elects to tackle this situation using apparatus that will be familiar to anyone who has either watched the film *Withnail & I* or is a repellent weirdo.

When the doctors call it is all set up, but with Michel waiting his turn, another testee is spotted behaving unusually as the flask is passed to him. All the riders present are summarily ordered to lower their shorts: a tube is discovered, one end taped to an intimate place, the other connected to a rubber bulb in his armpit containing somebody else's urine, and Michel's humiliation is complete. He is immediately thrown out of the race, and as a taunting postscript the genuine sample he subsequently provides passes the test.

I'd been wondering about Pee-Pee and Pollentier for some days, and wondered about them again as the D909 rose gently between the wet, black, coal-face cliffs of the Gorge de l'Arondine. There was no one about; the road was straight; the milk was going the way of all ingested fluid and I thought: this'll do.

During my idle speculations on the subject I'd always imagined the short-rucking would be the hard bit, but the wrongheadedness of this assumption became quickly apparent. Pulling the shorts up to get at the old budgie perch was one thing; getting them to stay there was another. Wobbling lewdly about the rainslick tarmac I realised the problem was my continuing inability to remove both hands from the bars simultaneously. A fearsome elastic tension is Lycra's defining quality, and by assigning four fingers of my right hand to keeping this at bay I was left with only a thumb – rightly belittled as the least articulate of the major digits – for the delicate and demanding directional operation. The ensuing scene is not one I am ever likely to recall with enthusiasm. It started raining heavily as I wound disconsolately past the copper-belfried church at la Giettaz, and if I say that I greeted this downpour with muted joy you will have some idea of the extent to which I had failed to master Charly Gaul's initiative.

It was a shame, really, because la Giettaz seemed the most perfect example yet of an Alpine village: shockingly precipitous outlook; proper wooden chalets; even a sanatorium where uniformed nurses wheeled blanket-kneed pensioners up the mountains. A couple even had a light-hearted race with me – well, light-hearted for them anyway. There wasn't room for more than one incontinent sporting legend on these hills.

With my morale still damp and soiled, I got in a spot of bother up the col d'Aravis. Paul Kimmage often comments how form varies from mountain to mountain, how you can grovel up one then fly up the next, and now I understood what he meant. The streams that had been wallowing gently over boulders as smooth as elephants' backs were now darting violently between sharp rocks and vaulting over waterfalls, and as the hill steepened I began to struggle, head bobbing, fingers fumbling at the gear levers. 'Allez! Allez!' shouted two girls as they laboured past in a 2CV; two whimpering 'k's later I was applauded sporadically over the muddy, misty col by a family drinking something nice and warm outside the now-traditional summit café. Distracted with exhaustion, I almost overcooked it on the descent, flirting with a barbed-wire fence at incautious velocity, once more filling the wet, green valley with bungee-jumper shrieks as the back wheel slipped in the verge-side mud.

Still, the main point was that I got to la Clusaz twenty minutes ahead of schedule, which allowed me plenty of time to decide that this was the sort of ritzy *glühwein* resort where Fergie would come skiing, and to down two Ricards and a lager in the square by the church. In consequence I was half asleep at the table when the family arrived, and soon fully so as Birna drove west between mountains with the silhouettes of crowned monarchs. I awoke as we arrived at what I instantly understood would be the most expensive hotel I have ever paid for out of my own pocket, with a lobby full of silver-haired Blake Carringtons in ironed leisure-wear and immaculate, deck-chair-strewn gardens running down to its own private stretch of Lake Annecy's crenellated, aristocratic shoreline.

'It isn't that bad,' said Birna, seeing my features sag into a very close approximation of the funereal depression portrayed during the aftermath of that ill-fated excretory experiment. And at fifty quid for the lot of us, it wasn't. Remembering how ludicrously cheap French hotels tended to be, it occurred to me that the Beau-Site in Talloires showcased the best attributes of the surrounding nations: Swiss service, Italian view, French prices.

Ahead was the last day of mountains, and if I did survive, I realised now it would only be by the skin of my teeth. I hadn't seen another bike for almost two days, or a single name daubed on the tarmac, and at breakfast I found out why. 'Is not so many vélo 'ere,' said the black-tied young waiter at breakfast. 'Too many montagnes. I préfère ze, uh, sliding sports: snowboard, wakeboarding.' Still savouring this last word – there is something wonderful about hearing a recalcitrant French mouth bully itself round a many-syllabled English word – I took another messy mouthful of croissant and asked if anyone would be watching the Tour when it passed down the road. 'Yes, of course, I watch it always – but I do not 'ave ze . . .' and here he thumped a fist dramatically to his chest . . . 'ze *art* for vélo. It's very . . . difficult, very 'ard sport.'

'Yes,' I said, toying vaingloriously with my jersey zip and gazing through the French windows as a thick mist squatted down on to the mountains. 'Yes, it is. And you prefer the wakeb . . . what was it again?'

Tiny drops of cloud were already clinging to exposed flesh when the family waved me off at la Clusaz. It wasn't going to be easy. Between here and our scheduled meeting at Evian lay 130k of badness, up and down a 5,000-foot mountain before the Alps went out with a wet and lonely bang up the hors catégorie col de Joux-Plane. This name had always sounded like something out of a nursery rhyme, conjuring gay images of bunting and maypoles, but the chanting children were all bundled over an echoing precipice when I unfolded the Michelin. The frail white line that traced its circuitous path on the map had a messy, doodled look, one that suggested Friday-afternoon cartography, a sort of that'll-do approach to a road no one would seriously consider following. Three small hands waved sadly through the drizzled windows, and I realised for the first time what a rubbish holiday this was for my children: thrown around the back seat all day in a Dramamined stupor, then being kissed awake in the late after-noon by a filthy, tearful cripple.

La Clusaz, le Grand-Bornand: what made one village masculine and another feminine? Maybe it was the legacy of my own gender-related tower/tour travails, but I was starting to become genuinely angered by this linguistic imbecility. At la Clusaz the night before I'd asked for 'un bière', only for the fat-faced patron to chide, '*une* bière'. With my tongue loosened by pastis and fatigue I'd leant back in my slatted chair and muttered, 'Tell you what, René, bring one of each: maybe they'll get it together and make me lots of little baby bières.'

My experiment in town-sexing was made more difficult by the thickening fog. The last haul up to the category-one col de la Colombière was so lonely that slugs were making it all the way across the road; the bleak, cloud-hazed patches of browned snow and muddy moorland were the sorry remnants of a majestic panorama that I only got to see on the postcards in the col-topping café. Here I drank a double espresso and dripped sweat and mist on to the table, then briefly caught my craw in the zip again before heading off for the descent, followed into the fog by the amazed gaze of the patron's young daughter holding a vigil at the window.

Clenched with cold I almost died on the way down, my approximate, frost-fisted control of the handlebars edging me on to the wrong side of the road just as an oncoming car ghosted out of the fog. Only when the pine-shingled hovels gave way to all-weather tennis courts was I sure I'd made it; when I glanced back up, the mist-swirled peaks looked ablaze, and if they had been I'd have gone back up there to thaw. Pedalling desperately to try and generate some body heat I sped through Cluses, a jarring outbreak of dark satanic mills, then hurled myself at the third-category hill outside. It started to rain and my speedometer stopped working; a learner-driver side-swiped me and the two slices of fruitcake I'd nicked at breakfast had somehow vanished from my jersey pocket. A closed bridge, a dispiriting detour, cuckoo-clock balconies and then, running on empty and with the first bonk-of-England madnesses marching over the horizon, I was in Samoëns, looking for lunch, the road to the Joux-Plane and any mislaid parts of my brain.

There wasn't a lot to do in Samoëns, not at 3.30 on a wet Wednesday in June, and while sitting in a pine-panelled bar dispatching a parade of fried and fatty foods I watched a lot of people not doing it. Sturdy housewives waddled aimlessly past. A pouchy-eyed man with a low brow and a bobble hat came in and gruffly ordered a Lucifer Flambée, which I saw described in my bill of fare as 'bière et alcool'. More sturdy housewives. A driver delivering dustbins to a hardware shop sat in one of the wheel-barrows on display outside and his mate gave him a quick and noisy ride round the square. After another dozen housewives, a man cycled past one-handed, guiding a second bike with his right hand, which still impresses me now, though probably not as much as it did then if a hazy memory of open applause has any basis in reality. As bobble hat was ordering his second Lucifer, two pairs of purple cycling shorts swooshed in through the door, and when after a few more fistfuls of chips I realised that the heads above these shorts were issuing English voices I looked behind me to see a young couple, as fresh-faced as *Blue Peter* presenters, helmets on the table, writing postcards and drinking hot chocolate. Without thinking I rose and approached.

'Sorry,' I said, apologising for my appearance as well as for the fact that I hadn't decided what I was about to say, 'but I noticed your legs there and I just need to know what you're doing.'

As conversational icebreakers go this was rather a *Titanic*, but it is a tribute to the overlooked good manners of England's youth, or at least its hearty, active Home Counties subset, that the pair looked up with eager, open faces rather than the wary, sod-off glowers demanded by the situation.

'Yuh – well, we're just doing a bit of a tour,' began the male, who I have no choice but to describe as a boy. 'Ten days. We flew into Geneva last night and just got down here. It's great – you can take your bikes for free on BA. What about you?'

'Well – you could call it a bit of a tour. The Tour. The Tour de France.'

'Cool,' said the girl in neutral tones, scratching a shoulder blade through her grey fleece top. Minimal departures in the bump department aside, she could quite easily have passed for her boyfriend. 'It's a shame the weather's so awful – the scenery's supposed to be amazing. Dad used to come skiing here in his bachelor days.'

'I suppose that would have been in the Seventies,' I said with a small, wry snort she clearly missed.

'. . . Er, yuh, well, he met Mum in '79 so . . . yuh. Seventies.'

Oh, children, children. A solemn and ruminative silence fell over us, and to break it the boy said, 'Yuh – we're off to Morzine next.'

'Mmmm? Oh. Yeah. Me too. How you getting there?'

'Only the one way, I think. The Joux-Plane.'

'Well, there we go. That's my route. Because it's part of the Tour de France, which I'm doing. All of.'

'Cool. Well, in that case maybe we could all . . .' and here he exchanged very quick but very eloquent glances with his girlfriend, 'Well . . . good luck. Pretty grim up there, by the looks of it.'

Almost immediately they clattered out into the wet wooden street with brisk waves, postcards half-written and hot chocolates half-drunk. I could understand their reluctance to accompany me up the Joux-Plane, or rather I couldn't, the heartless little bastards. Did I really look that grisly? I suppose they just wanted to ride up hand-in-hand and have a celebratory wholesome snog at the top. Ten minutes later, feeling very, very tired, I was zipping up my rain top and remounting without enthusiasm.

As befitted what was, after all, the steepest climb in the 2000 Tour – 8.4 per cent for 12 kilometres – the road out of Samoëns thinned and rose almost immediately. Soon I was out of the saddle and into the mist. Farms as messy and hopeless as hillbilly homesteads were left behind and now there was nothing but fir trees and pot-holes and my breath piping seamlessly into the fog. The non-functioning speedometer had been getting on my tit end all day, but now that blank, unaccusing display was a solitary source of comfort.

'Hey!'

Almost asleep in the saddle, I clumsily uncleated a foot and looked up in bleary alarm. It was the two cyclists.

'Hey!' Having been descending towards me at speed, they brought their matching green tourers to a squeaky, unsteady halt alongside. 'It's closed. The pass. "Route barrée".'

I looked at them like a kindly old country parson being informed by heavenly messengers that God despises him, and always has done. 'Closed? But . . . closed why? Why closed?'

'No idea. Big gates across the road with a no-entry sign. Closed. Route barrée.'

I tried to come to terms with the situation, but immediately knew that in the absence of opiate drugs such an endeavour was doomed. 'Closed,' I said, in a blank and broken whisper.

'Yuh – bad news. It's at least a 40k detour back to the D road up the gorge.'

I peered into the unhelpful mist above. It was cold – actually, very cold now that I had stopped pedalling – but surely there couldn't be enough snow up there to block a road. And if there was, couldn't I just shoulder the bike over it? I didn't have to think very long about those additional 40 kilometres to know that even quite a sizeable risk of lonely death was worth taking to avoid them.

'I'm going to give it a go.'

'Yuh? It's got to be another 6k to the top and . . .' Levering his forearm at a radical angle to denote the forthcoming gradient, the boy appraised my age and condition in a glimpse that damned and sympathised in almost equal proportions.

'And it's absolutely *bitter*,' said the girl, rubbing her thermal gloves. Why didn't I have thermal gloves?

'I don't have any choice,' I said with off-hand bravado. 'It's on the route – the Tour route.'

'Cool,' said the boy, consulting a ridiculous chronometer the size of a cartoon alarm clock. 'OK, well, uh, best of luck again. Maybe see you in Morzine for a hot toddy.'

I had listened politely to details of the girlfriend's father's premarital holiday habits and they hadn't even had the common decency to recognise the ongoing enormity of my achievement. Twice I'd tolerated this, excusing it as a conversational oversight. The third time I did not.

'I doubt it, actually, because I'll be there before you and I'm going straight on to Evian,' I said briskly, pulling my chinstrap tight and preparing to leave. 'Anyway, I'm sure you can think of plenty of other ways of warming each other up.'

I was quietly pleased with this parting shot for the thirty seconds of histrionic puffing it took me to reach the next bend, at which point I realised that it wasn't *her* father's holidays, but *their* father's. They were not boy and girl but brother and sister.

Though few made themselves apparent at the time, there were several beneficent side effects to this regrettable riposte. One was that for valuable minutes I had preoccupations beyond the rigours of the climb; another was an increased determination to overcome whatever hazard had closed the road and so make good my escape from sibling outrage. A rather sketchier third was that my veiled accusation might indeed have forestalled an incestuous atrocity: they wore the same clothes, after all, and rode the same bikes – and, let's face it, there's no smoke without fire.

Cows were now wandering about the foggy road, inciting an injection of speed as efficiently as any injection of speed, and straining up through a dense fir copse I was almost unsaddled by a police car descending out of the mist at idiotic velocity. As the driver completed an extravagant evasive manoeuvre, his passenger just had time to frown at me, shake his head and cross raised forearms in unequivocal mimicry of the looming blockade.

I pressed on into the cloud. Although my dramatic 'mine not to reason why' avowal to the siblings had, I now understood, been that of a pompous nob-end, it was true to say that I did feel a moral and spiritual obligation to conquer the final mountain. To bunk off would be to cast a depressing symmetry upon my climbing career; by defeating the Joux-Plane I could look back on an almost unbroken rising arc of achievement.

The obstacle that had repelled the illicit lovers was hardly as fortified as they'd made out, just a single crowd-control barrier flung half-heartedly across the road: 'Route barrée' in word, maybe, but hardly in deed. A bit further on were a couple of exclamation-mark triangles, and an additional no-entry sign with a dented yellow 'CHAUSSÉE DEFORMÉE' propped beneath it. Negotiating an unimpressive landslide round the next – small bits of Christmas tree and a few buckets of mud slopped over the road, the tarmac nibbled daintily away at one side – I felt enormously smug. Up, round, back, up: half a dozen twists and fifteen minutes later I was leaning my bike up against a signpost with a tin Savoy flag riveted to it, willing self-timer flash to overcome fog so that future generations would not be spared the inspiring image of their intrepid ancestor standing haughtily by his machine before the enamelled legend 'Col de Joux-Plane (Altitude 1700 m.)'.

I couldn't see much but then it didn't seem there was much to see: wet tussocks; mud; the occasional mothballed ski-lift creaking eerily overhead, lost in the clouds. An anticlimax in a way: I'd been thinking all day of the weary jubilation as the Tour riders eased over the Joux-Plane, possibly bloody, certainly bowed, but not beaten. For perhaps half a dozen of them the race would still be on in earnest; for the other 120-odd survivors, this might as well have been the finish line, the remaining stages to Paris just a procession, maybe the chance to sneak a cheeky stage win but no more. If you survive the mountains you survive the Tour, and if you survive the Tour you are a Giant of the Road.

Of the seven HC climbs, I'd pushed up half of the first, bunked off the second and been chauffeured along the last stretch of the third in a drugged-up coma. But the remaining four had all been conquered in a fashion that by my standards at least was very possibly heroic. Giant of the Road might be stretching it a bit, but wheeling along the flat crest of my final Alp I was King of the Hill. A short and inglorious reign, however, because then I went round a corner and discovered, as I attempted to follow it, that the road had fallen down the mountain.

I suppose I might have died. Had the visibility been more than two bike lengths I'd certainly have been going a lot faster, and in this manner would have plunged majestically into the gaping, mist-shrouded chasm rather than keeling gently over into its muddy but benign upper reaches: done a Thelma and Louise, in other words, rather than a Laurel and Hardy.

Hauling ZR back on to the tarmac and palming filth off my legs, I understood that this might have been what all the barriers were about. The Alps, once taller than the Himalayas, were shrinking every year; in a demonstration of the puniness of man's efforts to shore up the mountains, the rain had sluiced away a large piece of Joux-Plane, taking a load of road as it did so. The chaussée hadn't been deformed so much as amputated. For fifty feet, the remaining usable section of tarmac was a ragged ribbon stitched haphazardly to the mountainside, never wider than a mantelpiece and sometimes considerably narrower. With one foot on the muddy slope and the other on what was left of the road, I hoisted ZR in red, numbed hands and carried her to safety like the hero in an adventure film, albeit one scripted by Fishwife Productions.

I was shaken, and soon I was shivering. During some of the more exciting descents I had become acquainted with the phenomenon known as 'brake fade', the point at which the hardened rubber pads, overheated by continuous application, would begin to judder and hiss before abruptly adopting the speed-retarding qualities of buttered fish scales. Such an unlikely physical transformation always struck me as impressive as anything in the Old Testament, or the tiger who ran so fast round a bush that he turned into ghee.

That a bicycle constructed from materials which not many years ago would have been described as 'space-age' should suffer from this alarmingly fundamental malaise still strikes me as more than a little crap, but at least I had learned how to remedy it. By alternately pressing the front and rear levers, the pads were given a chance to cool down: milking the brakes, I called it.

When the road plunged eagerly back through the tree line I began to milk – left, right, left, right – but it was freezing, and you can't freeze milk, and as the cold fog rushed over my wet, red fingertips at 65 k.p.h. I was quickly stripped of all digital mobility. The brakes could be on, or they could be off, but switching between these two was no longer an available option. My knuckles had become locked in that mystical extremity where fire and ice merged, the split second after you brush your toe painfully against a bath tap and can't tell whether it was the blue one or the red. It was all I could do to scream my way through the next few bends until the gradient temporarily flattened and I was able to judder to an agonising halt.

Descending a snowbound peak in the 1989 Giro, Paul Kimmage had to stop by the road and pee on his hands to get some heat back in them. I would have if I could. For a moment I just stood there in the fog, fists in opposite armpits, ears in shoulder blades, an armless, neckless freak howling unlikely scenarios involving most of the Christian religion's big names. Then, abruptly inspired, I crouched and clasped the friction-heated wheel-rims, enjoying up to two seconds of relief before the surprisingly enormous temperatures started to melt my fingerprints off.

I hopped and stamped and slapped myself like a bereaved Iranian, but it didn't help. My rouged wrists were still festively dew-dropped, my feet pulsed with hot pain like recently de-toed stumps, and had Crystal Gayle not wanted a worldwide hit she could have done a lot worse than recording the touching homage 'Don't It Make My Brown Knees Blue'. I forced myself to take a swig from the bidon and when the contents hit my teeth I thought they'd all fall out. It distantly occurred to me that, as the road was closed, third-party assistance would only be available when it opened, and then in the form of a desultory search for my clenched corpse.

The blasphemy had gone, replaced by less mentally demanding wet-throated, guttural bull noises, when I remembered what lay at the bottom of the bar-bag, beneath pills and pump and plastic spoon. Our friend Emma had given it to me, at least partly as a joke, and I had just got the punchline. I very much doubt that anyone, except perhaps an unusually jaded sexual pervert, has ever unscrewed the cap of a tube of Deep Heat with such a graphic display of lurid glee. In one clumsy splurt I liberated the entire contents, then smeared all exposed flesh and gasped in masochistic ecstasy as the fiery white cream penetrated my brittle carapace.

It didn't last long, but then it didn't need to. Four bends later, again beginning to clamp my shrieking fists around the liniment-lubricated levers with all the dextrous precision of a wino at dawn, I came upon a huge mound of smouldering hay piled up in a lay-by. Untroubled by the scant respect this smoking apparition paid to both logic and meteorology, I sat on it and, upon discovering that to do so was lovely, stayed sitting on it for perhaps fifteen minutes. Then I remounted, and moments later found myself swishing out of the fog, around the facing set of Route Barrée gates and into the predictably architectured ski town of Morzine. The first human I'd encountered since the gesticulating gendarme, an Alpine executive digging his ornamental log pile out of a landslide, surveyed me with excusable wariness: pit ponies, surely, weren't meant to cycle, particularly not fatally neglected specimens slathered in shaving foam. And why was this one smiling?

Down the wide main street I cruised, able at last to stoke up the inner fires with frenzied pedalling. Leaving the pine cladding and treble glazing to absorb a looming night of incestuous outrage, I whisked down the valley to Lake Geneva.

Rolling into Evian I saw a primary-school teacher up a ladder in her classroom, struggling to affix some jolly mural, and then I realised it was gone seven o'clock, and that this must mean that the people of Evian were good people. It was exactly what I wanted, undemanding and comfortable, with a ponced-up, casino-cluttered promenade along the lake that could wait until tomorrow. We'd booked a hotel in advance, and the family had already checked in. 'Good God,' said Birna, exiting the lift and seeing the receptionist grinning desperately at The Amphibian Formerly Known as Tim. She wouldn't let the children see me until I'd been hosed down in the bath, but when after two changes of water they all rather sweetly filed in with offerings of chocolate and lollipops I felt like one of those black-and-white Tour legends being interviewed in the tub. It was beginning to look as if I might be becoming rather great.

Fourteen

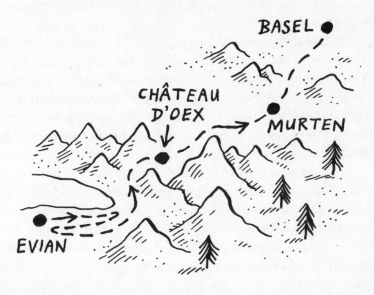

The Tour de France invariably makes a foray into neighbouring countries, usually for commercial purposes or the less rational motivation referred to earlier, the one that says: 'Hey: look at all these sexy guys on bikes and stuff! Don't you wish you were French?' The Tour has even been to Britain a couple of times, most entertainingly in 1974, when for six hours the riders pedalled disconsolately up and down an unopened bypass outside Plymouth in a stage intended to promote the export potential of French artichokes. The Tour director forgot his passport and was shadowed by undercover Customs officers all day; hardly anyone else turned up and the following morning's *Daily Mirror* rhetorically enquired: 'Tour de France: can 40 million Frenchmen be wrong?'

Anyway, the 2000 Tour had embraced the raw artichoke of cross-border co-operation more fondly than any of its predecessors. On this basis it was a slight shame for my friend Paul

Ruddle, who had abruptly arranged with Birna just before she left to meet up with us in Evian and cycle with me for three days, that his Tour de France would take place almost exclusively in Switzerland.

Not that this or much else seemed to be troubling him when he arrived with Birna from the airport. He'd been up until 3 a.m. crating his bike to British Airways' exacting standards, but you'd never have guessed it from the greedy eagerness with which he surveyed the hills on Lake Geneva's eastern flank as we set off to the multi-storey to unload and assemble his bicycle, a hybrid mountain bike/tourer.

I wouldn't wish to embarrass Paul by mentioning his scarily successful career as a City high-flyer, but there we go: I just have. A man who had made his name with flawless judgement and an associated reluctance to suffer fools gladly was an unlikely volunteer for my tour; as he had also just completed his first marathon in three hours, and was still running up to a hundred miles a week, it was difficult to see what Paul hoped to achieve in my company. It really was astonishingly kind of him to sacrifice what for a City man is probably an entire decade's holiday allowance, but having thanked him in these terms I began to see that my worst fears were being trumped. As well as being the physical apotheosis of the adjective 'toned', he also knew what he was doing.

'You're pretty good at that,' I said, watching in the harsh car-park light as Paul slipped wheels into axles and bolted on pedals, handling the spanners and hex keys with a juggler's flourish.

'Used to work the odd weekend in a bike shop when I was a kid,' he said, closing an eye and chewing a lip as he assessed the alignment of his front brakes. Here was further evidence of the many-siblinged upbringing in Northern Ireland that had prepared Paul for most of life's challenges.

'How many odd weekends?'

'About four years' worth.'

On the plus side, this meant at least three *drrr-thwick*less days; on the minus, my self-styled status as team leader was already looking tenuous. Having treated the subterranean parkers of Evian to an unexpected buttock festival, we slipped into Lycra, threw anything unwanted into the Espace and prepared to depart.

'Actually, sod this,' blurted Paul, tearing off the maroon helmet which he'd promised his wife he'd wear and flinging it into the car as I was about to close the boot. 'I just can't be doing with that.'

'Because it looks stupid?' I asked, running a self-conscious finger around the even more conspicuous circumference of my own headwear.

'That's right,' said Paul, and off we went.

I understood that Paul was not the sort of person who fell off bicycles. Mentally spooling through a montage of my own experiences of horizontal cycling, in particular the many featuring slow-motion topples in a variety of urban and rural settings, I accepted the different logic of our parallel situations. Although Paul had no interest whatsoever in watching sport, I recalled that he was always good at doing it. He couldn't tell you who the England manager was but could wipe the floor with me at keepie-uppie. The name Tiger Woods would ring only the faintest bell in Paul's mind, but in his hands a golf club could propel a ball with prodigious accuracy and distance. And though I now understood that the words 'team jersey' made sense to him only in terms of Channel Island offshore-banking consortiums, it was no surprise to look behind and see Paul pedalling lazily past Evian's relentlessly manicured ornamental lakeside gardens with both hands behind his head.

It got worse when we met up with Birna and the kids. 'Did Paul tell you what happened to him in Singapore last week?' I didn't think this story would involve a fine for destroying a bus shelter, and I was right. Apparently, Birna told me as Paul coughed with embarrassed modesty, he had been working out on a hotel exercise bike with such devastating potency that the machine had exploded. 'It didn't *explode*,' said Paul quietly. 'Just sort of . . . caught fire and melted a bit.'

'Oh, come on,' said Birna with a distasteful leer, looking as if she might be about to grab part of Paul's leg between her thumb and forefinger.

We'd gone about 15k up the busy lakeside road when Paul's mobile rang. I was wondering how many multimillion deals we'd have to broker in lay-bys along the way when he passed it to me. It was Birna.

'Anything unusual in your back pocket?' she said, and even before I patted my kidneys for new lumps I knew that there was. The car keys.

In the high sun, the great blue lake glittered almost painfully as I barrelled back to Evian while Paul waited at a waterside café. Half an hour later I met Birna outside the casino and voicelessly handed over the keys, wearing an expression normally associated with the latter stages of cholera, then set off to cover those 15 waterside kilometres for the third time in a little over an hour. But then two cyclists in pink jerseys whisked past me without a sideways glance, and though this seemed to be another bad thing, it actually proved to be rather a splendid one.

Road-race cycling is founded on physics, and in particular the laws of air resistance which dictate, as I may well already have mentioned, that on a flat road a rider tucked behind another can maintain the same speed as the leader while exerting 20 per cent less energy. The tactical implications of this affect all aspects of the sport. One-man breakaways are invariably doomed; the peloton, sharing the wind-breaking effort at the front, can maintain far higher average speeds for far longer. And by letting their leader tuck in behind them, a team can give him if not a free ride then a very cheap one, towing him along, keeping him fresh for the final climb or sprint.

It was this latter aspect that interested me most when, after an out-of-the-saddle rotary frenzy, I somehow managed to get up to the rear wheel of the second pink cyclist. His friend was pedalling hard; he was doing so steadily; I quickly established, to my considerable delight, that I could maintain my speed and position with only the occasional desultory revolution.

I can only describe this experience as sensational. Wheel to wheel we swished towards Switzerland, and I realised that at last my knowledge of the sport could gain me an important advantage over a horribly well-conditioned new team-mate. It should not be too difficult to persuade Paul to go at the front, letting me idle in his slipstream like the leader I so richly deserved to be; he would unwittingly tow me along to the end of the day, and as the Espace loomed in the hotel car park I'd ease gloriously by. Twenty per cent less effort – even better results than a skinful of EPO. The next morning, confused by his own exhaustion and my chirpy freshness, it would be a simple matter to break Paul's spirit. A 'Keep it going, marathon man' here, an 'Are you sure you're OK?' there and he would soon accept the new hierarchy: me as boss, him as cowed and humble domestique.

Oh yes. This was all most satisfactory. Ruddle would carry my water, read the map, complain in restaurants, wash my kit. Such was the natural law of the Tour. Ninety per cent of all professional riders completed their careers in the service of an élite few, and were humbly happy to do so even for risible rewards. In 1986, Paul Kimmage was paid £700 a month by his team; two years earlier, the average professional was on about £400 at a time when trade unions were campaigning for a national minimum wage of £450.

Every rider had to serve their time in the ranks. A young Eddy Merckx was ordered to cede certain victory in the 1967 Paris–Nice to his team leader – the leader was Tom Simpson, and Paris–Nice his final win. Paul might be the better raw talent (might? *Might*? The only machines I ever damaged through overzealous physical attention were ones that had erroneously retained my small change), but he had not earned his stripes. Where was he when Moore toiled through the endless forests of Aquitaine or crested the mighty Galibier?

And, oh, how wearisome that stripe-earning process might prove to be. Merckx ruled his domestiques with a rod of iron: another of his famously ponderous catchphrases was 'You have to put your own interests above camaraderie.' Louison Bobet once dispatched a domestique on an epic quest for refreshment: he finds a bar, but has no money; the heartless patron insists on payment; he runs outside and begs the requisite coppers from locals; runs back in, purchases the water, runs back out and remounts; after scorched and agonising toil – by now the peloton is over eight minutes up the road – he pants back to his leader, tortured by the cool bottle whose contents he dare not even dab to his own cracked lips. 'Where have you been?' tuts Bobet as his mobile factotum breathlessly un-stoppers the bottle for Monsieur Louison's convenience; then, peering at the label, shrieks, 'And you know very well I *hate* that brand!'

But even Bobet, even Merckx, even I in my wildest dominatrix fantasies, could never quite aspire to the autocratic excesses of René Vietto, France's first King of the Mountains. Some months before the 1947 Tour, troubled by a septic toe, Vietto asked his doctor to remove the offending digit: 'Take it off,' he breezed. 'I'll be lighter in the mountains.' Extreme behaviour, I think you'll agree, but for René this was only the warm-up act. Training for the Tour, he sidled up to his trusted deputy Apo Lazarides and had a quiet word. Apo was an unusually impressionable fellow; the year before, leading the peloton by a country mile up the Izoard, he was seized with a fear of imminent attack by wild bears and stopped to wait for the rest to catch up. Behaviour such as this may have made him vulnerable to René's more lunatic whims: though we may never know what was said between the pair, the fact of the matter is that Lazarides also set off from Paris in 1947 one toe short of a shoe-full, and walked with a limp until the day he died.

I broke out of formation with a cheeky 'As you were, men!' then arced round to the lakeside bar. Paul was sitting under a parasol, bike propped against the quay wall, shades on, surveying the glorious vista. In one hand he held what was full enough to be his second beer, and in his other – this was better than I dared hope – smouldered a small cigar. 'That was quick,' he said with a happy, lazy smile, and I felt a twinge of regret for what I was going to do to him. But it soon passed, and I heard myself say, 'Well, you've got time for another, then.'

'What – beer or cigar?'

'Well, Switzerland starts just up the road and everything's going to treble in price,' I said, squinting at the white-crossed red flags hanging limply on their poles by the distant border post. 'Better make it both.'

Evian was hardly Detroit, but crossing the frontier the contrast was astonishing. Fresh, flat tarmac slipped smooth and silent under our wheels; the fields looked as though they had been ploughed by craftsmen working delicately with small trowels. We didn't see any roadside rubbish for an hour, and even then it was a can of Italian beer.

But at the same time the cycling experience was diminished. In France, riding two abreast is accepted practice, but as I chatted to Paul about this and that – this being the importance of smoking a lot of cigars while cycling, and that being the added benefits of doing so while riding at the front – we were furiously honked at four times in ten minutes.

That the perpetrators were invariably hidden behind smoked glass which shook to the amplified beat of the power ballad was the first indication of an unlikely truth: the semi-rural Swiss male fancies himself as a bit of a lad. Over the next two days we saw hundreds of strutting young men proudly displaying the tight jeans, rolled-up jacket sleeves, flicked-back tonsorial splendour and threadbare moustache of the prize arse. Additionally, every town seemed to have its own sex shop – sadly, not one of these was called The Alpine Horn – and though at first we thought it was a one-off customisation job, repeated sightings eventually persuaded us to accept that Volkswagen had officially released a special Swiss edition of its best-selling product and entitled it the Golf Bon Jovi.

The road levered upwards, and looking ahead I saw spots of perspiration moistening my domestique's back as he fumbled with his gears. Settling comfortably behind him, I recalled a recent conversation that only a stern sense of duty prevented me from sharing with my domestique. 'The col des Mosses? Ooooh, that's quite a climb. I'm going to give it a go one day – maybe next July.' I'd been discussing my itinerary at the breakfast table with an American who seemed involved in some way with the running of our hotel, but because he was both older and balder I hadn't been overly concerned. The col des Mosses was only a category two, after all: the Tour's last big hill, maybe, but only a hill.

Between neatly terraced vineyards we climbed, boy racers screaming round hairpins in their Golf Bon Jovis. It was quite a haul. Paul's shoulders were rolling, and I suddenly recalled that he'd had four hours' sleep, and remembered my own travails up that first big hill near Poitiers all those weeks ago. Only later did I establish the precise beastliness of the col des Mosses: an ascent of over 1,000 metres in 17.5 kilometres, not as steep as some category ones, perhaps, but more drawn out than many HCs.

When the road hugged up against the side of what soon became a horrible gorge cliff, occasionally hiding itself under a rockfall-deflecting concrete canopy, I had no choice but to accept that this was all a little more extreme than expected. Then, suddenly, there was an abrupt bend and the road leapt idiotically across the void, reaching the opposite cliff by means of an apologetic little bridge.

218

That this hadn't happened once throughout the Alps had long been a source of mystified delight, but it was happening now. Paul pulled over with an awed exclamatory sound and started rooting about in the bar-bag for his camera; I welded my gaze to the front wheel and sped rigidly across to the other side. My team-leader slipstreaming tactics were summarily abandoned, and inspired partly by guilt at my self-serving awfulness, partly by a colon-cramping fear of looking back until that big hole in the ground had gone away, I pedalled determinedly onwards.

By the time I did peek behind, Paul was a barely animate white speck in a grim panorama of concrete and blasted rock. How pathetic he looked, and what a fiend I felt. It occurred to me that this might have been the first time I had tried to take advantage of a man by plying him with beer and tobacco. I had hogged his slipstream and clogged his lungs, and now he was in trouble. Waiting in the late-afternoon shadows, I unsuccessfully assembled dishonest explanations for my action. 'Sorry,' I said, when at last he gasped up to me, and as he sweated out a look of slightly aggrieved bemusement I knew that the ridiculous team-tactic fantasy was at an end. 'I'll go in front for a bit,' I continued, pulling alongside him, 'but, you know, at a reasonable pace. It's . . . supposed to be easier if you ride behind someone, apparently, because of the, um . . .'

'The wind resistance,' panted Paul, who I later remembered had some sort of scientific degree in which sound knowledge of real facts about our world played a more important role than they had in my own university course, wherein a reasonable pass could be guaranteed by pathologically random use of the phrase 'on a broadly macro level'.

Despite my constant assurances that this was the last climb of note, the face that Paul wore as we creaked into the mountain-top pastures was not that of a man on holiday. Hungry, tired and now freezing bloody cold we crested the green col side by side in a cool dusk whose advanced status was explained when Paul flatly pointed out that my watch, mortally bollocksed in the Joux-Plane mists, was underestimating the time by a factor of two hours. It was gone 9 p.m., easily the latest I had been on the road, and neither for the first time or the last we were rescued by Paul's mobile phone. It rang as we started the descent, and fifteen minutes later we were wedging bicycles between sleeping children in an Alpine lay-by.

The hotel in Château d'Oex was grand but scarily empty, and had I been alone I would not have wished to select the phrase 'skeleton staff' in describing its paucity of personnel. Birna nobly baby-sat, giving Paul and me the opportunity to sit alone under the smoking room's distant ceilings, marooned on sofas the size of bouncy castles while the Turkish waitress supplied us with rather too much wine. 'It'll be better tomorrow,' I said, unfolding a large map.

'Yes, it will,' he said, 'because instead of going from here to here to here' – I watched him trace the Tour's dilatory route across to Lausanne and up to Lake Murten – 'we're going to do this.' And with the firm authority of a seasoned decision-maker he snipped off two sides of a sizeable triangle.

'Great,' I said, or rather belched. Paul had served his time as a domestique; the balance of power was shifting and I wasn't about to resist.

I went down to breakfast the following morning with blood all over my face. Sunburned crevasses on my nose and lips had been opened up by the previous evening's chilled mountain-top mist, and were still leaking as I set about the buffet with the gusto of the slightly hungover. Surveying a table groaning with cooked meats, cereals, fruit and cheese, I realised how deeply poxy French breakfasts were, how even in a flash French hotel you only got a couple of croissants and a foil-topped preserve. Breakfast was One of the Good Things About Switzerland – not, let's face it, an unwieldy list. The only entries I'd managed so far were the nice little crests on car number plates and public conveniences that were both clean and not peopled by brazen cockwatchers – surprising, perhaps, in the land that spawned Oscar Plattner's Flying Circus.

Groggy with calories, we agreed the meeting place and left my family to occupy their final full day abroad. It was a glorious morning for Paul and me, a glorious day in fact: an endless parade of sun-dappled, chuckling brooks; of wild flowers and tailwinds; of doe-eyed cows in verdant pastures and doe-eyed blondes in Mercedes convertibles. We raced narrow-gauged trains through narrow-gauged villages, rattling along at such effortless speed that we only noticed that the gorges and peaks and cliff-top castles had gone when we sneaked off the Tour route at Bulle and looked behind us.

'I suppose that's the end of the Alps,' said Paul, and he was right. I'd never realised how flat are vast tracts of the Swiss landscape. For the next two days the worst you could say was that it rolled, but even then only gently. With the mountains gone the cyclists returned, again generally retired ones, and in our new co-operative relaying formation we fairly flew past them all with a taunting vigour that Paul seemed to find uncharitable.

'It's dog eat dog with these old blokes,' I insisted stoutly as we ate big pieces of meat by a fountain in Payerne. 'Give them half a chance and they'll make you suffer.'

He looked at me the way he had when I'd deserted him halfway up the col des Mosses, then ordered a further pair of beers.

Swiss people generally prefer not to say anything at all, but of those who do, only 18 per cent speak French. Unastonishingly the Tour route had been designed to meet most of them, and for the last day and a half the towns Paul and I had pedalled tended to kick off with a La or a Le and take in at least a couple of acute accents. Murten seemed to mark some sort of boundary. Beyond it were a sea of achs and umlauts and reckless overuse of the letter z; just before it everything was confused – there were villages whose names started off French but lost their nerve right at the end: la Corbaz, Greng, Faoug.

Murten itself was the front line, and the German-speakers had dug in deep. Along its meticulously preserved medieval streets, a chevron-shuttered shop-front stood out between the witch-hat towers and Gothic script and flagstoned fish shops. 'BOUCHERIE/ CHARCUTERIE' read the gilded glass sign above, but decades of rust crusted the shutter padlocks and the upstairs windows were cobwebbed and flaky. The butcher had clearly been Murten's final Frenchman, and it was tempting to picture him being drummed out of town by a baying Teutonic lynch mob. But this was not the Swiss way. All that day I'd been surprised to notice that the French-Swiss villages welcomed visitors with one of those blue 'Commune d'Europe' signs ringed with the EU's stars. I would have thought Switzerland was about as likely to apply for EU membership as to host the start of the next round-the-world yacht race, but there these signs were, presumably a symptom of some fundamental socio-political split cleaving the French community from its dominant German-speaking counterpart. In almost any other country this would have expressed itself in an ugly orgy of ethnic cleansing; here, they'd settled for a light dab with the cultural duster.

The hotel was excellent, partly because of the turrets and stone staircases and terrace overlooking a watery sunset, but mainly because my room had a huge circular bed with a headboard stereo encased in a sort of limestone and leatherette inglenook. So proud were the proprietors of this splendidly misplaced feature that they'd put a huge photograph of it outside their dungeon-style front door. 'Something is missing from this picture . . .' teased the multilingual caption beneath it, following up with a strident 'YOU!' that conjured images of Lord Kitchener frog-marching alarmed honeymooners up the stairs.

I was asleep in my pants, spreadeagled in the Leonardo da

Vinci/*Man Alive* position with the telly on, when my family walked in. 'Baron Austin von Powers, I presume?' said Birna, and glancing blearily from face to happy face as the host of the Austrian edition of *Who Wants To Be A Millionaire?* barked and spat from the end of the bed I understood that they had enjoyed their day and that, more than this, they were relieved that it had been their last. Much of their afternoon, I was breathlessly informed, had been spent in a water-slide park, and I realised that this was the sort of thing they should have been doing all along. Birna's gesture in bringing the children out was one of the nicest things anyone had done for me in many years, but, in the final analysis, when Cliff Richard sang about going on a summer holiday, it is surely no accident that his lyrical inspiration was drawn from jaunty shoreline entertainment rather than the tortured suffering of a parent.

The restaurant prepared a small and expensive supper, brought to our table by a nice girl from Norwich who had been in Switzerland just long enough to acquire an Australian accent. In the last day and a half not a soul we'd asked had been aware that the Tour would shortly be passing their front door, and the waitress did not break this duck. 'Well, it'll be nice to see all those well-toned legs,' she said, wiggling a wrinkled nose cheekily at Paul, then turning to look me up and down, haughtily intoned, 'Of course, they're all on *drugs*.'

If there is any group more fond than our children of creating unproductive noise at the crack of dawn it must surely be the world's German-speakers. No sooner had I drowsily entombed Valdis in a soundproof chamber of eiderdown and leatherette than a huge and ugly symphony of human and mechanical activity struck up in the cobbled street outside. I raised a rusted eyelid and whimpered at the clock under the telly: it was 6.49. A short time later Kristjan folded back our diamond-painted shutters and peered outside. Had the medieval high street been transformed into a glittering steel and glass mall? Was there a shiny new aircraft carrier in the car park? No. 'I think there's a man painting the dustbins,' and he was right.

The family farewells were fond but frenzied – if Birna hadn't put her foot down she might easily have missed out on one of Eurostar's four-hour cancellation festivals in Paris – with Paul turning in another flawless performance in his final cameo as gooseberry. At the risk of being beaten about the face and neck with a narrow-heeled shoe, I wish to state that one of the very saddest aspects of their departure was the ceremonial return of the panniers. I managed to offload some of the spare clothes and binned a couple of *procycling*s, but saddling up ZR was still a dockside experience of depressing proportions.

'This would have been fun up the Alps,' I said to Paul, testing the weight with a laborious hoist of the back wheel. He wandered over and gave it a tentative heave before pedalling off down the cobbles.

'Swap if you like,' he said, after I rolled alongside.

'OK,' I replied. 'We'll do it when we stop next.'

Idling out of Murten, we paused at a grocer's and Paul went in to buy water. Sitting with the bikes under an awning, the displays outside every other bank and chemist telling me it was already 28°C, I wondered what he'd meant by this. I placed a hand under his pannier rack and lifted, or rather didn't. Jesus. His bike loudly identified itself as a Saracen, and those wheezed uphill comments about it being built like a tank suddenly acquired a more resonant significance.

'Shall we change over here, then?' Paul breezed towards ZR and started eyeing its svelte alloy bits greedily.

Without actually pushing him away, I abruptly clamped both arms on the bars and began to blather about the difficulty of adjusting the saddle.

'No problem,' said Paul, with a wry smile. 'We'll do it at lunch.'

On a pendulous cycle-path route to Solothurn I took the lead, and soon established that not only did Paul's bicycle strain leadenly up hills, but even downhill, even in my slipstream, he had to pedal to keep up as I freewheeled. Our whole cycling relationship had been founded on the unspoken assumption that I was much better than he was. Now we both saw that this was not the case.

Feeling the same sense of exposed inadequacy that I had when Kristjan discovered Daddy was not battling for yellow with Lance Armstrong, I knew insubordination was inevitable. As a low range of mountains petered out to our left beyond the wide and lazy River Aare, I called back, 'Those must be the foothills of the Jura.' There was a small noise from behind, the kind of brief, desolate hum I make when someone tells me something about horse-racing.

We were now deep in the sort of rural suburbia that the nation seemed to specialise in, all hoovered lawns and remote-control garage doors. 'The word "Jurassic" is derived from Jura,' I continued stoutly, ignoring another bleak whimper, 'on account of the . . . well, the old stones.'

A middle-aged man in a shellsuit was carefully threading chevroned hazard tape round a newly weeded flower-bed, which struck me as unnecessarily Swiss of him. Schoolchildren and mothers were all striding along quietly and correctly, and I realised that the whole scene was like something from an architect's model: the unnaturally green grass and brutally marshalled vegetation, the gleaming, geometrically parked BMWs, the orderly people and orderly houses. The architect Le Corbusier had been born in Switzerland, I remembered, and so could perhaps be forgiven for failing to predict that the real-life global inhabitants of his fatefully influential modular concrete estates would not behave in this fashion, choosing instead to interact with their environment by weeing in lifts and throwing tellies off the roof.

The same sort of thing had regularly occurred to me while

indulging my fascination with Swiss breakfast television, which consisted of a scrolling roster of live, fixed-camera broadcasts from mountain-top weather stations, devoid of humanity and soundtracked with yodelly accordion. Try that in Britain and after two days you'd have trouserless students sidling into shot. Mind you, after three you'd have a bloody civil uprising.

'The architect Le Corbusier . . .'

'Why do you keep doing that?'

'Sorry, I'm just trying to be . . . to sound as if . . .'

'No – *that*. You just did it again.'

'What?'

I looked back and Paul gave me a pained look, then, like Joyce Grenfell being compelled to utter a foully racist epithet, whispered, 'Spitting.'

How awful, and how true. After the first hour of cycling I was always seized with an urgent physiological need to expectorate, and though in the initial days I would check for witnesses before stringily anointing the hedgerows, repeated contact with flobbing Frenchmen and televisual evidence of the Giro peloton in full phlegm had together inspired complacency. Three weeks on I didn't even know I was doing it.

'But every sportsman . . .' I began, and ended, then began again. 'OK, I mean I know it's not *great*, but it's like . . . well, like, I wouldn't want to sit on a French loo seat, but in Switzerland . . .'

I had absolutely no idea what I was trying to say, but whatever it was it certainly hadn't helped.

'Oh, Tim,' said Paul, genuinely upset, 'you've got to *hover*.'

We lunched in Solothurn, outdoors by the Baroque cathedral, watching student cyclists judder over the cobbles as we waited for beer and pasta. Both took an age to arrive and proved sadly insufficient, so having quickly dispatched them we went to the restaurant next door and ordered them all over again, watched with interest by our first waitress.

By the time we'd finished Paul had developed an obsession

226

with a topless man wearing denim shorts of a type more generally associated with garage-calendar blondes, sporting the facial hair ensemble of Magnum PI. For twenty minutes he strolled about the stalls opposite us, speculatively appraising plastic sandals and running his hands over his torso.

'Who the fuck does he think he is?' said Paul. Susceptible as I am to contracting the emotional neuroses of others, I was soon leading the vile mutters. When the man bunched fists on hips and fixed the sky above the cathedral with a lingering, blinkless stare, I knew it was very important that we leave Switzerland quite quickly.

We had to anyway. I'd felt rather a bully during the previous day and a half, chivvying Paul along when he stopped to take photos, driven by a kilometre-clocking restlessness borne of three weeks of almost constant daylight pedalling. But he had a plane to catch from Basel tomorrow morning, which meant getting there tonight, which meant another 90 kilometres. This was more than I had managed in any single afternoon, but I wasn't about to tell Paul that, any more than I was about to remind him about swapping bikes.

The road turned to face the Jura's foothills, but mercifully only went over their big toe. The Côte de Oberer was just a category-three hill, yet still proved steep and hot enough for us to be overtaken by three teenage girls whom we only managed to reel in via an idiotically menopausal effort. But the descent was a cracker: barrelling down towards a wheat-sown plain of almost prairie-like dimensions we slipstreamed a moped, waited till his buzzing engine began to sputter, and then gloriously forced our way past, whipping his two-stroke arse at 60 k.p.h.

I was probably going almost as fast when some sort of insect somehow flapped unscathed into my undone neck zip, and before succumbing to a frenzied tattoo of slaps and scratches managed to pierce flesh in two places. Having screeched to a messy halt in a petrol-station forecourt, I tore off almost all of my clothes while continuing to flay my torso like the Incredible Hulk's agonised alter ego in the very early stages of transformation. When, at length, Paul's hilarity subsided just enough to permit intelligible speech, he was able to give a detailed account of the memorable facial expressions this spectacle had elicited from passing motorists.

At the top of the category-three climb I'd phoned a hotel near Basel airport, speaking with a shifty little Beavis who began each sentence with a *sotto voce* snigger so repellent that I couldn't face asking him for directions. The folly of this omission became clear as we wound through Basel's unending industrial suburbs in an 8 p.m. sunset. We'd put a bellyful of kilometres under our belts – 125, with clearly more to come – and it had stopped being fun some time ago. Through underpasses, around gyratory systems, alongside marshalling yards – there wasn't much to see, and there wasn't much to say.

Jostled by tram and hassled by truck we were soon lost. Having established a rapport with the hotel, no matter how unsatisfactory, it was down to me to sort this out, and reluctantly taking Paul's mobile I called on all my long experience of the indecision-making process. 'Huhmmmhuh-huh,' cackled Beavis almost silently as we stood at a roaring intersection. 'Church . . . hmm-huh . . . tram . . . huh-hmmm.'

'Listen,' I shouted above the Friday-night roar of a thousand Golf Bon Jovis, 'we're at the junction of . . .' – a hopeless glance at eight lanes of traffic '. . . we're at a big road wi . . . hello? Hello?'

Paul looked at me expectantly. 'Church-tram,' I announced confidently, in a way that explained I'd done my bit and that it was now up to him to make sense of this runic statement.

I sort of knew he would, but it might have been nice if he'd taken a bit more time about it. Six minutes later Beavis's shoulders were shuddering soundlessly over our passport photos. Twenty more and we were settling down to the first of many glasses of red wine and awaiting a Châteaubriand, en route to waiter-winking levels of inebriated jocularity.

We drank to the 313 kilometres we'd done in three days, we drank to the sunset gilding the half-timbered toytown around our terrace table, to the shiny green trams gently clanking around the flower-filled roundabout and the well-scrubbed burghers of Basel queuing up neatly to board them. We drank to each other's lower legs, Paul to my knife-sculpted calves and I to his hawser-like Achilles tendons, and we drank to our resilient buttocks. 'I forgot to tell you to smear Savlon all over your perineum,' I said, and to this oversight we drank the heartiest draught of all.

One of the few good things about cycling all day is that even if you consume an unwise surfeit of alcohol at the end of it, it seems to be very difficult to generate a hangover. One of the very many bad things is that it is not impossible.

The night before, belatedly rinsing my kit, I had comprehensively flooded the bathroom while failing to discover how to drain the washbasin. In the morning I found that this operation was effected by a sturdy under-sink wand, and that the way to locate this wand was inadvertently to snag one's scrotum against it. The family had gone off with my toothpaste, obliging me to improvise unsatisfactorily with crushed Rennies, and the gusset of my shorts was still dripping wet.

Damp and hunched I'd taken my place in the breakfast room, where a waitress was barking 'Jacques! Deux oeufs!' into an intercom, although I couldn't see who they might be for as my only fellow guest was a giant ceramic rabbit. I'm not quite sure what it is with the Swiss, but seeing this conspicuous item in the corner of the room I was reminded that both the hotels we had previously patronised featured similar menageries: a porcelain St Bernard by the reception desk in Château d'Oex; a glazed Alsatian guarding a stairwell in Murten. The rabbit, however, was in a different league. As well as being surreally oversized, easily as large as a well-fed circus seal, it was arrestingly decorated with a huge floral garland hung in a flamboyant Hawaiian ruff about its glossy beige neck. A frozen glower of frustration demonstrated that it was aware not only of this humiliating accessory, but also of its own inability to remove it.

The rabbit was, in essence, the kind of object that demanded an act of fatuousness from all passers-by, and before Paul arrived I had attempted to negotiate its purchase.

'I must have him,' I muttered to the waitress, staring at her with the pallid intensity of the hungover and aiming a rigid but unsteady finger at the beast. 'If I were to tell you,' I continued as she began to smile with difficulty, wheeling out my favourite *Antiques Roadshow* catchphrase, 'that an inferior example was recently sold at auction to a rival collector for 68,000 . . .' but then I stopped, understanding from the waitress's expression that although this was by no means the first time that the rabbit's transfixing presence had obliged her to deal with an unfunny guest, never before had she been required to do so in English, and in a louder, clearer voice I said, 'Deux oeufs, s'il vous plaît.'

Paul arrived and with patchy enthusiasm we dispatched Jacques' oeufs. Our bikes had spent the night in a skittle alley in the hotel basement, and as I carried ZR back upstairs Paul called out, 'We could swap bikes here – the airport's just down the road.'

'Sorry?' I shouted, much too loudly, and hastily pedalled off without even cleating myself in.

The airport was in France, which meant ninety minutes of roadside filth and fond farewells before I rolled over the Rhine and into Germany, alone for the first time since the Pyrenees. As we'd crudely mummified Paul's bike with airport baggage tape and cardboard, I had suddenly become mired in the deep melancholy that is the wine drinker's morning-after lot.

'You've only got 500k left,' said Paul encouragingly, seeing my head drop as we reached the head of the check-in queue.

I nodded but could manage only an upside-down smile. We

shook hands and I thanked him again; then as he heaved his entombed Saracen across to the oversized luggage gate I called out in a small voice, 'Hey – swap bikes with you now.'

Fifteen

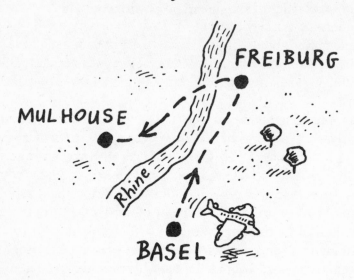

Germany did its best to comfort me, with blue skies and cherry trees and unbelievably cheap groceries, though I'd have traded them all for a tailwind. Along the westernmost edge of the Black Forest – the road went straight through the 'S' of Schwarzwald – it wasn't too bad, with the trees and hills shielding me, but the last 35k to Freiburg-im-Breisgau were attritional. Freiburg is the home town of Jan Ullrich, Germany's premier cyclist and effectively the world number two after Lance Armstrong, and after the ignorance and apathy of Switzerland it was good to be back among the converted. A home-made billboard bellowed 'Hier kommt sie durch! TOUR DE FRANCE am 20 Juli 2000 ab 11 Uhr!' across a field of maize, and all afternoon a succession of serious cyclists sped towards me with the wind in their wheels.

If the French want to know why they have not produced a Tour winner in the last fifteen years, I would advise them to visit Freiburg. It occurred to me on the way in that the oncoming cyclists were generally ten years younger than I am rather than thirty years older, and freewheeling up to the town centre I beheld that the main station was ringed with the largest collection of parked bicycles I have ever witnessed outside documentaries about China. Three to a parking meter, five to a tree, endless stacks in endless racks – there were tens of thousands of them, as sure a sign as any of a vibrant and youthful cycling culture.

The sprawling bikefields were the best thing about Freiburg – honestly, I took photos of them and everything. Elsewhere there was a sort of Hansel and Gretel cathedral, some uncharacteristically grubby nineteenth-century streets and a muted atmosphere that was Sunday afternoon rather than Saturday evening. The centre had presumably been flattened in the war, but it looked as though they'd only just remembered to start rebuilding it. Bronzed-glass office blocks were interspersed with huge empty lots, and above the heavily scaffolded station shot a high-rise hotel so new that the lift-call buttons were still sheathed in plastic. I know this because I checked in – fifty quid a night but I couldn't be arsed to find an alternative – and because the buttons in question were marked not with the usual up and down arrows, but the words 'Ab' and 'Auf', which meant as little to me as they did to the many dispirited refugees I accompanied from the basement to the eighth floor and back, and back.

I showered and changed and wandered off into an evening that stank of brewing thunder. An American-themed restaurant promised 'Live Euro Fussball und Great Beer' but delivered neither, though I didn't really care. I was tired, and tomorrow was a big day: the time trial, against the clock, contre le montre, when for 58.5 flat-out kilometres I'd see what I was made of, how the mountains had built up my physical and mental strength. With my family and Paul around I'd occasionally found myself diverted from the job in hand, but now I was focused. The lullaby that night was not the rush of glacial meltwater but freight trains and ding-dong station announcements and the tortured shouts of madmen. I didn't mind a bit. No mosquitoes, no rosé wine, none of those holiday-style distractions. And I was in Germany. That alone concentrated the mind wonderfully. You can't be on holiday in Germany.

If the Tour hadn't been decided already, it would be after the time trial. The race of truth, they call it – no tactics, no team-mates to fetch and carry and hide behind, just a special lightweight bike and a silly aerodynamic body condom and an hour and a bit of hammering on the pain barrier.

I slept for thirteen hours and then at breakfast, elbow to shellsuited elbow with a throng of face-stuffing Germans, I shovelled in a mountain of meat and eggs. I was taking this seriously. I'd traced the route on to the map: straight back down the Rhine, across it into France, down into Mulhouse. I retrieved ZR from the luggage store, flexed and twitched and slapped my legs, then went straight up to the check-out desk and smashed a brass reading light. As well as being embarrassing, this rather broke my concentration. 'I'm so sorry,' I said to the receptionist as she swept pieces of low-energy bulb into a pile using a postcard of the cathedral, 'I really don't know how that happened.' With an open face and a slow-motion sweep of the elbow she showed me. 'Thank you,' I said. 'Now I see.'

I'd been hoping the previous day's wind would have held, blowing me down the floodplain, but along with the sun it was gone. It was one of those flotation-tank days, still and humid, the air so stale it felt second-hand and so thick that it soaked up the noise, filtering the roar of nearby traffic into a muted, earplugged hiss. I rolled slowly along the pavement cycle lane, occasionally glancing around for a strip of bunting or a sheaf of flags that might announce I had reached the Leopoldring, the stage's start line, until while crossing a junction I looked up and saw that Leopoldring was the name of a road, and that I was already on this road. Buttocks! It was like turning up late for an exam. Adrenalin hosed into my heart and I shot off far too fast, almost immediately having to shriek to a stop at the next traffic lights. Waiting at traffic lights – this wasn't very professional. I'll be sticking my bloody arm out to indicate in a minute, I thought, although actually it was less than that.

Bursting with frustration I slalomed on to the cycle path. There'd hardly been a single cycle path in France, though by according cyclists equal road rights they didn't really need any. But they were everywhere in Germany and Switzerland and they hated it if you didn't use them. Usually I did, but they had a habit of whistling away into the woods or skirting even minor inter-sections with a seven-sides-of-an-octagon detour, and with my average speed down at a risible 22.9 the last thing I needed was extra kilometres. I'd averaged 27.7 for my 16-kilometre pro-logue, and if I couldn't do better than that now then all that had happened since would have been in vain.

Away from the roundabouts and traffic lights and out across the flat fields and stuffy, muggy forests, things began to pick up. I was grinding along in top gear, starting to taste metal but keeping the rhythm, and then with my AVS up to 26 I rounded a corner at substantially greater speed and found the path abruptly taped off and guarded by two girls with clipboards sitting on camp stools. To cut a short story shorter, I stopped. The one who had been bold enough not to hurl herself backwards off her stool looked at the dirty, hot wheel near her head, then up at its pilot. 'Sorry,' I panted, noting for the second time in half an hour how rude it was to apologise in a foreign language.

For a very small moment I attempted to mash my dozen or so words of German into an appropriate query, but had only got as far as 'Quick, Mr Captain: forward through technology!' when a lazy peloton appeared ahead. As its lead members reached us and broke off towards a neighbouring industrial estate, the girls ticked boxes and wrote down numbers; I deduced that this was some sort of sponsored cycling event and in a flurry of clumsy recleating set off in pursuit.

In something of a fury of pent-up pedalling I careered past the backmarkers, and was up to 45 k.p.h. when I hit the front past the final light-industrial unit, holding off a surprised trio of leg-shavers in matching courier-firm jerseys. Ignoring an indistinct cry of alarm from another set of marshals I bumped up the kerb and rejoined the cycle path, leaving everyone to continue their laps in peace. Feeble Sunday-morning amateurs.

A rollerblader didn't hear me coming and almost came a cropper, then the route branched off along a tiny road flanked by overgrown pillboxes. It was quiet now and again I put my head down, staring at the sun-bleached hairs on my brown knees. I bared a lot of teeth and gritted them hard, knowing that although I'd never get anywhere near the 50 k.p.h. the pros would average – *average* – along this route, at least I could put in the same agonising effort. Through quiet villages I glanced at my distorted reflection as it whizzed across the convex mirrors outside every concealed entrance, trying to keep my hands off the brakes even before sharp corners or zebra crossings, promoting the main-tenance of momentum above accident prevention in my list of priorities. The AVS was up to 31 k.p.h. when, with 38k covered, I raced across a junction towards the Rhine and the French border. And in fairness, it was 32 when, just under twenty minutes and just over 10 kilometres later, I crossed the same junction for the third time. I was lost. Looking at the straight-forward route on the map, it didn't make any sort of sense, but then by this stage nor did I.

Suffering more types of distress than I had ever experienced simultaneously I shouldered ZR and slipped and careered madly down a muddy embankment to the service station I'd noticed alongside the motorway beneath me. A man with a huge, hairy face was filling up his old Transit van. '*Frankreich? France? France?*' I jabbered, feeling my legs beginning to seize up. '*Da?*'

he said, in some sort of thick accent, and hurling ZR against a rack of antifreeze I ran into the shop. '*Frankreich?*' I yelped at an old couple perusing the biscuits; the husband nodded slowly and raised a thoughtful hand to his white stubble, but before it got there I was in the beverage aisle, sweatily buttonholing a man in a boiler suit who could only respond to my question with one of his own, and a teenage girl who didn't even manage that. Tears were welling up when I turned to see a shirtless youth with a towel over his shoulder, and before I could say anything he'd said, 'The road to France, yeah?' in fluent Lancastrian. I nodded and panted through his straightforward instructions – naturally enough, my mistake had been in following a fingerpost labelled 'Frankreich' – and with a breathless sound intended to express gratitude ran back outside and remounted. But not for very long. Those nascent twinges of muscle discomfort suggested that my legs might be taking advantage of this respite to formally register their complaint, and the unlubricated paroxysm that accompanied my first revolution caused the unwelling of those stockpiled tears and a clumsy dismount.

Seeing this, the Transit man jogged over with a look of concern. He placed one hand on my shaking shoulder, the other on ZR's crossbar, and displaying a characteristic intuition for le mot juste said, 'Da?'

What a kind man, I thought, what a good man, and then, because fatigue had changed parts of my brain, I thought how confused and upset he would be if I opened one of those bottles of antifreeze and poured it down his shirt.

'Da,' I replied, and oddly began to feel better. After all, 48k was only ten shy of the total; despite the intrusions of traffic management I'd covered three times my prologue distance at a significantly higher speed. It was all right. Five minutes later I went back into the shop and spent my last deutschmarks on two cans of Red Bull and some toothpaste I would shortly discover tasted of crushed Rennies. As I gingerly remounted again, the guy with the towel emerged and intriguingly disappeared into a flat-tyred caravan that was clearly a long-term feature of the quiet end of the enormous lorry park. Then, in no particular hurry, I went back to France.

Sixteen

Mulhouse was the end of the time-trial stage, but the next one started from Belfort, 45k to the west, or rather 60k by the time I'd become imaginatively lost amid the teenage snoggers in a maze of dead-end allotments. Under melting leaden skies and with a beastly wind pushing the whole countryside in my face, those late-afternoon kilometres tolled by with agonising sloth. Looking at the map now I can still remember every town: Reiningue where there was a cow loose in the maize fields; Bernwiller where I was respectfully applauded by an exiting congregation; Balschwiller where a crow pecked horribly at two roadkilled fox cubs.

Grovelling along it occurred to me that although these disordered assemblages of roofless barns were unthinkable over the Rhine, every town without exception bore a stridently German name. Crossing the Rhine–Rhône canal, now a good 50 kilometres inside France, I spotted a roadside shrine of some antiquity dedicated to 'Herr Jesus Christus'. Until 1919, all this land, the area known as Alsace-Lorraine, had been German territory. Seeing a memorial to 'Nos Enfants, 1914–18', I realised that the enfants in question would have been wearing spiky-topped helmets and laying down their lives for the Kaiser.

Reasoning it would at least be flat I followed the bleak canal for a bit, the bullrushes bent double towards me. But then the towpath ended and it was back across the damp, darkening hills, past an ostrich farm, past a dozen spaced-out ravers sitting by their cars in a lay-by, past an old bloke tipping the rain off his patio furniture and waving at me so cheerily that despite myself I got up on the pedals and gave him a bit of a show.

It was almost night when, with 131 kilometres on the clock, I wound wetly into Belfort past the floodlit bulk of a mighty red fortress that stared down at the town from a steep hill. A jumble of distant, amplified sounds and rain-blurred floodlights suggested that something was going on.

The upside of my visit coinciding with the Fourteenth World Festival of University Music was the looming opportunity to eat huge kebabs in a bracing sea of lithe young bodies. The downside was that the only hotel with any rooms left was called The Grand Hotel of the Golden Cask. The receptionist, presiding over a colonnaded lobby that led, eventually, to an opera-house double staircase, watched me wheel ZR towards her across the marble with an expression that eloquently betrayed an internal debate pitching human charity against decorum. It was the sort of dilemma you might face, I suppose, upon seeing the caretaker being extravagantly unwell while slumped on the pavement after your office party.

'La Tour de France passe par ici?'

It was the only time it ever worked. Her long face lit up, and in English so astonishingly good that I instantly forgave her for using it before I did she began to hold forth, or possibly even fifth.

240

'Yes, absolutely, the Tour is departing from here for its . . .' and here she slipped in the savouring smile of someone about to say something clever in a foreign language '*penultimate* stage on July the twenty-second. You are interested in the event?'

I explained my quest, and when I had finished she tilted her head, smiled a different smile and said, 'Chapeau!'

I could have kissed her.

Anyway, there followed some additional banter on Belfort's own cycling hero, Christophe Moreau, whose reputation had been tarnished somewhat during the most notorious drug scandal of recent years, the Festina affair, but who had since (another proud grin) 'cleaned the slate' and was now riding well. Finally, she said, 'Oh, but you must be starving hungry,' then helped me stow ZR in a laundry room and gave me a room key. Stepping beneath a ceiling where cherubs distantly frolicked in cumulo nimbus and into a corridor where a discarded champagne bucket lay outside every other door, I couldn't quite understand how this place was only eight quid a night more expensive than Freiburg's spartan station block. There were chocolates on the pillow and everything.

I put on trousers and espadrilles and went out to perform the aforementioned kebab dance before a North African band with large support among France's drunken-piggyback community. Then my legs started to concertina and in half an hour I was stumbling up to bed.

As a public service, I would like to advise visitors to Belfort with an interest in hydraulic equipment, agricultural materials or mattresses to avoid room 124 of the Grand Hôtel du Tonneau d'Or. These headings all appear on page 188 of the local *Yellow Pages* kept in the room, a page whose distressed remains I currently have before me. Although in later years I may easily wish to stuff a futon with maize husks and mount it on elevating pistons, my interest that morning was focused more on the page overleaf, 187, and the section headed *Masseurs*.

It was all part of a grand scheme that I'd hatched with Paul during our last night, one whose detailed refinement had filled an empty head during many subsequent hours in the saddle. This scheme required me to complete the penultimate Belfort–Troyes stage, at 254.5 kilometres the longest in the 2000 Tour, in one day. I'd done the mountains, but had yet to confront the Sisyphean demands of a huge, long day on the flat. Of course, 2,673 kilometres in twenty-seven days wasn't bad – in fact, every time I did the maths I found it very hard not to raise at least one arm above my head – but the most I'd managed in a single 24-hour period were the 151 wind-assisted kilometres to Agen. Farcical prologue and truncated time-trial aside, I hadn't ever done what the real riders did in a day, and this was a wrong I felt a need to right.

Setting off at 3 a.m. would of course be the key tactic, but a physical tune-up, my 2,700-kilometre service, was also impera-tive. 'You honestly will need to have a massage,' Simon O'Brien had said, and though he might easily have done so in anticipation of shameful misunderstandings involving the purveyors of executive relief, I had begun to agree with him. Mr Boardman's stretches could do only so much for legs with a combined age of 72.

Covertly examining page 187's listed practitioners over an expensive croissant was a deeply traumatic experience. I could almost hear Simon sniggering as I ran a finger down the names. What would Francis Yoder get up to when I was face down on the trolley? Did I really want to hear Patrick Baumgartner cracking his oiled knuckles? And one only had to say the words 'Denis Klingelschmitt' to conjure a hellish inventory of complex and expensive 'extras'. In the end, slightly depressed at my own pre-dictability, I went back up to room 124 and, feeling my features pucker into a compact gurn of lust, dialled the number shared by Dominique and Delphine Masson.

However, the call was answered by neither of Belfort's sassiest twins, but a bored-sounding man. Oh. 'Good morning. I am on a bicycle and my legs need attention,' I said. It was a phrase I had honed during a sleepless dawn; not until now did I appreciate that its only appropriate home was in a conversation on an obscure premium-rate service. I had to say it twice more before the man answered, using a great many words whose gist, as I understood it, was that though 'les Massons' had recently left his practice, he himself would be happy to attend to me, though not until tomorrow, today being the 'Pentecôte'.

I wasn't too sure about this last part, but it didn't sound great. The impression was of a hood-wearing cult that forbade the rubbing of foreign flesh on the second Monday in June. Why had the Massons left? Had they known too much? I wasn't going to wait an extra day so that some daubed, chanting fiend in a ram's mask could nail me to a candle-bordered altar.

Only when I'd been wandering about in the windy sun for an hour did I realise that even by French standards there were a lot of closed shops, and that this – combined with the fact that it was a Monday – suggested 'Pentecôte' might be Whitsun, and that today might therefore be a bank holiday. This meant another night in an expensive hotel and a further excruciating conversation with the Masson-murderer to arrange a massage appointment for 9 a.m. on Tuesday, but that was OK. The festival was still on and an extra day's rest would prepare me well.

Belfort was hungover. I'd heard the music banging on until dawn, and now there was vomit in the streets and a lot of traffic cones sticking out of a river so shallow that the ducks weren't so much swimming across it as wading. A Grace Brothers-style department store, a horse butcher with the bust of a donkey nailed proudly over the door, a grubby Fascist-looking station ringed with grubbier kebab shops – Belfort was hard to love, but at the same time you couldn't hate it. The sky was blue and already there were intimations of a holiday atmosphere.

As the crowds began to gather in the two brasserie-ringed

squares that were the festival's focus, I gazed up at that dominating sandstone fortress. It was this mighty edifice, I had been severally informed by the tourist leaflets, that had allowed Belfort to hold off the advancing Germans during the 1870 war in which the rest of Alsace was annexed. I knew the commanding officer, Denfert-Rochereau, from the names of any number of squares and streets and metro stations throughout France, and contemplating the huge red lion that growled out from the fortress-supporting cliff in commemoration of his siege-resisting exploits I understood something about the hero-worshipping culture that begat the Tour. It was perhaps no coincidence that those cycling nations with the noblest Tour traditions also shared a romantic attachment to their sons and daughters who had defied the odds with acts of extraordinary valour in other fields, an enduring and powerful national affection for those rare few who achieved the apparently unachievable. Whoever just said 'Belgium?' is in detention for a week.

The wind dropped and the heat was soon stultifying. Very glad that I hadn't tried to cycle 254 kilometres in these conditions, I ambled drowsily about the old town, watching lizards flash up walls, skirting round the bovine groups of riot police who set off up the street in a clomping rush every time someone dropped a bottle in the distance. Away from the squares the Moldovan ululations and death metal and jazz melted together like a badly tuned radio, but everywhere the atmosphere was wonderfully civic, partly no doubt because of the complete absence of entrance fees. All the public buildings were opened up as venues, and in the crowds outside pram-pushers mingled with pot-smokers, couples in their Sunday best joining crusties in their Wednesday worst at the kebab queues. I enjoyed it, and would have enjoyed it even more if I hadn't been compelled by nascent blisters to wear socks inside my espadrilles.

England were playing Portugal in that night's Euro 2000 game, and as the sun dropped below tomorrow's hills I walked into a bar manned by two crones, one quite old and one very. From the pink ceiling dangled the vast screen that had lured me in, and being the only customer, by the time I'd finished my first beer I had learned a great deal about this item and its life to date.

Good, isn't it, said the barmaid. Yes, I said. Mother paid 49,000 francs for it, said the barmaid. In Spain, said the mother. Because of the longer guarantee, said the daughter. But during the last World Cup the extra business paid for it twice over, said the mother. Are you interested in the Tower of France, I said. We cleared almost 20,000 francs on the night our boys beat Brazil, said the daughter. The tuning is difficult, said the mother, but it brings the customers in. Bicycles, I said. And it was tax-deductible, said the daughter. Look, England are winning 2–0, I said. It's all go in Belfort these days, said the mother. First these student musicians, said the daughter, and next month the Tour de France. Yes, I said. Christophe Moreau, said the mother, that's him in the photo up on the wall. That little beard didn't do him any favours, said the daughter, but he's a nice lad. Lives just down the road, said the mother, opposite the Novotel. Five bedrooms and a swimming pool, said the daughter. Look, Portugal have scored a goal, said the mother. And another, said her daughter. Oh, look at our friend, he's upset, let's give him a drink, said the mother. Here you are, said the daughter, a nice Dubonnet. Thank you, I said. You English love Dubonnet, said the mother. Do we, I said. Yes, said the daughter. I'm cycling to Troyes tomorrow, I said. Do you like my blouse, said the daughter. It's 254 kilometres to Troyes, I said. Oh no, dear, said the mother, I don't think so. Philippe once did it in two hours, said the daughter. Not on a bicycle he didn't, I said. A bicycle, said the mother, I don't think anyone goes to Troyes on a bicycle. I do, I said. Don't you like Dubonnet, said the daughter. Yes, I said, I'm just tired. Yes, said the mother, and aren't your hands hot. And your cheeks, said the daughter. We could tell you were a sportsman as soon as you came in, said the mother. The legs, said the daughter. Stand up and show us again, said the mother. Come on, there's no one else here, said the daughter, it's just a bit of fun. Wait, said the mother, you have a small wound on your neck. Come here, little wounded soldier, said the daughter, and I'll make it all better. Well, there's no need for that, said the mother, she was only trying to help. Excuse me, said the daughter, but don't think you can just leave without paying. I have paid, I said. Not for the Dubonnet, said the mother. Typical English, said the daughter. And Portugal scored again.

The festival was sweeping up its glass when I trudged slowly back across the squares to my hotel. Roadies were messing about with the instruments as they cleared the stages, and as I flopped on to my bed and clicked on the weather forecast there was an ominous drum roll from outside: circling wind and thunder-storms. Then the phone rang. It was reception. 'Monsieur Moore? I 'ave a message about your . . . massage.' Please don't say it like that. 'Is change for ten surty. Good night.'

The bad thing about the delay was that it severely com-promised my marathon itinerary. Even without a stop I'd be hard pressed to cover 254 kilometres in less than ten hours. The good thing was that it bequeathed me one and a half hours for additional preparation.

With my usual ruminative lunch no longer an option, early the following morning I stocked up with what I hoped might comprise 254 kilometres' worth of sustenance: five Mars Bars, one litre of apricot nectar and two of Yoplait Energie, a pack of Fig Rolls and a set of 'Baker Street' fruit cakes – the Holmes, which apparently had some butter in, and the Watson, which was slightly less turquoise. Then I retrieved ZR from the laundry room and cycled up the hill to a petrol station, where, before the curious gaze of staff and clients, I paid 10 francs to blast her abused and filthy flanks with a high-pressure jet of hot, soapy water. Finally, having temporarily redeposited ZR at the hotel, with a sense of foreboding in its own way more wretched than that I felt when the Pyrenees first hove into view, I trooped dismally into an Yves Rocher beauty salon and quietly asked a lady in white clothes to depilate my legs.

It had to be done. I'd spent too much time thinking about it: why they did it, how, when. Through all the countless hours I'd spent surveying my hairy knees as they rose and fell, rose and fell, I'd felt I was looking at the legs of a pretender. Now I'd done the mountains and got the tan, and if I wanted to be taken seriously by my masseur, the hair would have to go.

They were very nice in the salon. Some of the questions I had feared were asked (did I want a full-leg wax or a half; was I aware that the process might involve some discomfort), but most were not (did I mind if passers-by were herded in to watch; was there a long history of cross-dressing in my family; would it matter that as the first depilatory client after the Pentecost I was obliged by local tradition to retain an unshaved area on each shin in the form of an inverted crucifix). As Martine ushered me into her quiet depilatorium I explained my relief that such a procedure was clearly commonplace amongst Belfort's male population. Hardly, she said as I removed rather more clothing than I felt comfortable about. I was the first man they'd ever had in.

I knew it was going to hurt, but actually the pain was no worse than the last time I tore off a pair of gaffer-tape trousers after they caught fire. After the first Velcro-parting rip my eyes clamped shut while my mouth did the opposite.

Filling her second bucket with strip after waxed strip of flayed follicles, Martine confessed that she had once depilated her father. He was 'almost' a professional cyclist, a man who covered 500k a week for years, but after one shin's worth of her follicular yanking he yelped off the trolley and hobbled away in search of his razor. Christophe Moreau, now there was a super-hard man. He wouldn't have made a squeak, not even at this bit – ow ow ow STOP NOW – where I frenziedly pluck out any remaining individual hairs with these tweezers.

247

A razor, I thought. Why hadn't I just shaved my stupid legs with a razor? And why had I bothered anyway? Martine had assured me it was nothing to do with aerodynamics: part of the reason was to facilitate the massage process, but from what her father had told her the main intention was to reduce the risk of infecting the regular and serious leg abrasions that are the cyclist's lot. How awful, I'd thought; what a ghastly rationale. Shaving my face every morning was dull enough, but imagine if I did it not for presentation purposes, but because at some stage during the journey into work I would inevitably headbutt a postbox.

Walking out of the salon it felt strange to have thanked and paid someone for such an experience, though not as strange as my bald leg flesh felt as my trousers swished freely over it. I'd ordered a cab to take me from beauty salon to massage parlour and, gratified that even such an itinerary did not apparently mark me out in his eyes as a 'john', felt brave enough to ask the driver to wait. Thanking God and – behold the sound of crawling flesh – last night's predatory pensioners that I wasn't going into a massage parlour stinking of stale booze, I walked through an unassuming door and into an unassuming surgery.

Later I was told that in France, massage has none of the stigma attached to it by the British, and is indeed widely available on the health service. How I would have appreciated this knowledge as I took my place in the vet-smelly waiting room next to a scabrous old tramp reading a well-thumbed *Marie-Claire*. His turn was called by a pale-eyed young man of ominous appearance and he slowly rose into an arthritic hunch. In moments the sound of heavy skin being roundly belaboured thundered out of a half-closed door. When the old man began to protest wearily it was slammed shut.

'Monsieur?'

I'd been in two minds about staying, and they'd both decided to make a run for it when a cheerful man in his forties popped a curly-haired head round the corner. In moments I was, for the second time in less than an hour, lying face-down on a trolley with my trousers on a chair and my pants wedged up my crack, waiting for a hired stranger to get cracking on me.

'Alors,' he said, offloading a wristy squirt of cold white cream on to my hairless, goosebumped thighs. I'd noticed since returning to France that my ability to sustain conversation with the natives had improved exponentially, and also that I kept wishing it hadn't. Even two weeks ago I could have just bitten the headrest in agonised semi-silence; now I felt obliged to formulate considered replies as he systematically worked me over. The backs of my calves weren't too bad, permitting me to explain my quest in an almost normal voice, and to return the genuine excitement this seemed to cause him with appropriate modesty-conveying noises. For a brief moment we were two middle-aged men exchanging sporting anecdotes in a wholly humdrum fashion; then, as we moved on to discuss the region's cycling stars, he pressed his thumb into the nearside tendon beneath my right knee and with a stridency normally used to invoke the name of Mr Gordon Bennett I shrieked, 'CHRISTOPHE MOREAU!'

Thus ended my meaningful contribution to the debate, along with any residual fears that I might inadvertently develop an erection. My vital signs were still some way from normality when, working his way up, my cheerful tormentor manually encountered a contorted ganglion of muscle tissue in the underside of my left thigh. 'Aaah,' he said, and so did I, only with a generous helping of silent 'G's and many additional punctuation marks. After ten minutes he speculatively prodded my spine, and having issued a short sound at the upper limit of a human being's audible spectrum I frenziedly shook my head. The legs were one thing; if I'd wanted my back done I'd have . . . I don't know, had it waxed.

'Eh bien,' he said, towelling down his hands as he assessed my slathered bald bits, 'c'est pas mal. Vous avez . . . trente-six, trente-sept ans?' Those were awful words to hear. I'd thought he had been generically impressed by my achievement, but I had been wrong. I understood that all the kind words and encouragement I'd received in recent days had been rounded off with an unspoken coda: Not bad for an old man.

While Birna was packing I'd bundled most of my Tour books into her suitcase, weary of the humbling heroics of Messrs Cannibal and Badger. All I had left now were Paul Kimmage's brutally poignant *Rough Ride* and a novel Birna had brought out with her, *The Yellow Jersey*, featuring none other than the 'legendary fictional cyclist' Terry Davenport. An account of a slightly seedy 36-year-old Englishman making an improbable comeback in the Tour, this had been heartwarming bedtime reading for the last week. After the disqualification of most of the Frenchmen for doping offences (hissss!), and having literally beaten off a mob of Belgian bullies with his bike pump (hurrah!), Terry finds himself wearing the eponymous shirt, to the sporting world's astonishment, with only two days left. The night before, still unsettled by the groping grandmothers, I had snuggled up in bed to cheer myself with Terry's triumphant ride up the Champs-Elysées.

It is difficult to imagine that the literary editor of *Bicycling* magazine is a busy man, but without wishing to contest his presumably irrefutable verdict of *The Yellow Jersey* as 'the greatest cycling novel ever written', I have to say that after reading the first page I felt I could predict with some confidence what would happen on the last. How wrong I was. What no doubt sets *The Yellow Jersey* apart from the other cycling novels weighing down the nation's shelves are the wholly unexpected calamities of its abrupt denouement. On page 282 Terry is within sight of the Tour's most famous victory; then he gets really tired, and, eschewing the gnarled determination that has carried him through far more lurid crises, on page 283 he suddenly gives up. He is sitting in the back of the team car trying to come to terms with this turn of events, when someone hands him a letter from his girlfriend's mother. He opens it on page 284 and learns on page 285 that Bobbie has abruptly announced her engagement to a younger man who 'looked loaded and had a big car outside'. The end.

I was deeply shocked, but the moral was clear: the Tour was a young man's game, and if you tried to beat him at it you'd get really tired and give up. Then he'd drive off with your girlfriend in a big car. The end.

As I shuffled brokenly outside, the old tramp strode past me with a spring in his step. It was as though our bodies had been swapped. Still feeling as if my legs were leaking some vital life-force through their scooped-out, fingered pores, I was driven back to my hotel where I got myself jerseyed and cleated and Savloned up, then grabbed ZR and asked the receptionist to photograph rider and steed at the foot of the sweeping staircase. It was 11.10 a.m., and I knew that one way or another I would still be cycling long after it got dark.

My body seemed to heal with use. Reaching the brow of the first of the day's many rolling hills, I was beginning to believe that massage might after all be a beneficial treatment rather than a punishment, and my enhanced control of the bike now permitted mobile refuelling, the in-saddle consumption of fig roll or Mars Bar. At Ronchamp the route left the big road and for the final time I followed the Tour back to its rural origins, beating a track through forgotten hamlets where man made no sound but his best friend made plenty, places with waist-high weeds in the churchyards and dumped-car farms and mad and ancient names like Esboz and Quers.

Luxeuil was a market town of the old school, the banners across its narrow streets advertising another Day of Blood and – how I laughed – a looming Festival of Nocturnal Cycling. On any other day I'd have stopped here for my coffee; instead, with a practised air I slyly palmed a ProPlus from my jersey pocket and washed it down with chlorine-tainted apricot nectar.

The huge storms that brought down 20 million French trees in the last week of 1999 had been at their fiercest around here, and where I transferred from Michelin Map 243 to 241 every copse and thicket had at least a couple of prostrate victims, soldiers who'd passed out on parade. I thought of the forecast wind and wondered where it had gone. The sky's morning pallor had been burned away and now it was really very hot; looking down at my schoolgirl's knees, I could already see the tan reddening up.

It's never good when, as lorries overtake, you find yourself deliberately edging out in order to get nearer that cooling gust of cleaved air. Soon I could think only of fluid, an obsession fortified by the fact that, with 165k left, my remaining supply of solids consisted, in toto, of Holmes and Watson. Simon O'Brien had recommended fruitcake as the ideal long-distance sustenance, but then he wasn't to know that the recipe posthumously endorsed by Victorian England's favourite crime-fighting duo could find little space for fruit, and less for cake, in a list of ingredients that began and ended with stained lard.

The 100k was up and at just past 3 p.m. I waved flaccidly at the rust-pitted, crutch-toting invalid silently urging me to enjoy my stay at Bourbonne-les-Bains, a gentleman whose striking resemblance to Josef Goebbels suggested a spa-town heyday even more distant than I had become accustomed to. Then, horribly, the road pitched itself directly up the last set of double chevrons I would face. The Côte de Chagnon was only a category four, but long before I creaked over its unremarkable summit I was mumbling to myself like the mother of a recalcitrant toddler: 'Come on, come on – no, I've told you already, you're not getting any warm Yoplait until you've finished up your Watson.'

The last day before Paris was supposed to be a mobile party. Paul Kimmage's account of the ride into the capital was of singing and linked arms and the playing of practical jokes, but riding into Dammartin I felt less end-of-term and more first-day-back. Here I crossed the Meuse, and was reminded by an accompanying sign that I'd just entered the true north of France: the last big river I'd bridged, just before Bourbonne, had been the Saône, which went on to meet the Rhône at Lyon and thence flowed out into the Mediterranean. But the Meuse went the other side of whatever flaming hill I'd been ridging, winding its way up to the Channel. If I'd been near Troyes this would have girded me up for the final stretch. But a dizzy, unfocused peer at the itinerary confirmed what I'd feared: I was less than halfway there, and it had gone four o'clock.

The promised wind was belatedly building up and pushing me into the verge. The sun started to nestle down near the horizon, blinding me if I looked up and even, as was more common, if I looked down, reflected into my eyes off the steam-cleaned chain and sprockets. The road settled into a depressing routine, ribboning up and down a parabolic succession of large green humps; as dusk fell, the troughs between these filled with gnats and midges and other toothsome windborne snacks.

With my shadow twice the width of the road I climbed up to Chaumont, a railway town whose International Poster Festival had climaxed yesterday, its empty streets a testament to the citizenry's sullen realisation that there would consequently be no reason to emerge from their homes for another year. The sun had gone but its last silvered rays, Zorro-slashed with jet-fighter vapour trails, were still bright on the horizon as I swept giddily out of town on the N19. The 150k was up; soon I had passed my daily record and as I entered uncharted territory the last Plasticened palmful of Holmes broached my feebly protesting lips.

All I wanted now was a sort of controlled bonk, the semi-delirious accumulation of distance by a body too knackered to complain, slackly governed by a brain too knackered to notice if it did. I needed to be taken down to a place where nothing was real, where everyone had Eddy's legs, Lance's lungs and Tommy's drugs, and the Tour de France's final hill, the category four Côte d'Alun, took me there.

I couldn't tell you much about how I got up and less still about how I got down. At its foot lay Colombey-les-deux-Eglises, de Gaulle's former (and, in a less active sense, current) home and the place where in 1960 ol' Big Nose halted the entire peloton for a photo opportunity with the yellow jersey. For days I'd been wondering what kind of a show this ultimately French village would be putting on for this ultimately French event, but the next time I squinted through the gloom at my map and itinerary was at Bar-sur-Aube. I'd passed through Colombey 15 kilometres back and hadn't even noticed.

If it hadn't been a week away from the year's longest day, it would have been pitch black long before I rolled past a sign welcoming me to Troyes, city of art, history and gastronomy. As it was, the full, dark weight of night only dropped around me as I dumbly uncleated outside a McDonald's – gastronomy be damned: if anyone had ever needed food fast, it was me, then. It was 10.17 p.m.: I had been cycling for over eleven hours, twice what it would take the pros. The stage was supposed to be 254.5 kilometres but looking at my computer under a streetlight I registered that somewhere along the way I'd picked up another 3.2k. All I'd noticed during the last 50 kilometres had been a lot of long names – Montier-en-l'Isle, la Villeneuve-au-Chêne, Saint-Parres-aux-Tertres – and a horrid smell of Poupou-sur-les-Fields. I had travelled through five French departments and across huge swathes of two Michelin maps. Not bad for an old man.

Feeling almost totally disembodied I clicked spasmodically across the tiles like Mrs Overall, the food chain's heavily oiled final links piled up on my tray. It was Tuesday and the only other clients were students, who accepted my appearance with a nonchalance that cheered and depressed in equal measure. Having filled my face in the most literal fashion I remounted with predictable difficulty and set off for the finest hotel Troyes had to offer.

It didn't take long to find, snug up against the cathedral in a theatrically spotlit alley. But then it took even less time for the very kind and very young night receptionist to send me back into the night with some desperately awful tidings. A conference was in town. No room at the inn, nor at the three others she telephoned on my behalf. 'Try ze steshun,' she said, handing me a map of Troyes as I tried to get my face to do something grateful.

The station was not nearby, and as suspected its semi-industrial ambience made it the natural home of the city's tawdriest overnight accommodations. A couple of them had 'complet' signs outside the reception window, but one didn't, partly because the reception window was on the first floor. This probably needn't have required me to wheel ZR right through the busy ground-floor restaurant and over the feet of a dozen diners, but I could feel coursing through my veins a sort of drunken recklessness, an ugly, animal determination. Man need bed. Give man bed. I shouldered my bike up the stairs, panniers and all, to be greeted by a tall, skeletal crow of a woman grimly shaking her head and one hand.

Still not quite understanding how this was happening to me, or why it had to happen to me now, I found a phone box and rang Birna. The blathering torrent of self-pity was by this stage a staple of our telephonic encounters, and she listened patiently as, dispensing with respiration or punctuation, I stated that I was in a town with no hotels, that she had the hotel book, and that having cycled 94,000 miles I had forgotten how to speak French. 'You want me to find a room for you, then call you back,' she précised slowly, and with the now traditional lack of grace I agreed.

Five minutes later the phone box rang. 'I've found you the last room in Troyes,' said Birna. I made a little noise like a puppy being reunited with its mother. 'But there is one problem.' And then having its tail stamped on. 'It's not actually in Troyes.'

The lady Birna had spoken to at the Holiday Inn Forêt

d'Orient said her establishment lay 13 kilometres from Troyes. In theory this information should have led me to explore further avenues. It was a warm night; I could have dossed down in a park. I kept feeling that in my condition I shouldn't have cared where I slept. But I did. I cared passionately. I had done something exceptional and I wanted a reward. 'Tell them I'll be there in half an hour,' I muttered, and having scribbled down directions off I went into the night.

Thirteen was a lot of kilometres, particularly because – and you're going to love this – they involved retracing my journey right back up the N19. On passing the outlying hypermarkets I entered a dark world whose secrets were not about to be revealed by my feeble little flashing lights. Intended, as I now realised, solely for urban commuting under street lamps, these were memorably inadequate in the rural environment. The moon was more use. It was terrifying. My only fellow road users at this hour – and by now it was gone midnight – were enormous double-trailer lorries avoiding motorway tolls, roaring past with a what-the-fuck-are-you-doing-out-here blast of their foghorns.

I was relieved to turn off the N19, but not for very long. The trees rose up about me and blocked off the moon; if the roads hadn't been almost dead straight I'd never have made it. I could barely make out the fingerposts at all and, when I did, the only way to read them was to shin up the pole and hold my flashing light an inch away from the lettering. An owl hooted. I ran over something pulpy. There were other sounds. I hadn't seen any signs of life for an eon. The suggestion that somewhere in this wooded wilderness lay a Holiday Inn was an outrage against logic. Wolves – certainly; vagrant lunatics – odds-on; a solitary cleated foot emerging from recently disturbed soil – well, the night was young.

Thirteen was a lot of kilometres, but it wasn't quite as many as 22, which is what I learned I had covered from Troyes after an incongruous pair of illuminated roadside globes welcomed me up the drive of the Holiday Inn Forêt d'Orient. That made it 279.7 for the day. I fumbled and bumbled through the dark ranks of BMWs and clumsily manipulated ZR through the automatic doors. Two sturdy young men were bent over a pool table in the downlit gloaming; behind them a bald barman stood washing glasses. To my left the night receptionist was already eyeing me with something beyond interest, and as the three other faces angled towards mine I slapped my free hand against my left buttock and in a surprisingly mellifluous singsong, said, 'A welcome sight at *any* time.'

And ten hours later I was back in Troyes.

Seventeen

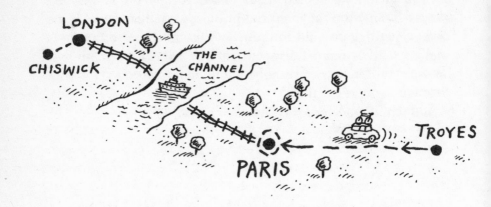

It was interesting to note how unremarkable I felt waiting on the platform for the 11.39 to Paris. Cyclists from Lance Armstrong to Terry Davenport invariably discovered at least one inner truth about themselves in the eye of some desperate ordeal. 'I met a guy up on that mountain who I grew to kind of like, and do you know who that guy was? That's right: it was me.' That sort of thing. But looking back over the already slightly unreal events of the past twenty-four hours, the only epiphany I could claim to have experienced was this: some mornings, even five croissants are not enough.

Though actually there was something else. Wheeling ZR back out through the Holiday Inn's automatic doors and into the misty sun I'd seen a roomful of sales-conference delegates staring bleakly into their Styrofoam cups as a bald man drew pie charts on an overhead projector; one of them turned to me as I cleated up and as our eyes met we both understood an important truth:

however wretched my day might be, even if it meant going back to Belfort and back his was going to be far worse.

Troyes had not surprised me by looking rather better by day: haphazard, half-timbered streets opening into well-scrubbed, geometric boulevards, a Gothic cathedral, market squares – a proper French town; the kind of place you wouldn't mind being twinned with, especially because every time the maire came over you'd be able to go on about the post-Agincourt Treaty of Troyes that recognised our own Henry V as heir to the French throne.

There were two tourist offices, and lured by window displays of bikes and jerseys and ville d'étape posters I visited them both. I didn't expect much, and I didn't get it – not even a souvenir bidon. But at least this time the ignorance was cheerful, and the lady at the second place did endeavour to help by telling me I'd got my helmet the wrong way round, even though I hadn't.

It was here I learned that it might indeed be possible to take my bike on the train, and so at least vaguely emulate the Tour riders, who would transfer by Orient Express to Paris for the final stage, a circuitous roam about the capital followed by the traditional mad scramble of laps up and down the Champs-Elysées. After painstaking ticket-office conversations and timetable consultations, I established with as much certainty as any tourist can hope for that the 11.39 to Paris Est was a service on which accompanied bicycles could be carried free of charge.

The 11.39 was one of those Sixties efforts with a windscreen that sloped the wrong way, the only sort I'd imagined being allowed to take a bike on, but it creaked up to the almost deserted platform on the dot and with difficulty I bundled ZR aboard.

'Eh! Non! Eh! Monsieur! C'est interdit!'

There were rapid footsteps and further cries and suddenly two inspectors were outside on the platform, gesticulating at the driver and yanking my door handle. Someone had already blown a whistle and there we were, having a tug of war through an open

259

door with ZR as the rope. I'd been wondering when the monstrosities of yesterday would catch up with me, and now I knew. There was little physical resistance and less mental: a four-armed yank and ZR was on the platform; a slight shove from an onboard official behind and I joined her.

'Oh, c'est joli, le maillot,' said one of the inspectors, dusting off my jersey as the train awoke with a long, rusted yawn and moved slowly away. 'Un rétro?'

His kind, trustworthy voice was so unexpected and disarming that I somehow found myself quietly discussing Merckx, Simpson, Bernard Thévenet and other Peugeot riders of yore when by rights I should have been well entrenched in a physical confrontation whose final scene would see me bellowing the terms of the Treaty of Troyes as the gendarmerie dragged me down the platform by my ankles. As the pair gently escorted me out of the station I did halfheartedly draw their attention to my pocket timetable, and in particular the little bicycle symbol next to the 11.39, but they both just smiled and nodded like uncles being shown their small nephew's inept artwork. It didn't really matter. There was an Avis office almost next door and in half an hour I was shooting past fields of lilac opium poppies, a handlebar in my ear, hairless thighs sticking to the hot upholstery of an Opel Corsa.

In one way it was a shame not to be cycling into Paris, not to see the Eiffel Tower taking shape on a hazy horizon and gradually reeling it in with each portentous turn of the pedals, but in most ways it was not. Everyone was getting sweaty and bad-tempered as I approached the outskirts – it was no place to be on a bike. The signs warned pedestrians to cross in two stages, but the way things were going it was more likely to be two pieces. After turning off the périphérique ring road it got worse, and the apparently straightforward task of finding a hotel and parking the car required me to commit several dozen motoring offences, from illicit U-turns to driving the wrong way down a one-way street. On the pavement.

The hotel, near the Place d'Italie in the city's unfashionable south, was unsatisfactory to the point of outrage. It looked no worse than grubby from the outside, set in a street behind an enormous hospital and flanked by the sort of dirty-windowed, faceless government offices you could only imagine being responsible for the most obscure bureaucratic pedantries: issuing crab licences, approving artichoke export quotas, plotting the wholesale assassination of environmental activists.

A big-faced man with a moist neck made me pay up front before entering my name with difficulty in his soiled register of the damned; as I trod carefully towards the lift he issued a two-tone grunt of dissent and without looking up thumbed at a dark stairwell. My fourth-floor window overlooked a forgotten courtyard full of dead pigeons and an avant-garde installation entitled One Hundred Years of the Fag End. Inside, the view wasn't much better. The wardrobe was the size of a child's coffin and contained a vegetable. Rolling back the tramp's blanket on a bed of institutional design, I beheld a pillowcase that might have been used to filter coffee. But of course it hadn't: after all, what's the bathroom towel for? Still, clicking off the Bakelite switch with wet hands I wished I'd used it. The shock was so violent it flung me halfway to the bed – not bad seeing as the bathroom was a shared one right down the end of the corridor.

But do you know what? I simply didn't care. I didn't care because it reminded me of the tawdrily romantic hotels I'd patronised during my first teenage visit to Paris. I didn't care because it was cheap. But mainly I didn't care because I was setting out into a flawless summer evening with a bottle of pink champagne inside me, and because having put it there in a very small number of minutes I was already strangely untroubled by the negative aspects of my environment, and because the reason I had put it there was because I had done it. I had gone all the way round an enormous country, all the way across Europe's hugest range of mountains: 2,952 kilometres, with almost 10 per cent of them in a single historic day. I had done all these things, and here was the bit I still couldn't get over as I jostled out into the zigzagging scooters and the apple-polishing Turkish grocers and the mincing old women walking their Pekineses: I had done them on a stupid bloody bicycle.

Feeling smug and splendid and world-famous, I promenaded luxuriously up to the Place d'Italie. It was remarkable that somewhere so humdrum by Parisian standards – this was just one of the minor étoiles, those vast roundabouts where boulevards converge – could seem the epitome of Continental sophistication in British terms. The nearest equivalent in London would be some brutalist concrete nightmare, a gyratory wasteland such as the Elephant & Castle. But here there was space and light and the huge glass wall of a daring new cinema complex and cobbles and ashlar and bars with outside tables: a proper urban focus for a proper urban community.

Sweden were playing Turkey and the local supporters of the latter team were out in force, filling the bars to the rafters and standing on chairs outside to get a view of the telly. It was all terribly exciting. I had a peek through one door and in seven loud seconds established that far post was 'deuxième poteau' and that Ross from *Friends* was playing on the left side of the Turkish midfield. And it was good to hear that even in such an environment, 'ooh la la' remains the exhilarated Parisian's default expression.

I found an outside table at a bar that wasn't showing the game, next to two old men almost inevitably playing chess. Lovers were sitting on the statues around us, stroking each other's warm faces in the 9 p.m. sun, and as my tall glass of cold beer arrived I surveyed the scene with the avuncular fondness of the reasonably plastered. But then, succumbing to this same group's vulnerability to wild swings of emotion, I suddenly felt a profound sadness. A snapshot photographed by my eyes the previous day was belatedly developed in my brain, and as it took shape I found myself looking at three teenage girls silently sharing a Coke outside a bar flanked by abandoned homes in a decaying rural town strung carelessly along both sides of a thundering main road.

How could you expect any young person to put up with a life like that when they could be having a life like this? The girls were mentally thumbing a lift from anything that passed – they even plotted my weary passage through their lives with glum envy – and one day soon someone would stop and pick them up and they'd be off. It was tragic to think that when the Tour first visited Londun or Obterre, or Carpentras or Chaumont or a thousand semi-derelict towns in between, each had been as vibrant as this in its own modest way, each had its own thronging Place d'Italie. But industrialisation and social mobility and any number of other demographic phenomena had lured people away to the cities, and even those rural towns that weren't just slinking off to die alone were doomed. They'd pay their million francs and string up their bunting and resurface their mini-roundabouts, but when the Tour came to town, that one day of sex and speed would only serve to highlight the snail-paced, strait-laced parochialism of the other 364.

I made my way back to the hotel, as wistful as it's possible to be with a leaking kebab in your mouth. The traffic was still insane at 10.30 and I knew that my final trans-Parisian stage would be feasible only at dawn, and that consequently I should go to bed straight away.

Bed was one thing; sleep was another. The sackcloth sheets were too short for the mattress and against my shaven shins the horsehair blanket felt like the rough grope of a lust-fogged drunk. That was how it started. The night before I had fallen immediately into a fatigued coma; only now, as the bedding rasped against my silken skin, did I notice how peculiar it felt to have hairless legs. Suddenly I couldn't keep my hands off them. Wobbling the firm, smooth bulk of those enormously bulked-up calves, as meaty and sculpted as granite chicken breasts; prodding and tracing the outlines of the entirely new front-thigh muscles that spilt over my kneecaps like double chins; stroking the thick and toughened tendons, still sore from the (how could it only have been yesterday?) massage.

It was like a variant of that joke about the reason men didn't have breasts: because if they did they'd just stay in and play with them all night. I kept expecting to be slapped in the face. Even after I finally stopped fondling myself and dropped off it wasn't over – twice that night (and there'd be many more such nights in the weeks ahead) I awoke with a start: what the bloody hell was this knobbly-kneed woman doing in my bed?

When it happened the third time I couldn't get back to sleep. My legs were now twitching spasmodically, wondering why they weren't pedalling – the legacy of a day spent cycling 279.7 kilometres followed by one sitting in traffic jams and getting drunk. With daylight sneaking in through the filthy curtains I creaked stiffly out of bed and stood before the wardrobe mirror. Even at this time of day, even with a slight hangover, it was a spectacle so frankly ludicrous that I barked out a single, mad guffaw.

Those legs, still blotched from their therapeutic ordeals, looked like champagne flutes: wrist-thin at the ankles, they progressively flared out on their way up to a set of mighty hams, thunder thighs indeed. Halfway up these the smooth, red-brown pint-of-best tan abruptly gave way to varicose magnolia and Puckish wire wool, as if I was wearing hairy white shorts. My similarly bleached torso, graced with its new – and hideous – stomach hairs, was topped by a zip-scarred neck and a gaunt, broiled head with singed and flaking extremities; from its sides dangled two thin arms whose tan-line apartheid had been brutally enforced. I might never leave my mark on the Tour, but that didn't matter. It had left its mark on me.

The final chlorinated bidon, the final night-dried Lycra taken down from the final hotel curtain rail, the final fistful of vitamins, the final slathering of the arse. Du pain, du vin, du Savlon – as silly and vile as they might be, I knew I would miss my routines. At 5.30 a.m. I clacked down four flights of dark stairs, dropped my key on the empty reception desk, bullied free several recalcitrant bolts and locks and stepped out into what I could already see, with a sort of mournful glee, was going to be a gorgeous day.

Any European city where a man can walk down a major thoroughfare at dawn wearing a string vest with his head held high is OK in my book. He walked past with a brisk nod as I leant against the car finishing my breakfast – three cellophane packets of biscuit crumbs stolen in rather better condition from the Holiday Inn. ZR stood ready beside me, assembled with practised hands; I chucked the panniers in the boot, cocked a leg and rolled off down an empty boulevard.

I never expected to do the whole stage – the route before those laps of the Champs-Elysées was monstrously complex, its details still a mystery after prolonged, albeit fizz-fuddled, consultation of a detailed map of the capital. Forty-eight kilometres would do me fine: that would probably be enough to experience the trademark sensations – heat, fatigue and fear – and, rather more importantly, certainly enough to bring up the momentous 3,000k. Gathering speed among the occasional taxis and police vans, I barrelled up the boulevards towards the Eiffel Tower, starting point of the 2000 Tour de France's twenty-first and final stage. I swished past a bus with three people on, washed-out ravers silently wondering how it had all come to this; someone was playing a synthesiser four floors up; from a side street came a ragged, drunken roar: 'Jean! Jean!'

I got to the Eiffel Tower as an enormous sun took shape behind it. The Eiffel Tower is one of the world's best things, and rolling to a halt in the centre of its four iron feet I had it all to myself. I remembered that picture of Hitler standing in front of the Arc de Triomphe, grinning with disbelief that all this was his, and grinned with disbelief. I had made it to Paris. With my gleaming exoskeleton legs I looked the part, and now I felt it. Giant of the Road might be pushing it a bit, but cycling off across the Pont d'Iena I felt a twinge in my joints that could only have been growing pains.

The sky went from cream to blue as I rolled along the Seine, past houseboats with a view to die for, past joggers, past hot-dog vendors already warming up their Westlers at 6.15. At the fourth bridge down I turned left and headed out across the vast, cobbled no-man's-land of the Place de la Concorde. A plumb-lined kilometre to my right stood the scaffolded bulk of the Louvre; to the right, the same vista eased up to the tiny, sunlit keyhole that was the Arc de Triomphe, over two kilometres up the Champs-Elysées.

'There are no tired legs on the Champs-Elysées,' they say, and though Paul Kimmage rather took the romance out of this by pointing out the absence of random dope controls on the final stage, I could see why they said it. Feeling exhilarated and tireless, up the mile-wide pavement I slalomed breezily between waiters putting out the first chairs and tables. On the way back down – the Tour riders would turn in front of the Arc de Triomphe ten times – I picked up speed with alarming ease. Thirty-five k.p.h. felt like 25; as I swished past the gendarmes questioning a van driver whose forlorn vehicle sat, front wheels splayed out, across the central reservation I gave Eddy Merckx an inner wink and hit 50.

I did a couple more Champs-Elysées laps, then arced off back to the Seine, bumping over the grilles that blasted weird wafts of hot Metro air up my legs. Past Notre-Dame, all the way back up to the Eiffel Tower, and all the way back. For another hour it was wonderful, but by 7.30 the magic had gone. Commuters were Henri Pauling it into the underpasses; van drivers parped and revved, and when I took refuge in the cycle lane they followed me. Hot, hounded and hungry, I glanced down at the computer and did a quick perimeter tour of the Jardin des Plantes, and another, and another. It was enough. The 3,000 came up as I turned off the Boulevard Vincent Auriol, exchanged curt abuse with a jaywalking businessman and eased up to the car.

That was it. It was 15 June: I'd done nearly 1,900 miles in a month to the day. There should have been bunting and blondes and big bottles of bubbly, but I really didn't mind that there weren't. Eddy and Tom and my support crew had helped me up the Alps, and Paul Ruddle had helped me down them, but at heart mine had been a solo achievement, a 3,000-kilometre lone break-away, and I was happy to celebrate its climax in an appropriate fashion.

In the final analysis, you see, because of what I had done I was simply a lot better than almost everyone else. With others around there would have been churlishness and jealousy; who knows, maybe even a couple of tiresome fans. Stalkers couldn't be ruled out. I took off my hot, wet gloves, opened the hatchback and, with a suitably epic commentary turning slowly through my mind, Moore's respectful hands began to strip down the machine that had been his slave, his master, his confidant and tormentor throughout a journey where suffering and glory had stood toe to toe and . . . and so on.

With my features settling into a happy, glazed reverie poorly suited to urban driving I set off into the rush hour, eventually finding myself amid the canoe-roofed British motorists piling back to Calais. The French were setting out deck-chairs on the not enormously appealing beaches south of the ferry terminal, getting ready for summer, a summer of which the Tour would as ever be the cornerstone.

I parked in the hire-car compound, built my bike and packed her bags, then pedalled across the hot tarmac to the Avis office.

'Voilà! You are return!' It was the man who had helped me dismantle ZR a month before.

'I am,' I said, with simple dignity.

'Oh, your vélo . . .' he said, peering over his desk at ZR's cleat-chipped crossbar and smutted tyres, '. . . your vélo 'as been doing many mileages, non?'

'Three thousand kilometres.'

This information changed the shape of his face. 'Sree souzand? Oh, c'est bien fait! Some montagnes?'

'Well, yes. I was following the Tour de France.' I remembered telling him this before, and I remembered how he'd reacted when I'd done so. He seemed to have forgotten.

'So . . . le Mont Ventoux?'

'Yes.' Well, near enough.

'L'Aubisque?'

I issued a sort of puff and rolled my eyes in an expression of partial conquest, hoping he wouldn't ask about Hautacam. He didn't.

'L'Izoard? Le Galibier?'

That was better. 'In the same day.'

'Eh bien,' he said with a smile, then pinched the brim of an imaginary trilby and raised it. 'Chapeau!'

Two hats in three days – it was a good feeling. And ten minutes later I almost made it a – woo-hoo – hat trick, defying the gloomy predictions of the girl at the ticket desk by covering the vast acreage of tarmac between her office and the ferry in less than the ninety seconds she had given me to get there before the ramp was raised. After an all-hands-on-sundeck crossing I whisked through the customs at Dover, waved past by officers who clearly couldn't imagine an earnest sportsman like that shoving a condom full of Kruggerands up his jacksy. More fool them!

On the way out, the route from station to ferry had seemed a white-knuckled, knee-buckled roller-coaster of mountains; on the way home, I honestly didn't even notice the change in gradient. The same Victorian guard's van and the same rattling progress, the scenery dribbling by when the noise and commotion implied an indistinguishable blur of greens and browns. We went through Staplehurst, and as I said this name to myself I somehow knew that my former sloth was already beckoning, that my endeavour had not been a turning point in my life, just a memorable detour, and that a lot of this might be because cycling around Avignon had something about it that cycling around Staplehurst did not.

And two hours later I was cycling up my road, oblivious to the highway hazards that had so unsettled me as I'd set off for London Bridge. Birna opened the door and smiled, then looked down at the flesh between shorts and socks and stopped.

'Oh, you *haven't*,' she said.

Epilogue

I can't pretend it was unpleasant to reacquaint myself with activities not focused either on doing an enormous amount of physical exercise or recovering from it, but it certainly was odd. No longer did each day begin with a wake-up gut-punch of nauseous fear at the wretchednesses ahead; no longer did it end with a dead-eyed vigil at the dinner table, wordlessly watching bits of wasp and Alp and sun-flayed nose drop into a half-eaten plate of pasta. Nevertheless, it was at meal times that I had most trouble. Breakfast had to be relearned as a time to sip tea and read the paper, rather than an industrial process centred on funnelling a kilogram of Bran Flakes down my gullet straight from the packet; at lunch and supper I searched in vain for the tureens of Coca-Cola and the side orders of chips. I no longer got drunk before reaching the fat bit of the wine bottle, and no longer avoided a hangover if I proceeded down to the dimpled bottom. The weather forecast had lost its status as the day's most significant media event, and the nutritional information on food packets played a diminished role in my nocturnal ponderings.

For the first few nights my legs itched and twitched from lack of exercise; once I'd had to get up and run on the spot in the bathroom for ten minutes, and once I very nearly went for a bike ride. After two weeks my legs were stubbling up and those muscles beginning to waste, fruit rotting on the bough. ZR was outside the back door with the kids' bikes, a spider's web under the crossbar, its chain rusting in the late-June rain.

July was twelve hours old when the Tour started, and fourteen hours after that, with Michelin maps all over the bed and a sympathetic knot of anguish in my innards, I was embarking on the first of twenty-one nightly vigils, tuning into Channel 4's extended 2 a.m. highlights. The Futuroscope prologue was won by an incredulous 22-year-old Scotsman, David Millar, riding in his first Tour, but if I'd hoped to feel a chest-swelling affinity I would be quickly disappointed. On the flat stages at least, the cameras, their focus narrowed on the leading riders' faces, would show little that I recognised. Behind all those hoardings and gantries, the view beyond was obscured by massed ranks of picnickers waving merchandise thrown out by the advance caravan of publicity vehicles: yellow feeding bags, polka-dot caps, green cardboard hands as big as bin lids.

The corn was stiff and yellow and as the race turned south the maize was up to the riders' shoulders; inevitably, the sunflowers were out. The stage into Limoges was won by a Frenchman, the host nation's first win for two years, but he had an Italian name and a face like a proboscis monkey so they couldn't get too excited about it. An ageing Dutchman won the next after an epic breakaway and when Channel 4's Paul Sherwen interviewed him beside the podium he cried. They were averaging almost 50 k.p.h., and it kept raining. Paul's senior partner Phil Liggett said he'd covered thirty Tours and this was some of the worst weather he'd come across.

The race reached Dax, which in common with all the other villes d'étapes looked a lot better with the flags out, but when it set off towards the Pyrenees I wasn't thinking about bicycle-shaped flower-beds and the other fruits of their million-franc civic knees-up. Sitting there in the middle of the night, flanked by sleeping wife and rib-kicking infant daughter, this was what I'd been waiting for. Up until now it had all been tactical and fairly pedestrian; as the highlights zipped straight to the foot of the col de Marie-Blanque, I knew I was about to witness the extremes of human emotion. I wanted to see men soar where I had grovelled, knuckle down where I'd knuckled under; to see how it should be done. But I also wanted to see how it shouldn't, to see terrible pain and defeat, to enjoy the company of my fellow failures.

'A tough little climb, the Marie-Blanque,' said Phil, and it was tougher that day more than most. There was cloud and driving rain; a few soggy cardboard hands waving limply by the road but plenty more wind-filled golf umbrellas. It had been a gut-cramping bellyful of chilled fountain for me; for them it was a bidon of hot tea.

The Tour had suddenly gone into slow motion. For a week the peloton had flashed past spectators in a smudge of hissing metal and artificial colour; now fat, wet, flag-wrapped Belgians were able to waddle alongside the toiling riders, bellowing abuse or encouragement. Four men abandoned the race before the summit, and a fifth fell on the descent and was taken away in an ambulance, Lycra slashed, skin gashed. News that a rider had thrown in the towel was announced via a little on-screen graphic of a man energetically hurling his bike to the floor and storming off in disgust. None of those I saw being helped into their team cars, eyes glassing up like dying fish, looked as though they'd be up to that. Drugged-up men at the threshold of human suffering, mouthing agonised obscenities and peeing into their tight, greased gussets: an enticing image in certain circles, perhaps, but surely not the appropriate inspiration for a national romance.

I watched the ascent of the Aubisque like a man reliving a nightmare. The towns were transformed by the crowds and banners, but with slug-tennis rain keeping all but the very drunkest spectators at home I had a clear view of every fateful hairpin, tunnel and false summit. 'In these conditions, with the wind chill, your limbs get tetanised on the way down,' said Paul, and I instinctively flexed my knuckles and pressed them into my hot armpits.

'Blown to pieces' was a favourite refrain in a day of violent clichés; all around people were either putting hammers down or hitting walls. Lance Armstrong started the climb to Hautacam with fifteen riders between him and the leading Spaniard; he stood up in the saddle and, without a single facial indicator of expended effort, cruised haughtily past wobbling wrecks of men, leaving his rivals to fight distantly among themselves. Armstrong had the yellow jersey and a four-minute lead and as a contest the Tour was over.

David Millar winced over the line a creditable thirty-second, and with haunted eyes spoke of encountering 'The Fear' during his journey through 'a world of pain'. Then, without warning, there was the round, expressionless, shop-wigged face of Eddy Merckx. 'Deez climbs are not so hard,' he told Paul Sherwen in a slightly robotic monotone, turning away for the next interview even as Paul said, 'And that's from a man who knows a bit about the Tour de France with five victories in the event.'

Dammit all to hell, Merckx. Why did he have to say that? When the end credits began to roll it was like reading every clause and subsection of my Pyrenean surrender. Phil and Paul had explained perhaps a dozen times that the Tour was won and lost in the mountains. It was where Armstrong had won, and it was where I had lost.

The weather got worse when they reached Ventoux. There was snow on the summit and a terrible gale that had the trees waving desperately for help as Channel 4's Gary Imlach bellowed his report to camera. It was awful, the kind of occasion that blurs the boundaries between holidaymaker and refugee, and yet if Gary was to be believed an astonishing 300,000 people were camped out on Ventoux. Men in bobble hats and puffa jackets were out there, battling with flyaway flags and furniture; the drinks vendors had swathed tea towels over their beer taps and were instead doing a brisk trade in vin chaud. I liked professional cycling, I mused, but some people really, *really* liked it. Behind Gary a ramshackle peloton of plucky amateurs pedalled agonisingly through the narrow column left between placards and Peugeots and pastis-pouring pedestrians; one of the sturdy crowd-control barriers was blown over with a clatter and just in front of it a cyclist in a yellow jersey caught a gust in the chest and came to a halt, twisting a foot out of his pedal bindings just in time. It occurred to me that in all my weeks on the road this was the first yellow jersey I'd seen; that such was the hallowed, iconic status of this item only a heretic would dare to wear it; and that when he did, a divine blast of cold wind would come down from on high and smite him off his bike.

Then the coverage fast-forwarded, the cheers grew to a rowdy climax – how awful to have that noise following you around all day – and there was Lance Armstrong, wraparounds propped casually on his head, untroubled but for a sheen of sweat. As the camera panned back down the field we got to the sufferers, a fitful dribble of pained men. This was better; these were my people. The King of Belfort himself, Christophe Moreau, went by alone with his tongue hanging down to the bottom of his goatee. (In fact, Moreau was to have a glorious Tour, astounding himself and his many close personal friends in Belfort by finishing fourth overall as the leading Frenchman.) Then the rump of the peloton, men who'd given up and just wanted to get to the top in one piece, and there was David Millar, with blood running down his legs and a horrible vampire slash on his throat. He'd crashed earlier on, and while doing so had trapped the flesh of his neck in someone's chain, which still makes me feel ill even thinking about it. 'It only hurts when I breathe,' was his wry assessment of the after-effects. He finished, but many didn't. 'There are another ten riders in there today,' said Phil as the broom wagon rolled up past Tom Simpson's memorial. It was thirty-three years to the day.

The following stage, across Provence from Avignon to Draguignan, was undertaken at astounding speed. How *could* these people be the same ones who less than twenty-four hours earlier had been trapping their necks in people's chains and toiling up a mountain mired in most of the human body's least appealing secretions? But the stage after that was the killer, the one that most riders said they feared above all others.

Between Draguignan and Briançon lay 250 kilometres and three mountains over 2,000 metres; if there was a calvary, this was it. The smelly-bearded German Devil recognised this, waddling about the mountainsides in a soiled red leotard, and so too did his Italian nemesis: the Angel, all in white, fiddling with his feathery wings as he stood in wait on the roof of a camper van near the summit of the day's final peak, the col d'Izoard.

The preparatory climb out of Draguignan, up that awful parched road through those mountain-top firing ranges, was a route I knew like the back of my hand but not quite like the top of my knee. That's where I had the race with that mechanic, that's where those stupid Austrian bikers almost ran me down, that's where I bought all that Fanta and that's where I . . . offloaded it – a whole lifetime of suffering and sickness, at least deserving of a respectful hearse-speed drive-by, condensed into four dismissive minutes.

But it was the penultimate climb of the day that had me staring at the telly in dry-lipped anticipation. By the time they lowered their jersey zips at the foot of the col de Vars the riders had covered 167 kilometres in just under six hours of cycling; as the stage leaders passed the point where I'd been shamed by that rusted butcher's bike, the helicopter camera panned out to reveal a vast acreage of sheep-shit tussocks and gravel. In the shadows a grey, dry-ice mist was wisping about, giving the treeless geological rubble a sort of troll-valley Icelandic aspect.

At ground level it's all Thermos fumes and Italian chatter and that faint ski-crowd whooping – *hup-hup-hup-hup* – urging some emptied soul upwards. Then the road bends up and the camera is behind the leading group of seven riders, all rank outsiders hoping for a single day of glory. From this angle the brutal gradient of this section becomes clear, and with it the pain: all seven are standing up in the saddle, shoulders slowly rolling. The camera pulls alongside the last rider in the group, a Dutchman in the orange strip of Rabobank, and zooms in on his tortured features: every inhalation, and there are many, seems to crack another rib; every revolution, and there are not so many, heralds a complicated, discordant medley of distress. Up past a corrugated-iron chapel, up past more yells and gestures; he whisks a glove off the bars and in a ragged swipe smears stringy dreadfulness across his face and hair. This is where the crowds are hemming tightly in, parting just before the seven to leave a ribbon of pock-marked road barely wide enough for a bike. There are only two curves left and, as the other six begin to pull away, the muscles in that big Dutch head bulge and pulse in desperation: he's fucked if he's going to be dropped this close to a summit in the Tour de France. He sits down, then vaults up in the saddle again, aware perhaps that this is as close as he's ever been to fulfilling the fantasies of his youth, but probably not of the considerable excitement his efforts are causing in a dark bedroom in west London.

One more corner to go and now there are names and slogans rolling slowly beneath his wheels; he's not reading them but I certainly am. There's a PANTANI and an ULLRICH and a NO SAHAJA YOGA, whatever the blinking flip that is, and just before the summit, as Rabobank toils triumphantly up to rejoin the group, oh me oh my, oh joy of joys, there it is, clear and stark even as we cut up to the aerial shot from the helicopter, and I'm screaming at the telly as if my 500–1 shot is a nose behind the Grand National leader coming into the home straight.

The only two words I have previously admitted writing at the top of the col de Vars were 'The shame', ballpointed in tiny, go-away scrawl on a filthy, damp page of my training diary. But actually there had been a third. At Castellane I had purchased three litres of magnolia emulsion and a roller, and late that afternoon at the top of the col de Vars, watched by half a dozen German motorcyclists, I jumped out of the car and slathered five cream-coloured capitals on to the frost-cracked tarmac. Who does he think he is? said the Germans' faces, and even in the unsightly throes of my current excitement I knew it had been a fair point. Who had I thought I was? Not Eddy, who had no feelings; not Bernard, who had too many; not Tom, who had the ability to destroy himself, nor even the many also-rans who didn't. Firmin Lambot, older than I when he'd won in 1922, had done so on mud tracks and with cast-iron technology; yet his average speed over 5,468 kilometres – 24.1 k.p.h. – was more than I'd managed in any single day excepting that stunted time-trial. But maybe it had never been about times or speeds. Oscillating between destinies, I was honouring glory and failure alike: an ordinary man trying to find his place somewhere between the animals and the gods.

In typography of a size and stridency normally associated with phrases such as 'AMBULANCE – KEEP CLEAR', even in the late-afternoon gloom it had blared out to the heavens; today, with the mist burnt off by a garish sun, it had star billing, up in lights around the planet. As a billion viewers watched the world's greatest annual sporting event rolling over the top of another Alp, there, unavoidably, was the bland yet mysterious name